SENECA

IN TEN VOLUMES

VII

NATURALES QUAESTIONES

I

WITH AN ENGLISH TRANSLATION BY

THOMAS H. CORCORAN, PH.D.

PROFESSOR OF CLASSICS, TUFTS UNIVERSITY

CAMBRIDGE, MASSACHUSETTS
HARVARD UNIVERSITY PRESS
LONDON
WILLIAM HEINEMANN LTD
MCMLXXI

American ISBN 0–674–99495–7
British ISBN 0–434–99450–2

Printed in Great Britain

CONTENTS

INTRODUCTION

LUCIUS ANNAEUS SENECA was born about 4 B.C. (the exact date unknown) in Corduba, Spain, and brought to Rome as a child. His father was also named Lucius Annaeus Seneca, soon called " the Elder " or " the Rhetorician," whose writings are still read. His brother, Novatus, who was adopted and changed his name to Gallio, was the proconsul of Achaia at the time St. Paul was brought to trial. Seneca's nephew, son of another brother, became the famous poet, Lucan. Seneca " the Philosopher," or " the Stoic," or " the Younger " became the most powerful and famous of them all. Seneca, his brother Gallio, and his nephew Lucan all died on the orders of Nero.

Seneca's education at Rome imbued him with the great philosophical currents of his day and made him both an adherent of Stoicism and its principal innovator and teacher. He also became an innovator in Latin style, developing an abbreviated, to-the-point, and spontaneous method of writing and oratory which won him a large following, especially of young people, and some adverse criticism from his contemporaries and later Latin writers. His enormous popularity as a public speaker—by this time he was in the Senate—incurred the jealousy of the Emperor Gaius Caligula (as we are told, in the anecdotal fashion of Latin biography), who decided to put Seneca to death but was persuaded by a " female associate " that Seneca was in poor health and would die soon anyway. Numerous such anecdotes indicate that Seneca became a leader of young literary, and probably political, intellectuals, and, in addition, a leader of fashion and style in living.

He was so prominent that it was worth while to exile him. He was moving in high circles that included Julia Livilla, the sister of the late Emperor Caligula and enemy of Messalina, wife of the then emperor, Claudius. In A.D. 41 Messalina arranged the exile of Julia and Seneca on the rather common (and usually political) charge of adultery. Seneca, who was about forty-five years old, was sent to Corsica where he spent eight years in rather dismal exile but in continuous literary activity, producing the bulk of his moral essays and keeping his reputation as a writer and philosopher very much alive among the intellectuals at Rome.

In A.D. 49 Agrippina—who had replaced Messalina as the wife of Emperor Claudius—had Seneca recalled from exile to be the tutor of her son Nero. In addition to assuring the best possible education of the age for Nero, by the most eminent teacher of the time, Agrippina had political motives in attaching to herself and to the prospects of her son becoming emperor the enormous prestige and following which Seneca had among the Stoic intellectuals at Rome, a great many of whom were important political figures either by office or family connections.

Roman historians were puzzled about Seneca's responsibility for the character of Nero and for both the good and bad events of Nero's early reign. How much blame should be attached to a teacher because of his pupil's bad development is always a difficult question. After all, Judas Iscariot disappointed his great teacher. But Seneca became more than a teacher for Nero. Since Nero was just a teenager when he became emperor Seneca found himself very much part of a team in control of the vast Roman Empire. He had the important support of Burrus— important because Burrus was in charge of the emperor's private army, the Praetorian Guard, stationed at Rome. Seneca and Burrus early became involved in a power-struggle with Agrippina for control over the boy and consequently over the Roman Empire. For a time, Seneca, with the help of Burrus, seems to have been dominant—he even wrote Nero's speeches for him—and there resulted " the Golden Five Years of Nero's Reign " (*Quinquennium Neronis*) which were looked back upon later as the period in Roman history when the empire was governed best. But meanwhile, at the palace bad things were beginning to happen. Young Nero poisoned his half-brother Britannicus (son of Claudius), whom Agrippina threatened to take to the army as the rightful heir to the throne. In A.D. 59 Nero murdered Agrippina (on the second try, after an unsuccessful attempt with a collapsing boat) and then went on to a whole series of political executions. How much Seneca connived in the murder of Nero's mother, and of others, is unclear. After the death of Agrippina Seneca seems to have lost much of his influence—which is taken to mean that either he had agreed to her murder and so became odious to Nero or that he had been uninvolved and so became a disapproving embarrassment to Nero. There are ugly stories of Seneca exploiting his position to acquire enormous wealth, such as lending money to the Britons (which they did not want) at interest rates so exorbitant and unjust that, when he recalled loans, Britain revolted under the leadership of Queen Boudicca.

If Seneca had any power left after the death of Agrippina he lost it in A.D. 62 when Burrus died from ill health or Nero's poison. Seneca went into an unofficial retirement during which he was so fearful of being poisoned by Nero that he would eat only food he could find in the fields and drink only water from public fountains. Accusations that he took part in a plot to kill Nero, called the Conspiracy of Piso, provided the emperor with the justification for ordering his death. Although the validity of the accusations is impossible to determine it is reported that some of the conspirators planned, after killing Nero, to install Seneca as emperor. He might have made a good emperor and might well have averted the period of civil war and anarchy that broke out after Nero died. But in A.D. 65, three years before Nero's end, Seneca received orders from his pupil and emperor to commit suicide. His death was slow, awkward, and painful, but in the process he was able to revise a book, cheer up his wife and friends, and dictate a lecture which was later published.

Seneca's great fame is that of a philosopher and literary figure. Throughout his career of spectacular ups and downs he wrote prolifically, almost always touching on the problems of human existence in a world filled with wrong and with abrupt changes in personal fortune. Typically Roman, he searched for and found in a philosophical system the intellectual mechanism to enable him to accept a role in a world that offers sudden contrasts of good and evil, hope and despair, power and ruin, life and death. In his own career he saw more than enough of the world as it is, and he was able to pour his experiences into a collection of literary works that in his own time and for centuries afterwards provided men with the intellectually moral equipment for survival in a world and society that cannot be approved of. His writings are often tediously repetitive, disorganized, and hopelessly moralistic—at least for this generation—but he emerges as a man desperately striving to express himself as being both opposed to the evils of his time and yet capable of continuing to function within the system while maintaining his personal moral commitment. He disapproved of the world in which he lived yet he played a leading role in it, as was appropriate for a tough Roman pragmatist.

His extant works are the *Moral Essays* (sometimes broken down into the *Dialogues* and the moral treatises individually titled), the *Letters to Lucilius* (*Epistulae*), the *Natural Questions*, nine tragedies, and the *Apocolocyntosis* (a satire on Claudius—and some think not by Seneca). In addition, he apparently wrote monographs on such subjects as India and Egypt, and, as he says in the *Natural Questions*, on earthquakes. He wrote poems and, of course, orations. Some works extant today are incorrectly attributed to him, such as the tenth tragedy (the *Octavia*) and an imaginative collection of letters between him and St. Paul.

The work *Natural Questions* was written during a

period of great crisis in the closing years of Seneca's life. His reference to an earthquake at Pompeii provides the date of A.D. 62 or 63 (probably 62) for his Book Six, on earthquakes, which was one of the earliest books of the *Natural Questions*. He completed the entire work in a remarkably short time, obviously after many years of reading on the subject. Another reference in the *Natural Questions* indicates that he wrote the bulk of his *Letters to Lucilius* after he had completed some of the books of the *Natural Questions*, maybe all of them. Thus, Seneca started the *Natural Questions* not long before A.D. 62, and by the time he was forced to commit suicide in April, 65, he had completed the *Natural Questions*, the *Letters to Lucilius*, and the *De Providentia*.

The Lucilius to whom the *Natural Questions*, the *Letters*, and the *De Providentia* are addressed was not much younger than Seneca. The internal evidence of the *Natural Questions* and the *Letters* suggests that Lucilius was close to sixty and Seneca about seventy years old. Lucilius Junior had risen from rather humble origins around Naples and Campania to become the governor of the Roman province of Sicily, an office which he had evidently assumed shortly before Seneca started the *Natural Questions*. He was a writer and poet—Seneca quotes some of his verses and refers to others—and may, in fact, have been the author of the extant poem *Aetna* (dubiously ascribed in the manuscripts to Virgil).

Seneca's sources for the *Natural Questions* include almost forty authorities cited by him, of whom only five are Latin writers, the rest Greek ranging in time from the earliest Pre-Socratic thinkers, such as Thales,

INTRODUCTION

to Greek authors and lecturers of his own time. Of
course Seneca did not consult directly the writings of
all his sources, many of them famous for not having
left any writings. On the other hand he did not, as
some charge, rely solely on a single work dealing with
ancient scientific thought, even though there were
such works available to him, by Theophrastus, for
example, or by Posidonius. Too much can be made
of the fact that in cases where we have his source,
especially Aristotle's *Meteorologica*, Seneca is revealed
as rather less than exact in reporting verbatim what
his predecessor says. We know from what he tells
his mother in A.D. 41 (*Ad Helviam Matrem* 20.2) that
he had been interested in the subject of the *Natural
Questions* for at least twenty years before he wrote it.
During that time he must have read and remembered
more than one book by way of preparation. His
inaccuracies, or freedom, in transmitting the statements of his Greek sources need not prove that he
knew them only through a Latin intermediary. He
is just as inaccurate in quoting Latin poets. His
practice, and generally that of all ancient writers, was
to cite and quote from memory. Often Seneca's
poetry quotations differ in word-order and even
choice of words from our present texts and, in one
instance, he ascribes a line of verse to the wrong poet.
According to Quintilian (*Inst. Orat.* 10.1.128) Seneca,
a man of wide knowledge, used what we would call
" research assistants," or maybe just " librarians,"
who sometimes led him into error.

His method, in most of the books of the *Natural
Questions*, is to present a survey of the theories of the
major authorities on the phenomena under study.

INTRODUCTION

He can, and often does, agree or disagree with particular theories. His age evaluated theories by the arguments of analogy. To test a theory by controlled experiment was not a standard reflex and it would be inappropriate to expect it. His contribution, as he and his age saw it, was to present to the reader what had been learned (i.e. the theories) about phenomena, to demonstrate (sometimes, but not always) by analogy which explanations were seemingly wrong or foolish, to indicate (again sometimes but not always) which theory or theories he preferred (and he could accept more than one as an explanation), and to make moral observations on something suggested by the topic. Also, the study itself of what had been learned about natural phenomena was felt by Seneca to provide moral improvement.

The Prefaces (only to Books One, Three, and Four A), the preliminary remarks to Book Two, and the moral essays closing the books are vehicles for Seneca's moralizing and are structurally detachable from the treatment of natural phenomena. However, it must be kept in mind that to Seneca the moral observations are a logical part of the total work.

Because of the size and the nature of the *Natural Questions* a brief summary of each book should be useful at this point:

The phenomena treated in Book One belong to several classifications. Some are illusions in the atmosphere (rainbows, halos, and parhelia), others are real fires (meteors), and one phenomenon (comets) does not occur in the earth's atmosphere at all.

INTRODUCTION

Seneca is aware of the difference between illusions and real fires (cf. 1.15.6) and he is convinced that comets occur above the atmosphere in the vicinity of the stars. In fact, in his book on comets (Book Seven) he refutes theories that comets are caused by any atmospheric conditions. Evidently he includes comets, briefly, in Book One as simply phenomena among others that are seen in the sky. After a Preface on the values to one's self of studying divine things (i.e. celestial phenomena) from which the mind begins to know god and to transcend its own mortality, Seneca introduces the subject of this book which he specifies as fires (in the atmosphere). He explains that the fires occur by friction and that the earth exhales many particles capable of being ignited. He carefully emphasizes that such fires occur close to the earth; they are below the stars even though they may appear, as in the case of halos, to be around the stars. Then he treats specific phenomena, devoting several chapters to the theories about rainbows, what they are, what causes them, including objections to the theories, and concluding that a rainbow is a reflection of the sun in a cloud as though in a mirror. He passes on to Streaks, parhelia, and other lights in the sky, and comets. The theories of reflected images, presented throughout the book, induce Seneca to end with moralizing on man's evil use of mirrors.

Book Two, the longest book, deals with the physical nature and causes, and the interpretations by soothsayers, of lightning and thunder. He devotes eleven chapters of preliminary statements on the divisions of a study of the universe, on unities and composites,

the parts and the material of the universe, as well as
tension in the atmosphere (which proves unity) before
he gets to the subject of thunder and lightning.
These preliminary remarks give the impression of
providing a kind of outline of the total work; however,
the reader will find no such systematic organization in
the *Natural Questions*. Among Seneca's sources there
seems to have been little disagreement on the
obviously fiery nature of lightning, or that thunder
and lightning occurred in the clouds. Specific details
of the remote and immediate causes were disputed.
Seneca presents both the theories of his sources and
the main objections to them, passing through the
concepts of Anaximenes, Anaximander, Anaxagoras,
Aristotle, the Stoics, Diogenes of Apollonia, Posidonius, Asclepiodotus. Along the way, Seneca faces
the problems of explaining how the fire of lightning
moves downwards when fire by nature rises, and
of how fire is kindled in clouds, which are composed
of the opposite element, moisture. After describing
briefly the marvellous effects of lightning (to which he
returns in a later chapter) he takes up the subject of
divination, a category in any study of lightning in
his day. He delivers a logical discussion on what fate
is, how vows and propitiations fit into a scheme of
fate, and how fate is revealed by omens. This
section of the book includes a review of Etruscan
beliefs, credited in part to Caecina, a Roman writer on
Etruscan lore, and mixed with the teachings of
Attalus, who influenced the young Seneca considerably. Then he returns to the physical explanations
of thunder and lightning, especially by Posidonius
but including Clidemus and Heraclitus, and ends with

a statement of his own views. The last chapter draws from the study of thunder and lightning the moral resolve that death is eventually unavoidable in any circumstances and thus lightning should offer no special terror.

The subject of Book Three is, as Seneca states in the first chapter, waters of the earth, which he places in a different category from celestial waters that come from the clouds. In a rather long Preface he acknowledges his advanced age and the enormity of his project which he defines as a survey of the universe with the intention of passing this knowledge on to others. Actually, he means that he will make a survey of what is known or theorized about the universe. As always, he is capable of accepting more than one theory, on the assumption that one explanation may be correct but another even more correct. After this statement of method he goes on in the Preface to stress the truly important reason for studying nature, and that is the moral improvement to be gained from such a study. It makes a man able to endure adversity and calamity, avoid evil, be free from personal vices, etc. As he says, " What is important in human existence is to have seen the universe in your mind." After the Preface he outlines the problems to be investigated: what causes terrestrial waters and how are they produced? He establishes classifications: still waters, running waters, hot, cold, etc., and decides that topography determines the kind of water. Then he arrives at a very old question: since the rivers flow into the ocean, where do the rivers get their supply of water, why is the ocean not affected by the continuous inflow and the land not affected by the continuous outflow of water? Seneca reviews five theories: (1) water returns from ocean to land by hidden routes, (2) rivers are supplied by rainfall, (3) rivers come from underground reservoirs, (4) air, which is an element, under the ground changes into water, which is another element, just as (5) the element earth can change into water. He objects only to the rainfall theory. Rivers can be affected by earthquakes, landslides, and trees and crop cultivation; rainfall can also affect rivers but cannot make a river. That rivers consist of water and that water is one of the four elements is not a theory to Seneca but a fact which leads to the reasoning that it is in a sense pointless to question where an element comes from; it exists as a part of nature and is thus in inexhaustible supply. As in his explanation of earthquakes in Book Six and probably in his explanation of the source of Nile water in the lost portion of Book Four A, he is preoccupied with the concept of vast caverns and veins of air and water under the earth. Rivers come from these underground reservoirs and move through the earth in a way analogous to the passage of air and moisture through the veins and arteries of the human body. Reports of live fish dug out of the ground induce Seneca to deliver his moralizing attack on luxury practically in the middle of this book rather than at the end as he commonly does in the other books of the *Natural Questions*. In this case, the luxury is the fad at Rome of watching the changing colours of a surmullet as it dies on the banquet table. He returns to the existence of underground reservoirs and explains the various types of water (classified according to taste, odour, medicinal properties, heat, etc.) by the nature of the earth through which the water passes, or by the earth or air elements from which the water was transmuted. The last four chapters contain a description of the cyclical deluge and destruction of the human race and animals, after which living creatures will be re-created along with a mankind innocent of sin, an innocence which will last only as long as the men are new.

We have perhaps the first half, maybe a little more, of Book Four A, on the Nile, which is listed in the manuscripts as the Seventh, Eighth, and even Tenth Book, and is missing entirely from the class of manuscripts called *Quantum* (which puts the book on Lights in the Sky at the beginning of the work). Seneca very probably ended his *Natural Questions* with this book on the Nile. Attempts have been made to reconstruct the lost portion by guesswork and with the help of Joannes Laurentius Lydus, who wrote in Greek a work titled *On Months*, about the time of Justinian, which is thought in one part to give a résumé of Seneca's references to ancient authors on the Nile. Lydus' résumé, which is reproduced by Oltramare, is very brief and gives no indication of how Seneca used his sources. Perhaps Seneca explained the flooding and the source of the Nile in connection with the vast reservoirs of subterranean water which he had discussed in Book Three and at length in Book Six. What we have of the Nile book starts with a rather long Preface to Lucilius, whom Seneca advises to be on guard against flatterers and to follow the example of Junius Gallio, Seneca's brother, whose virtues are praised considerably. After giving almost equal praise to Lucilius, Seneca offers to take his mind off his duties in Sicily by telling him about the Nile. The Nile chapter begins with a high-light description of the progress of the river from wastelands and swamps to Philae, on to Memphis, and finally to the sea which it reaches by seven mouths. The account is enlivened by a story of shooting the rapids and of a battle between crocodiles and dolphins. Then Seneca starts to present the theories about the Nile flood and the objections to them. The rest of the book has disappeared. Presumably it contained Seneca's own theory, or theories, and very likely concluded with the moral reflections common to the other books.

Book Four B was probably placed by Seneca at the beginning of the *Natural Questions*. Only the last chapters have survived, probably less than a third of the whole. The title may have been *Clouds*, and the book dealt with what the clouds supposedly discharge: rain, dew, hail, frost, snow, etc. However, *Hail and Snow*, or variations, found in some manuscripts better describes the contents. In the parts of the book that remain he adopts the theory that hail is formed in a frozen cloud. He ridicules attempts to ward off hail by incantations. In the closing chapters he presents arguments to justify the theory that snow is formed near the earth. The book ends with Seneca moralizing against the luxury of cooling drinks with ice and snow. It is easy to appreciate the attempt to assemble a seemingly complete book from the Nile fragment with its Preface and the Hail and Snow fragment with its moralizing conclusion.

Book Five, the shortest in the *Natural Questions*, is unusual because Seneca makes almost no reference

INTRODUCTION

to his sources, other than Democritus (with whom he disagrees) and Varro. Further, the book shows considerably more unity than the others, which makes it seem likely that Seneca is following a single source for Book Five. His constant use of Greek names for the winds indicates that his source is Greek, with the exception of Varro in Chapter Sixteen where Seneca accompanies the Greek names with their Latin equivalents. He opens the book with an orderly definition of wind as simply moving air, objects to Democritus' definition of wind as atoms bumping against each other in a small space, and takes up the theories on the formation of winds: air ejected from subterranean caverns, exhalations of particles from the earth, and an analogy with human flatulence. Although he accepts as a " truer " explanation the theory that wind is the result of particles emitted by the earth he feels that it is a still better explanation to say simply that air has the ability to move itself and so become wind. A discussion of types of winds (gulf breezes, etesian winds, cloudbursts, whirlwinds, subterranean winds) and theories about them is followed by a listing of the names of winds and the division of the sky into zones and sectors. The moralizing conclusion deals with man's misuse of winds by building ships to sail to war.

Seneca introduces Book Six with the news to Lucilius that he has just heard about the earthquake in Campania, the one that struck Pompeii, Herculaneum, and even part of Naples. As a young man he had published a work on earthquakes and now he can find out whether he has learned anything new or at least become more diligent in his research. He dwells on the peculiar terror earthquakes cause; but death is death no matter from what source and it attacks us from all sides at all times. In fact, he describes so many causes of death that he begins to worry lest he is adding to the anxiety of his readers instead of comforting them. A knowledge of earthquakes, Seneca says, will remove the irrational fear of them. He examines the theories that connect earthquakes with one or more of the four elements: water, fire, earth, and air. His own belief is that earthquakes are caused by air in subterranean caverns and passages. He describes briefly the amazing effects of earthquakes: pestilence, the fear that causes insanity in some people, statues split in two, the peculiar movements of buildings, the disappearance of entire cities, and the separation of land-masses. His moralizing conclusion is intended to eliminate the fear of death. Seneca feels that the old theories are rough and inexact but he wishes to give proper credit to their inventors and to acknowledge the laudable efforts of early philosophers. Some of the theories (for example, air as a life-giving principle and the vibrations of air in underground caves) he seems to include merely because they are well known and so belong in any list of theories. He is sturdily convinced that great caverns and passageways exist under the earth and that these are filled with air and water which can cause earthquakes. He inclines towards air as the main cause.

In Book Seven Seneca believes that comets are permanent celestial bodies which observe a regular orbit, in the manner of the planets. They are not illusions or temporary fires in the atmosphere. Long

INTRODUCTION

before Seneca, the Pythagoreans had developed a similar theory; however, Aristotle and Posidonius placed comets wrongly in the category of atmospheric phenomena. Seneca is often accused of uncritically following Posidonius, and like all ancient " scientific " writers he relied a great deal on Aristotle, but on this point he disagrees strongly with his illustrious predecessors. It is perhaps unfortunate that Aristotle and Posidonius were such powerful authorities that their views prevailed over Seneca's, with the result that comets were long misunderstood. Book Seven begins with the almost apologetic argument that comets are explainable by the ordinary laws of the universe and, although rare, are no more remarkable than the regular behaviour of the more carefully recorded and comparatively prosaic stars and planets. Seneca promises that a study of celestial phenomena may help us to understand whether the universe moves around the earth or the earth moves while the universe stands still. He devotes considerable attention to presenting and refuting the theories of Epigenes, who believes comets are atmospheric fires produced by a whirlwind sort of action. Seneca is equally critical of the belief that comets are illusions created by light from planets in conjunction. He introduces and refutes the theories of Artemidorus, whose " whole account of the universe is a falsehood " and who believes that light from unknown planets mingles with light from the stars and projects the illusion of a comet. Next, Ephorus is attacked for reporting that a comet once split up into two planets. Apollonius' theory that a comet is a star (or a planet) is rejected by Seneca whose conviction is that a comet is not a star or a planet but a kind of third type of permanent body in the universe. Zeno's concept that a comet is produced by the combined rays of stars, or the idea that comets are created by the reflections of neighbouring planets, and the Stoic theory of comets as mere atmospheric fires—are all dismissed by Seneca on the grounds that the long-lasting, regular movement of comets proves they have their own position in the universe. The orbits of comets need not be the same as those of planets for them to be considered permanent bodies; however, since comets occur rarely it should not be surprising, Seneca points out, that knowledge of their orbits is scanty. Also, there is no reason to conclude that comets are not eternal and in the same category as stars, even though comets and stars have differences in appearance and movement. The concept that because a comet predicts future events it is therefore different from a star is rejected by Seneca with the argument that a comet forecasts not immediate events but events for the entire year and is thus a part of the laws of the universe. In much the same way he attacks as inaccurate the idea that the slow speed of comets proves they are heavy with earthy matter (unlike the stars). In his conclusion, Seneca asserts that much remains to be discovered about many things in the universe, including comets; however, we are more interested in vice and luxury than in acquiring knowledge, and there is so little interest in philosophy that many things which were once discovered are being lost.

This work *Natural Questions* contains obscurities, contradictions, cross references that cannot be found,

INTRODUCTION

and promises of discussions that never occur. Yet there is no reason to suppose that the work is not substantially as Seneca meant it to be (except for the lost portions of the Nile book and of the first part of Book Four B), nor is there any reason to believe that he failed to complete it. Evidently the inconsistencies did not bother him and they very likely did not bother his readers.

One of his most confusing devices is the use of an imaginary questioner. It provides a kind of class-room atmosphere with Seneca lecturing and parrying questions from seemingly anywhere in the room. He uses the device also in his *Dialogues*, where it makes some sense, and in his *Letters to Lucilius*. Although the questioner lends a certain spontaneity to the exposition of theories in the *Natural Questions* it is often difficult to determine where the question ends and the answer begins or to decide whether the question or objection is being made by Seneca himself, or by Lucilius, or is anticipated from the reader.

Another puzzling feature of Seneca's style is the absence of any specialized " scientific " terminology, although in our own age of over-jargon in every field such a lack of technological vocabulary on Seneca's part seems almost refreshing. Any suggestion that a modern scientist be included in a team to translate the *Natural Questions* should give all admirers of Seneca the shudders. To render his vocabulary in modern space-age terms would misrepresent Seneca and be unfair to him. He has much to offer if a translation keeps his knowledge correctly in his own time.

This text follows the Second Edition (1961) of

Oltramare's Budé text (originally 1929) along with close consideration of Gercke's definitive 1907 Teubner text (which Oltramare found so admirable he needed to do little by way of alteration), with the help of William Hardy Alexander's *Text Emended and Explained* and his idea of correcting the text partly on the basis of clausular rhythm.

The more than fifty manuscripts of the *Natural Questions*, dating from the twelfth to the fifteenth century, fall into two major divisions called *Grandinem* (the Φ family) and *Quantum* (the Δ family) according to the first word of the first book in each series. *Grandinem* lacks the end of the Nile book and the first part of the book on Hail and Snow. *Quantum* has lost the entire Nile book and Book Three after *efferantur* in Chapter 25.6.

A long tradition opens the *Natural Questions* with *Quantum* as the first word of Book One (*Lights in the Sky*) and starts *Grandinem* in the middle of Book Four even though that order is clearly incorrect, as can be seen from Seneca's own cross references within the *Natural Questions* (for example, Book One was written after Book Seven; cf. 1.15.4). The study of the Nile was the last book of Seneca's original work and, in all probability, was considered Book Eight. Only the first half is extant. Joined to it by tradition is his study of Hail and Snow, which begins with the word *Grandinem* and was probably the first book of the *Natural Questions* that Seneca published. Only the second half has survived. The two halves together produce one book out of what was in fact two books at opposite ends of the original work. The expediency is to refer to Book Four as Four A (*The Nile*) and Four B (*Hail and Snow*). There is nothing to be gained by changing the established order. Except for Seneca's occasional cross references each book is independent of the others in treating separate natural phenomena. It is suspected that he may not have had any advance plan for the sequence of books.

Of the *Grandinem* family the most important manuscripts are H, which Gercke considers best; E; K, which is admired; and P, which Oltramare considers helpful. The *Quantum* family has A, B, and V. Somewhere between the two families is the manuscript referred to as Z, which Gercke collated and Oltramare gives special attention to, using Z to corroborate H which, as Oltramare says, has obvious errors and numerous gaps and interpolations even though it is the best manuscript. In spite of the efforts of scholars to improve matters, the condition of Seneca's text remains in many places most uncertain or quite unrecoverable. Again and again one has to be content with conjectures which, while often giving the general sense of a passage, must not be taken as certainly Seneca's actual words.

The designations for manuscripts, here given in alphabetical order, come from Gercke and Oltramare:

A   Leidensis, thirteenth century
B   Bambergensis, twelfth century
E   Berolinensis, thirteenth century
F   Mertonensis, fourteenth century
G   Montepessulanus, thirteenth century
g   Guelferbytanus, thirteenth century (a large number of mixed MSS.)
H   Parisinus, twelfth to thirteenth century

INTRODUCTION

J   Sancti Johannis Oxon., thirteenth century
K   Cameracensis, twelfth century
L   Leidensis, twelfth century
λ   (used by Gercke and Oltramare to desig-
       nate the group of MSS. JKLOM)
M   Excerpta Parisina, thirteenth century
O   Leidensis, fourteenth century
P   Parisinus, thirteenth century
S   Montepessulanus, thirteenth century
T   Parisinus, thirteenth century
V   Vaticanus, twelfth to thirteenth century
Z   Genevensis, twelfth century

REFERENCE WORKS

THE texts of Erasmus (1515), Fortunatus (1522), Pincianus (1536), Muret (1585), Gronovius (died 1671), and others whose works exist only in rare-book collections are not listed here even though their names appear in the *apparatus criticus*.

William Hardy Alexander, "*Naturales Quaestiones*. The Text Emended and Explained," *Univ. of California Publ. in Class. Philol.*, Vol. 13, No. 8 (1948) 241–332.

V. Capocci, *Chi era Seneca?* Turin (1954).

L. Castiglioni, "*De Naturalium Quaestionum Codice Veneto Marc.*, XII 141 (Cod. Lat. 1548)," *Miscellanea G. Galbiati* I (Milan, 1951) 167–201.

—— "Contributo alla storia del testo delle *Naturales Quaes-tiones* di Seneca," *AFLC* 18 (1952).

H. W. Garrod, "Notes on the *N.Q.* of Seneca," *CQ* 8 (1914–1915)

A. Gercke, *Senecae NQ Libri VIII*, Teubner; Leipzig (1907).

INTRODUCTION

P. Grimal, *Sénèque, sa vie, son oeuvre, sa philosophie*, Paris (1948).

R. M. Gummere, *Seneca the Philosopher and his Modern Message*, " Our Debt to Greece and Rome," Cooper Square Publications; New York (1963) (Reprint).

Fridericus Haase, *Senecae Opera*, Vol. 1, Leipzig (1852).

I. Lana, *Lucio Anneo Seneca*, Turin (1955).

Concetto Marchesi, *Seneca*, Giuseppe Principato; Milan-Messina. 3rd edn. (1944).

A. L. Motto, " Recent Scholarship on Seneca's Prose Works, 1940–1957," *CW* 54 (Oct.–Nov. 1960, Jan. 1961) 37–48; 70–71; 111–112.

—— " Seneca's Prose Writings: A Decade of Scholarship, 1958–1968," *CW* 64 (Jan.–Feb. 1971) 141–158; 177–191.

Paul Oltramare, *Sénèque. Questions Naturelles*, 2 vols., l'Association Guillaume Budé, " Les Belles Lettres "; Paris (1961).

René Waltz, *La Vie de Sénèque*, Paris (1909).

SENECA: NATURAL QUESTIONS

BOOK I
LIGHTS IN THE SKY

LIBER PRIMUS [1]

DE IGNIBUS IN AERE [2]

Praefatio 1. Quantum inter philosophiam interest,
Lucili virorum optime, et ceteras artes, tantum
interesse existimo in ipsa philosophia inter illam
partem quae ad homines et hanc quae ad deos pertinet.
Altior est haec et animosior; multum permisit sibi;
non fuit oculis contenta; maius esse quiddam sus-
picata est ac pulchrius quod extra conspectum natura
posuisset. 2. Denique inter duas interest quantum
inter deum et hominem. Altera docet quid in terris
agendum sit, altera quid agatur in caelo. Altera
errores nostros discutit et lumen admovet quo dis-
cernantur ambigua vitae; altera multum supra
hanc in qua volutamur caliginem excedit et e tenebris ereptos perducit illo unde lucet.

3. Equidem tunc rerum naturae gratias ago cum
illam non ab hac parte video qua publica est, sed cum
secretiora eius intravi, cum disco quae universi
materia sit, quis auctor aut custos, quid sit deus,

[1] *liber quintus* KT; *liber sextus* Z; *liber septimus* GHL;
[*Liber Primus*] *Liber Quintus* Oltramare.
[2] Most of the MSS. give no title. *De Discurrentibus* (*Ignibus*
understood) Z; *De Ignibus Caelestibus* g; *De Ignibus In Aere
Existentibus* Oltramare. *Pracfatio* was added by Fortunatus.

BOOK I

LIGHTS IN THE SKY [1]

PREFACE 1. Lucilius, my good friend, the great difference between philosophy and other studies is matched, I think, by the equally great difference in philosophy itself, between that branch which deals with man and that which deals with the gods. The latter is loftier and more intellectual, and so has permitted a great deal of freedom for itself. It has not been restricted to what can be seen; it has presumed that there is something greater and more beautiful which nature has placed beyond our sight. 2. In short, between the two branches of philosophy there is as much difference as there is between man and god. One teaches us what ought to be done on earth; the other what is done in heaven. One dispels our errors and furnishes a light for us to see through the uncertainties of life; the other rises far above this fog in which we wallow, and, rescuing us from darkness, leads us to the place whence the light shines.

3. I, for one, am very grateful to nature, not just when I view it in that aspect which is obvious to everybody but when I have penetrated its mysteries; when I learn what the stuff of the universe is, who its author or custodian is, what god is; whether he keeps

[1] Whatever the title which Seneca gave to this Book, its subject is "Fires" or "Lights" in the atmosphere.

totus in se tendat an et ad nos aliquando respiciat,
faciat cotidie aliquid an semel fecerit, pars mundi sit
an mundus, liceat illi hodieque decernere et ex lege
fatorum aliquid derogare an maiestatis deminutio
sit et confessio erroris mutanda fecisse . . . [1]

4. Nisi ad haec admitterer, non tanti [2] fuerat nasci.
Quid enim erat cur in numero viventium me positum
esse gauderem? An ut cibos et potiones percolarem?
ut hoc corpus causarium ac fluidum, periturumque
nisi subinde impletur, farcirem et viverem aegri
minister? ut mortem timerem, cui uni nascimur?
Detrahe hoc inaestimabile bonum, non est vita tanti
ut sudem, ut aestuem. 5. O quam contempta res
est homo, nisi supra humana surrexerit! Quamdiu
cum affectibus colluctamur, quid magnifici facimus?
Etiamsi superiores sumus, portenta vincimus. Quid
est cur suspiciamus nosmet ipsi quia dissimiles
deterrimis sumus? Non video quare sibi placeat qui
robustior est in valetudinario. 6. Multum interest
inter vires et bonam valetudinem.

Effugisti vitia animi; non est tibi frons ficta, nec
in alienam voluntatem sermo compositus, nec cor
involutum, nec avaritia quae, quicquid omnibus

---

[1] *necesse est eadem placere ei cui nisi optima placere non possunt. Nec ob hoc minus liber est ac potens; ipse est enim
necessitas sua.* These are two marginal comments (the second
a comment on the first comment) which should be eliminated
from Seneca's text (cf. Alexander p. 251).

[2] *tanti* Leo, Gercke, Oltramare.

entirely to himself or whether he sometimes considers us; whether he creates something each day or has created it only once; whether he is a part of the universe or is the universe; whether it is possible for him to make decisions today and to repeal in part any sort of universal law of fate; whether it is a diminution of his majesty and an admission of his error that he had done things which had to be changed.

4. If I had not been admitted to these studies it would not have been worth while to have been born. What reason would I have to be glad that I was placed among the living? In order that I might digest food and drink? In order that I might stuff this diseased and failing body, which would soon die unless it were filled continuously—and that I might live as an attendant on a sick man? In order that I might fear death, the one thing for which we are born? Well, you can have this invaluable prize —living is not so important that I should even get sweaty and hot. 5. After all, man is a contemptible thing unless he rises above his human concerns. But what greatness do we achieve as long as we struggle with ignoble passions? Even if we are victorious we conquer only monsters. What reason is there to admire ourselves because we are not as bad as the worst? I do not see why a man should feel pleased who is simply less sick than the others in the hospital. 6. Having good health is very different from only being not sick.

You have escaped the illnesses of the soul, Lucilius. You do not present a false front, your speech is not composed to suit someone else's policy, your heart is not twisted; you do not have greed (which denies to

5

abstulit, sibi ipsi neget, nec luxuria pecuniam tur-
piter perdens quam turpius reparet, nec ambitio
quae te ad dignitatem nisi per indigna non ducet:
nihil adhuc consecutus es; multa effugisti, te nondum.

Virtus enim ista quam affectamus magnifica est,
non quia per se beatum est malo caruisse, sed quia
animum laxat et praeparat ad cognitionem caelestium dignumque efficit qui in consortium deo veniat.

7. Tunc consummatum habet plenumque bonum
sortis humanae cum calcato omni malo petit altum
et in interiorem naturae sinum venit. Tunc iuvat inter
ipsa sidera vagantem divitum pavimenta ridere et
totam cum auro suo terram, non illo tantum dico quod
egessit et signandum monetae dedit, sed et illo quod
in occulto servat posterorum avaritiae. 8. Non
potest ante contemnere porticus et lacunaria ebore
fulgentia et tonsiles silvas et derivata in domos
flumina quam totum circumit mundum et, terrarum
orbem superne despiciens angustum et magna ex
parte opertum mari, etiam ea qua extat late squali-
dum et aut ustum aut rigentem, sibi ipse dixit:
" Hoc est illud punctum quod inter tot gentes ferro
et igne dividitur? 9. O quam ridiculi sunt mortalium termini! Ultra Istrum Dacos nostrum arceat [1]

---

[1] Oltramare supplied *nostrum* and restored *Dacos . . . arceat.*

itself what is has taken away from everybody else), nor extravagance (it squanders money shamefully only in order to get it back even more disgracefully), nor ambition (it will take you to high position only through degrading methods). As yet you have attained nothing. You have escaped many ills, but you have not yet escaped yourself.

That special virtue which we seek is magnificent, not because to be free of evil is in itself so marvellous but because it unchains the mind, prepares it for the realization of heavenly things, and makes it worthy to enter into an association with god.

7. The mind possesses the full and complete benefit of its human existence only when it spurns all evil, seeks the lofty and the deep, and enters the innermost secrets of nature. Then as the mind wanders among the very stars it delights in laughing at the mosaic floors of the rich and at the whole earth with all its gold. I do not mean only the gold which the earth has already produced and surrendered to be struck for money but also all the gold the earth has preserved hidden away for the avarice of future generations. 8. The mind cannot despise colonnades, panelled ceilings gleaming with ivory, trimmed shrubbery, and streams made to approach mansions, until it goes around the entire universe and looking down upon the earth from above (an earth limited and covered mostly by sea—while even the part out of the sea is squalid or parched and frozen) says to itself: " Is this that pinpoint which is divided by sword and fire among so many nations ? 9. How ridiculous are the boundaries of mortals! Let our empire

imperium, Haemo Thraces includat; Parthis obstet
Euphrates; Danuvius Sarmatica ac Romana dis-
terminet; Rhenus Germaniae modum faciat; Pyre-
naeus medium inter Gallias et Hispanias iugum
extollat; inter Aegyptum et Aethiopas harenarum
inculta vastitas iaceat. 10. Si quis formicis det
intellectum hominis, nonne et illae unam aream in
multas provincias divident? Cum te in illa vere
magna sustuleris, quotiens videbis exercitus sub-
rectis ire vexillis et, quasi magnum aliquid agatur,
equitem modo ulteriora explorantem, modo a
lateribus effusum, libebit dicere:

it nigrum campis agmen.

Formicarum iste discursus est in angusto laborantium.
Quid illis et nobis interest nisi exigui mensura cor-
pusculi?"

11. Punctum est istud in quo navigatis, in quo
bellatis, in quo regna disponitis [1] minima, etiam cum
illis utrimque oceanus occurrit. Sursum ingentia
spatia sunt, in quorum possessionem animus ad-
mittitur, et ita si secum minimum ex corpore tulit, si
sordidum omne detersit et expeditus levisque ac
contentus modico emicuit. 12. Cum illa tetigit,

[1] *regna disponitis* Fortunatus, Haase, Gercke, Alexander;
regnatis. † *Ponitis* Oltramare.

confine[1] the Dacians beyond the Ister; let it shut out the Thracians by means of the Haemus; let the Euphrates block the Parthians; the Danube separate Sarmatian and Roman interests; the Rhine establish a limit for Germany; the Pyrenees lift their ridge between the Gallic and Spanish provinces; between Egypt and Ethiopia let an uncultivated wasteland of sand lie. 10. If someone should give human intellect to ants, will they not also divide a single floor into many provinces? Since you have aspired to truly great thoughts, whenever you see armies marching with flying banners, and a cavalry, as though engaged in something grand, scouting now at a distance, now massed on the flanks, you will be glad to say:

> A black battle-line
> Moves on the plain.[2]

This army of yours is only a scurrying of ants toiling in a limited field. What difference is there between us and the ants except the insignificant size of a tiny body?"

11. That is a mere pinpoint on which you navigate, on which you wage war, on which you arrange tiny kingdoms—tiny, even though ocean does run to meet them on both sides. Spaces in the heavens are immense; but your mind is admitted to the possession of them only if it retains very little of the body, only if it has worn away all sordidness and, unencumbered and light, flashes forth, satisfied with little. 12. When

---

[1] Seneca defines some natural frontiers. Ister or Hister is the lower Danube, Danuvius the upper. Mount Haemus is Great Balkan.

[2] Virgil *Aen.* 4.404, describing ants.

alitur, crescit ac velut vinculis liberatus in originem
redit et hoc habet argumentum divinitatis suae quod
illum divina delectant, nec ut alienis, sed ut suis
interest. Secure spectat occasus siderum atque
ortus et tam diversas concordantium vias; observat
ubi quaeque stella primum terris lumen ostendat,
ubi columen eius summumque cursus sit, quousque
descendat; curiosus spectator excutit singula et
quaerit. Quidni quaerat? Scit illa ad se pertinere.
13. Tunc contemnit domicilii prioris angustias.
Quantum est enim quod ab ultimis litoribus Hispaniae usque ad Indos iacet? Paucissimorum dierum
spatium, si navem suus ferat ventus. At illa regio
caelestis per triginta annos velocissimo sideri viam
praestat nusquam resistenti sed aequaliter cito.
Illic demum discit quod diu quaesiit; illic incipit
deum nosse. Quid est deus? Mens universi.
Quid est deus? Quod vides totum et quod non
vides totum. Sic demum magnitudo illi sua redditur,
qua nihil maius cogitari potest, si solus est omnia, si
opus suum et intra et extra tenet.

14. Quid ergo interest inter naturam dei et
nostram? Nostri melior pars animus est, in illo

the mind contacts those regions it is nurtured, grows, and returns to its origin just as though freed from its chains. As proof of its divinity it has this: divine things cause it pleasure, and it dwells among them not as being alien things but things of its own nature. Serenely it looks upon the rising and setting of the stars and the diverse orbits of bodies precisely balanced with one another. The mind observes where each star first shows its light to earth, where its culmination, the highest altitude of its course, lies and how far it descends. As a curious spectator the mind separates details and investigates them. Why not do this? It knows that these things pertain to itself. 13. Then it despises the limitation of its former dwelling place. After all, how great is the distance from the farthest shores of Spain all the way to India? Only the space of a very few days if a good wind drives the ship.[1] But in the heavenly region the swiftest star,[2] which never stops and maintains a constant velocity, has a journey of thirty years. Here, finally, the mind learns what it long sought: here it begins to know god. What is god? The mind of the universe. What is god? All that you see, all that you do not see. In short, only if he alone is all things, if he maintains his own work both from within and without, is he given due credit for his magnitude; nothing of greater magnitude than *that* can be contemplated.

14. What, then, is the difference between our nature and the nature of god? In ourselves the

[1] Cf. Strabo 2.3.6, 102C from Posidonius, whose idea greatly influenced Columbus.
[2] The planet Saturn.

nulla pars extra animum est. Totus est ratio, cum
interim tantus error mortalia tenet ut hoc, quo neque
formosius est quicquam nec dispositius nec in
proposito constantius, existiment homines fortuitum
et casu volubile ideoque tumultuosum inter fulmina
nubes tempestates et cetera quibus terrae ac terris
vicina pulsantur. 15. Nec haec intra vulgum
dementia est sed sapientiam quoque professos con-
tigit. Sunt qui putent ipsis animum esse, et quidem
providum, dispensantem singula et sua et aliena, hoc
autum universum, in quo nos quoque sumus, expers
consilii aut ferri [1] temeritate quadam aut natura
nesciente quid faciat.

16. Quanti aestimas ista cognoscere et rebus
terminos ponere, quantum deus possit; materiam
ipse sibi formet an data utatur; utrum utro
sit prius, materiae supervenerit ratio an materia
rationi; deus quicquid vult efficiat an in [2] multis
rebus illum tractanda destituant et a magno artifice
prave multa formentur, non quia cessat ars, sed quia
id in quo exercetur saepe inobsequens arti est?
17. Haec inspicere, haec discere, his incubare, nonne
transilire est mortalitatem suam et in meliorem
transcribi sortem? " Quid tibi," inquis, " ista

[1] *aut ferri* EZ Oltramare; *auferri* HPABV Alexander.
[2] *in* supplied by Gercke.

better part is the mind, in god there is no part other than the mind. He is entirely reason. None the less, meanwhile, a great error possesses mortals: men believe that this universe, than which nothing is more beautiful or better ordered or more consistent in plan, is an accident, revolving by chance, and thus tossed about in lightning bolts,[1] clouds, storms, and all the other things by which the earth and its vicinity are kept in turmoil. 15. Nor does this nonsense exist among only the common people; it also infects those who say they have knowledge. There are some men who conclude that they themselves have a mind, indeed a provident one, evaluating situations, both their own and other peoples'; but the universe, in which we also exist, they presume is lacking in plan and either moves along in some haphazard way or else nature does not know what it is doing.

16. What value is it, do you suppose, to establish definitions, to learn about such things? For example, how powerful is god? Does he form matter for himself or does he merely make use of what is already there? Which comes first: does function determine matter, or does matter determine function? Does god do whatever he wishes? Or in many cases do the things he treats fail him, just as many things are poorly shaped by a great artist not because his art fails him but because the material in which he works often resists his art? 17. To investigate these questions, to learn about them, to brood over them—is this not to transcend your own mortality and to be admitted to a higher plane? You say: " What good

[1] In Bk. 2.12.1 ff. Seneca distinguishes between lightning flashes (*fulg-*) and lightning bolts (*fulm-*).

proderunt?" Si nil aliud, hoc certe: sciam omnia
angusta esse mensus deum.

1 1. Nunc, ut ad propositum opus veniam, audi quid
de ignibus sentiam quos aer transversos agit. Magna
illos vi excuti argumentum est quod obliqui feruntur
et praerapida celeritate; apparet illos non ire, sed
proici.

2 Ignium multae variaeque facies sunt. Aristoteles
quoddam genus horum capram vocat. Si me inter-
rogaveris quare, prior mihi rationem reddas oportet
quare haedi vocentur. Si autem, quod commodis-
simum est, convenerit inter nos ne alter alterum
interroget quod scit illum respondere non posse,
satius erit de re ipsa quaerere quam mirari quid ita
Aristoteles globum ignis appellaverit capram. Talis
enim fuit forma eius qui bellum adversus Persen

3 Paulo gerente lunari magnitudine apparuit. Vidimus
nos quoque non semel flammam ingentis pilae specie,
quae tamen in ipso cursu suo dissipata est. Vidimus
circa divi Augusti excessum simile prodigium.
Vidimus eo tempore quo de Seiano actum est, nec
Germanici mors sine denuntiatione tali fuit.

---

[1] Aristotle *Meteor*. 1.4.341b 3–4. Pliny (*NH* 2.90) says it is
a comet ringed in a kind of cloud of hair. Henceforth refer-

will these things do you?" If nothing else, certainly this: having measured god I will know that all else is petty.

1. Now to get to my proposed work. Hear what I think about those fires which the atmosphere drives across the sky. They move obliquely at very high speeds, which is proof that they have been driven by a great force. It is obvious that they do not move on their own accord but are hurled.

The fires have many different shapes. Aristotle calls one kind a Goat.[1] If you ask me why, you should first explain to me the reason some are called Kids. However, it is best for us to agree that one will not ask the other such questions, which he knows the other cannot answer. It will be more appropriate to investigate the phenomenon itself rather than to wonder why Aristotle has called a ball of fire a Goat. Actually, that was the shape of a fire which did appear, about the size of the moon, when Paulus was waging war against Perseus.[2] Also, we have more than once seen a flaming light in the shape of a huge ball which was then dissipated in mid-flight. We saw a similar prodigy about the time of the death of the deified Augustus. We saw another at the time when Sejanus was condemned. And the death of Germanicus[3] was announced by the same sort of sign.

---

ences to Aristotle will be to his *Meteorologica* and to Pliny will be to Pliny the Elder, unless otherwise stated.

[2] At the Battle of Pydna, 168 B.C.

[3] Emperor Augustus died in A.D. 14; Seianus was condemned by Emperor Tiberius in A.D. 31; Germanicus Caesar, son of Drusus who was brother of Tiberius, died in A.D. 19. He was famous for his German campaigns.

4   Dices mihi: " Ergo tu in tantis erroribus es ut
existimes deos mortium signa praemittere et quicquam in terris esse tam magnum quod perire mundus
sciat ? " Erit aliud istius rei tempus. Videbimus
an rerum omnium certus ordo ducatur et alia aliis
ita implexa sint ut quod antecedit aut causa sit
sequentium aut signum. Videbimus an diis humana
curae sint; an series ipsa, quid factura sit, certis
rerum notis nuntiet.

5   Interim illud existimo eiusmodi ignes existere
aere vehementius trito, cum inclinatio eius in alteram
partem facta est et non cessit,[1] sed inter se pugnavit;
ex hac vexatione nascuntur trabes et globi et faces et
ardores. At cum levius collisus et, ut ita dicam,
frictus est, minora lumina excutiuntur,

crinemque volantia sidera ducunt.

6   Tunc ignes tenuissimi iter exile designant et caelo
producunt. Ideo nulla sine eiusmodi spectaculis nox
est; non enim opus est ad efficienda ista magno
aeris motu. Denique, ut breviter dicam, eadem
ratione fiunt ista qua fulmina, sed vi minore: quemadmodum nubes collisae mediocriter fulgurationes

---

[1] Gercke adds *aer* before *non cessit.*

---

[1] Seneca does so below in his discussion of lightning, Bk.
2.32–51.
[2] Pliny 2.96: *trabes quas* δοκοὺς *vocant,* meteors.
[3] In Pliny (2.90) these are comets and meteors (2.96).
Aristotle 1.4.34lb 4: δαλοί, "burnt-out torches."
[4] Virgil *Aen.* 5.528.

You will say to me: " Are you then so greatly **4**
ignorant that you believe that the gods send in advance announcements of death and that anything
on earth is so important that the universe is aware it
is perishing? " Later on there will be an occasion for
me to answer that.[1] We will see whether a fixed
succession is supposed for all events and whether
some phenomena are so involved in others that what
has happened before is a cause or an indication of
what follows. We will see whether human affairs
are any concern to the gods; whether the sequence
of events foretells by definite concrete signs what it
is going to do.

For the time being, I guess this: fires of this sort **5**
come into existence because the atmosphere undergoes severe friction when there has been a tilting
of it to one side and there is no yielding, only
internal struggle. From this vexation are produced
fiery shapes, the so-called Boards,[2] Balls, Torches,[3]
and Blazes. When the air is more lightly shocked
and has less friction, so to speak, smaller streams of
light are discharged:

> And the flying stars
> Trail their tresses.[4]

Then the extenuated fires make a slender path and **6**
draw it out in the sky. So, no night is without
spectacles of this kind; for to produce them there is
no need of great atmospheric movement. Finally—
let me say it briefly—they are produced by the same
cause as lightning bolts are, but by less force. In
the same way as clouds, colliding moderately, produce flashes, but driven together with great force

efficient,[1] maiore impetu impulsae fulmina, sic quanto illas minus presseris [2] minoresve, tanto leviora lumina [3] emittent.[4]

7　　Aristoteles rationem eiusmodi reddit. Varia et multa terrarum orbis expirat, quaedam umida, quaedam sicca, quaedam calentia, quaedam concipiendis ignibus idonea. Nec mirum est si terrae omnis generis et varia evaporatio est, cum in caelo quoque non unus appareat color rerum, sed acrior sit Caniculae rubor, Martis [5] remissior, Iovis nullus in
8　lucem puram nitore perducto. Necesse est ergo, in magna copia corpusculorum quae terrae eiectant et in superiorem agunt partem, aliqua in nubes pervenire alimenta ignium, quae non tantum collisa possint ardere sed etiam afflata radiis solis; nam apud nos quoque ramenta [6] sulphure aspersa ignem
9　ex intervallo trahunt. Veri ergo simile est talem materiam inter nubes congregatam facile succendi et minores maioresve ignes existere, prout plus illis fuit aut minus virium.

Illud enim stultissimum, existimare aut decidere stellas, aut transilire, aut aliquid illis auferri et
10　abradi. Nam si hoc fuisset, etiam defuissent; nulla enim nox est qua non plurimae ire et in diversum videantur abduci. Atqui, quo solet, quaeque in-

---

[1] *efficiunt* HEABV.
[2] *minus pressit vis* Gercke.
[3] *lumina* Z Oltramare; *fulmina* most MSS.

produce lightning bolts, just so the less you compress clouds, or compress smaller clouds, the weaker the bolts they will emit.

Aristotle gives an explanation along these lines: 7 the terrestrial globe exhales many different particles, some wet, some dry, some hot, some suitable for starting fires.[1] It is not remarkable if the evaporation of the earth is of all different types and diverse, since in the sky, too, there appears not just a single colour of things. The red of the Dog Star[2] is brighter, that of Mars weaker, while Jupiter has no red, with its gleam extended into pure light. In the 8 great quantity of particles which the earth ejects and forces into the upper air it is necessary, therefore, that some nutriments of fire reach the clouds, which not only can burn in colliding but even when breathed on by rays of the sun. Even in our own experience, shavings sprinkled with sulphur attract fire from a distance. It is probable that such matter collected 9 among the clouds is easily kindled, and lesser or greater fires result insofar as there was more or less energy present.

Yet it is the stupidest thing to suppose that stars actually fall, or jump across, or that anything is taken or rubbed away from them. If this were so, the 10 stars would have perished. Yet every night very many seem to fall and to be carried off in different directions. Still, each star is found in its usual place

---

[1] Aristotle 1.4.341b 1.   [2] Sirius.

---

[4] *emittent* Z Oltramare; *emittunt* most MSS.
[5] *Veneris* Garrod.
[6] *ramenta* HG Oltramare; *stramenta* ABV; *sarmenta* Z.

venitur loco et [1] magnitudo sua singulis constat; sequitur ergo ut infra illas ista nascuntur et cito intercidant quia sine fundamento et sede certa sunt.

11 " Quare ergo non etiam interdiu transferuntur? " Quid, si dicas [2] stellas interdiu non esse, quia non apparent? Quemadmodum illae latent et solis fulgore obumbrantur, sic faces quoque transcurrunt et interdiu, sed abscondit illas diurni luminis claritas. Si quando tamen tanta vis emicuit ut etiam adversus diem vindicare sibi fulgorem suum possint, apparent.

12 Nostra certe aetas non semel vidit diurnas faces, alias ab oriente in occidentem versas, alias ab occasu in ortum.

Argumentum tempestatis nautae putant, cum multae transvolant stellae. Quod si ventorum signum est, ibi est unde venti sunt, id est in aere, qui

13 medius inter lunam terrasque est. In magna tempestate apparere quasi stellae solent velo insidentes; adiuvari se tunc periclitantes aestimant Pollucis et Castoris numine. Causa autem melioris spei est quod iam apparet frangi tempestatem et desinere ventos; alioquin ferrentur ignes, non sederent.

---

[1] *et* supplied by Gercke, Oltramare.
[2] *dicam* ABV.

and its size remains constant. It follows, therefore, that the fires are produced below the stars and quickly collapse because they are without support and without fixed position.

"Why, then, do they not also flash across the sky 11 in the daytime?" Well, would you say that in the daytime stars do not exist, because they are not apparent? Just as stars are concealed and obscured by the brightness of the sun, so the Torches also race by even in the daytime, but the glare of the daylight hides them. If, however, a great energy ever lights up with flashes so powerful that they are able to display their brightness even against the daylight—which sometimes happens—their fiery shapes are visible. Certainly our own age has more than once 12 seen Torches in the daytime, some being swept from east to west, others from west to east.

Sailors think it is a sign of storm when many stars fly across the sky. But if they are a sign of winds they belong in the region where winds come from, that is, in the atmosphere, which is right between the moon and earth.[1] In a great storm, so-called 13 stars[2] usually appear to settle on the sails. Sailors in danger then believe they are being helped by the divinity of Pollux and Castor. But there is reason for a more realistic hope, because it is obvious that the force of storm is being broken and the winds are dying down, otherwise the fires would be swept along and would not be settling.

---

[1] Pliny (2.102) discusses the terms *caelum* ("heaven," "sky"); and *aer* ("atmosphere," "air") as referring to a region below the moon, far below it.

[2] This is now called St. Elmo's fire,

14 Gylippo Syracusas petenti visa est stella super ipsam lanceam constitisse. In Romanorum castris ardere visa sunt pila, ignibus scilicet in illa delapsis. Qui saepe fulminum modo ferire solent et animalia [1] et arbusta; sed si minore vi utuntur,[2] defluunt tantum et insidunt, non feriunt nec vulnerant. Alii autem inter nubes eliduntur; alii sereno, si aer ad

15 exprimendos ignes aptus fuit. Nam sereno quoque aliquando caelo tonat ex eadem causa qua nubilo, aere inter se colliso, qui, etiamsi est lucidior ac siccior, coire tamen et facere corpora quaedam similia nubibus potest, quae percussa reddant sonum. Quando ergo fiunt trabes? Quando clipei et vastorum imagines ignium? Ubi in talem materiam similis incidit causa, sed maior.

1 2. Videamus nunc quemadmodum fiat is fulgor qui sidera circumvenit. Memoriae proditum est, quo die Urbem divus Augustus Apollonia reversus intravit, circa solem visum coloris varii circulum, qualis esse in arcu solet. Hunc Graeci halo vocant, nos dicere coronam aptissime possumus. Quae quemadmodum fieri dicatur, exponam.

---

[1] *et animalia* omitted in most of the MSS.
[2] *mittuntur* A²BV.

As Gylippus [1] was sailing to Syracuse a star seemed 14
to him to have settled on the very point of his javelin.
In Roman camps spears have apparently been
burning, obviously because the fires have fallen on
them. [2] Like lightning bolts they often strike
animals and trees, but if they employ comparatively
little force they merely flow down and settle.   They
do not cause damage or wounds.   Moreover, some are
thrust out between clouds, others from a serene sky if
the atmosphere has been ready to discharge them.
In the same way, it thunders sometimes in a clear 15
sky for the same reason that it thunders in a cloudy
sky, because the air collides internally.   Even if the
air is fairly clear and dry none the less it can con-
centrate and make a sort of substance similar to
the clouds, which produce sound when struck.
When do Boards occur, or Shields, [3] or the shapes of
vast fires? When the same cause, only more
powerful, acts on matter of this sort.

2. Now let us see what causes that bright light 1
which surrounds stars.   It is recorded in history that
the day the deified Augustus entered Rome on his
return from Apollonia [4] a circle of varied colours was
seen around the sun, colours that usually appear in a
rainbow.   The Greeks call it a " halo."   We can call
it, very appropriately, a " corona."   I will expound
how it is said to be formed.

[1] Gylippus was the Spartan commander hired by Syracuse
when it was being besieged by Athens in 414 B.C.
[2] Livy (22.1.8) and Pliny (2.101) describe this phenomenon.
[3] Like the one seen in 100 B.C. (Pliny 2.100).
[4] In 44 B.C.; when Octavius (later Emperor Augustus),
who was being educated at Apollonia in Illyria, heard of the
murder of Julius Caesar, he came to Rome where he was recognized as Caesar's heir Octavianus.

2   Cum in piscinam lapis missus est, videmus in
multos orbes aquam discedere et fieri primum angus-
tissimum orbem, deinde laxiorem ac deinde alios
maiores, donec evanescat impetus et in planitiem
immotarum aquarum solvatur. Tale quiddam cogitemus fieri etiam in aere. Cum spissior factus est,
sentire plagam potest; lux solis aut lunae vel cuiusli-
bet sideris incurrens recedere illum in circulos cogit.
Nam umor et aer et omne quod ex ictu formam
accipit in talem habitum impellitur qualis est eius
quod impellit; omne autem lumen rotundum est;
ergo et aer in hunc modum lumine percussus exibit.
3   Ob hoc tales splendores Graeci areas vocaverunt quia
fere terendis frugibus destinata loca rotunda sunt.
Non est autem quod existimemus istas, sive areae
sive coronae sunt, in vicinia siderum fieri. Plurimum
enim ab his absunt, quamvis cingere ea et coronare
videantur; non longe a terra fit talis effigies, quam
visus noster solita imbecillitate deceptus circa ipsum
4   sidus putat positam. In vicinia autem stellarum et
solis nihil tale fieri potest, quia illic tenuis aether est.
Nam formae crassis demum spississque corporibus
imprimi solent; in subtilibus non habent ubi con-
sistant aut haereant. In balneis quoque circa
lucernam tale quiddam aspici solet ob aeris densi
obscuritatem; frequentissime autem austro, cum
caelum maxime grave et spissum est.[1]

[1] Haase transfers *frequentissime ... spissum est* to Paragraph
6 below.

---

[1] Here Seneca uses the Latin word *area*.

When a stone is thrown into a fishpond we see the 2 water spread out in many circles, the first circle very narrow, then a wider one, then others still wider, until the impetus fades and is absorbed in a level of smooth water. Let us suppose something like this occurs also in the atmosphere. When air is compressed it can react to a blow; the light of the sun or of the moon, or of any star, encountering it forces it to recede in circles. Moisture and air, and in fact anything which is shaped by a blow, is forced into the same shape as that which shaped it. Now, all light is round. Therefore, air also struck by light will go into this round formation. For this reason the 3 Greeks called such shining lights "threshing-floors"[1] because generally the places set aside for threshing grain are round. Whether we call them " threshing-floors " or " coronas," we must not imagine that these lights actually occur in the vicinity of the stars. They are far away from the stars, even though they seem to encircle them like crowns. An image of this sort is formed close to the earth. Our vision is misled by its usual weakness and thinks that the ring of light is actually placed around a star. In the vicinity of the 4 stars and of the sun nothing of this sort can possibly happen because only tenuous ether exists there. For shapes are usually impressed only on dense and thick matter. On very tenuous matter forms do not have a substance where they can impose or maintain a shape. In steam-baths a halo of this sort is frequently seen around a lamp, because of the obscurity of the dense air. The same phenomenon occurs very often with the south wind, when the atmosphere is especially heavy and thick.

5 Nonnumquam paulatim diluuntur et desinunt. Nonnumquam ab aliqua parte rumpuntur et inde ventum nautici expectant unde contextus coronae perit: si a septemtrione discessit, aquilo erit; si ab occidente, favonius. Quod argumentum est intra eam partem caeli has fieri coronas intra quam venti quoque esse solent; superiora non habent coronas, quia ne ventos quidem.

6 His argumentis et illud adice numquam coronam colligi nisi stabili aere et pigro vento;[1] aliter non solet aspici. Nam qui stat aer impelli et diduci et in aliquam faciem fingi potest. Is autem qui fluit ne feritur quidem lumine; non enim resistit nec forma-

7 tur, quia prima quaeque pars eius dissipatur. Numquam ergo ullum[2] sidus talem sibi effigiem circumdabit, nisi cum aer erit densus atque immotus et ob hoc custodiens incidentem in se rotundi lineam luminis. Nec sine causa. Repete enim exemplum quod paulo ante proposui. Lapillus in piscinam aut lacum et alligatam aquam missus circulos facit innumerabiles; at hoc idem non faciet in flumine. Quare? Quia omnem figuram fugiens aqua disturbat. Idem ergo in aere evenit, ut ille qui manet possit figurari, at ille qui rapitur et currit non det sui potestatem et omnem ictum venientemque formam ex eo turbet.[3]

8 Hae de quibus dixi coronae, cum dilapsae sunt

---

[1] *vento frequentissime autem ... spissum est* Haase.
[2] Alexander would retain *illud* of both the Φ and Δ MSS. families instead of *ullum* Erasmus, Oltramare.

Sometimes halos gradually dissolve and fade away. 5
Sometimes they break on one side. Sailors expect a
wind from the direction where the circle of the halo
broke. If it has parted on the north side, there will
be a north wind; if on the west, a west wind. This
is proof that these halos occur in that portion of the
sky where winds also usually exist. The upper atmosphere has no halos because it has no winds.

To such arguments add this also: a halo is never 6
formed unless the air is stable and the wind inactive.
Otherwise a halo is not usually seen. Air which is not
moving can be driven, drawn out, and fashioned into
any shape. But moving air is not affected even by
light. It offers no resistance and takes no shape
because it is scattered layer by layer. Therefore, 7
no star will ever exhibit such an image around it
except when the atmosphere is dense and motionless,
and for that reason preserves the configuration of the
round light falling on it. Nor is this an unreasonable
theory. Remember the analogy I proposed a little
while ago. A pebble thrown into a fishpond, or a
lake, in short any still body of water, makes innumerable little circles; but it will not produce the
same effect in a flowing stream. Why? Because
swiftly moving water scatters every configuration.
The same thing happens in the atmosphere. Stationary air can be shaped, but air that is carried along at
high speed does not yield; it scatters every blow and
shape-bringing impression that comes from it.

When these halos, which I have described, have 8

---

[3] *exturbet* AV; *exturbat* B.

aequaliter et in semet ipsae evanuerunt, significatur
quies aeris et otium et tranquillitas; cum ad unam
partem cesserunt, illinc ventus est unde finduntur;
9 si ruptae pluribus locis sunt, tempestas fit. Quare id
accidat, ex his quae iam exposui intellegi potest.
Nam si facies universa subsedit, apparet temperatum
esse aera, et sic placidum. Si ab una parte intercisa
est, apparet inde aera incumbere, et ideo illa regio
ventum dabit. At cum undique lacerata et concerpta
est, manifestum est a pluribus partibus in illam
impetum fieri et inquietum aera hinc atque illinc
assilire; itaque ex hac inconstantia caeli tam multa
temptantis et undique laborantis apparet futura
tempestas ventorum plurium.
10 Hae coronae noctibus fere circa lunam et alias
stellas notantur; interdiu raro, adeo ut quidam ex
Graecis negaverint omnino eas fieri, cum illos historiae coarguant. Causa autem raritatis haec est
quod solis fortius lumen est et aer ipse agitatus ab
illo calefactusque solutior. Lunae inertior vis est
ideoque facilius a circumposito aere sustinetur.
11 Aeque cetera sidera infirma sunt nec perrumpere
aera vi sua possunt; excipitur itaque illorum imago

---

[1] Aristotle **3.3.372b** 16–35: a full description of how the
breaking of halos indicates coming weather.

dissolved uniformly and have faded symmetrically it
is a sign of quiet, calm, and motionless air.[1] When
they give way on one side, there is a wind on the side
where they are split. If they are broken in several
places, a storm is rising. Why this happens can be 9
understood from the explanation I have already
given. For, if the halo fades all round, it is obvious
that the atmosphere is even and therefore calm. If
the halo is cut away on one side, it is obvious that the
air is pressing in from that direction; and accordingly
that region will produce a wind. But one torn apart
and split on all sides indicates that force is being
exerted on it from all sides and that the atmospheric
disturbance is assailing it from one direction or
another. And so, from this agitation of air, with
repeated assaults and struggles in all directions, it is
clear that there will be a storm with several winds
participating.

Such halos will be seen generally at night around 10
the moon and other heavenly bodies; but rarely in
the daytime. Consequently, some Greeks argue that
they do not occur at all during the day.[2] However,
records prove that they are wrong. The reason for
their rarity in daylight is this: because the light from
the sun is too strong, and the atmosphere, agitated
and heated by the sun, is moving too freely. The
force of the moon's rays is weaker and so more easily
resisted by the surrounding atmosphere. The other 11
heavenly bodies are just as weak and unable by their

---

[2] It is impossible to know who these Greek authorities are.
Certainly Aristotle is not one of them: he says (3.2.371b 25)
that halos occur as frequently in the day as in the night. Halos
were recorded in 121 (an arc), 114, and 90 B.C.

et in materia solidiore ac minus cedente servatur.[1]
Debet enim aer nec tam spissus esse ut excludat ac
summoveat a se lumen immissum, nec tam tenuis aut
solutus ut nullam venientibus radiis moram praebeat.
Haec noctibus temperatura contingit, cum sidera
circumiectum aera luce leni non pugnaciter nec
aspere feriunt spissioremque quam solet esse interdiu
inficiunt.

1   3. At contra arcus nocte non fit aut admodum[2]
raro, quia luna non habet tantum virium ut nubes
transeat et illis colorem suffundat, qualem accipiunt
sole perstrictae.   Sic enim formam arcus discoloris
efficiunt.[3]   Quia aliae partes in nubibus tumidiores
sunt, aliae summissiores, quaedam crassiores quam
ut solem transmittant, aliae imbecilliores quam ut
excludant, haec inaequalitas alternis lucem um-
bramque permiscet et exprimit illam mirabilem arcus
varietatem.[4]

2   Altera causa arcus eiusmodi redditur.   Videmus,
cum fistula aliquo loco rupta est, aquam per tenue
foramen elidi, quae sparsa contra solem oblique
positum faciem arcus repraesentat.[5]   Idem videbis
accidere, si quando volueris observare fullonem; cum

[1] *versatur* ABVT.
[2] *nisi admodum* ABV.
[3] *accipiunt* V.
[4] *repraesentationem* ABV.
[5] *altera . . . repraesentat* omitted in ABV.

own force to penetrate the atmosphere. Their shape therefore is absorbed and retained in rather solid and somewhat unyielding material. Air should not be so dense that it excludes or rejects the light striking it, nor yet so tenuous or spread out that it furnishes no obstacle to the incoming rays. The proper condition occurs at night when with a gentle light the heavenly bodies tranquilly and smoothly strike and tinge a surrounding atmosphere which is thicker than it usually is in the daytime.

3. On the other hand, a rainbow does not occur at night, or very rarely,[1] because the moon does not have enough strength to penetrate clouds and suffuse them with colour, such as they receive when touched by the sun's rays. For thus do clouds produce the shape and varied colours of a rainbow.[2] In clouds some parts are swollen, others are hollow, some too thick to transmit the sun's rays, others too feeble to exclude them. This inequality mixes light and shadow alternately and produces the remarkable " multicolour " of a rainbow.

Another explanation of a rainbow is along these lines: when a pipe bursts somewhere we see that the water which is forced out through a tiny hole and sprinkled against the rays of the slanting sun presents the appearance of a rainbow. Watch a fuller, if you like, and you will see the same thing happen

---

[1] Aristotle 3.2.372a 21–29: a rainbow occurs at night due to the moon, but rarely—only once in over fifty years. He describes a moon rainbow (3.4.375a 16–20). Pliny insists (2.150) that rainbows do not appear at night regardless of what Aristotle says. But Aristotle was right.

[2] Or the meaning may be: "This in fact is the way in which people explain the multicoloured rainbow."

os aqua implevit et vestimenta tendiculis diducta
leviter aspergit, apparet varios edi colores in illo
3 aere asperso, quales [1] fulgere in arcu solent. Huius
rei causam in umore esse ne dubitaveris; non fit
enim umquam arcus nisi nubilo.

Sed quaeramus quemadmodum fiat. Quidam
aiunt esse aliqua stillicidia quae solem transmittant,
quaedam magis coacta quam ut transluceant; itaque
ab illis fulgorem reddi, ab his umbram, et sic utriusque intercursu effici arcum in quo pars fulgeat, quae
solem recipit, pars obscurior sit, quae exclusit et ex
se umbram proximis fecit.

4 Hoc ita esse quidam negant. Poterat enim verum
videri, si arcus duos tantum haberet colores, si ex
lumine umbraque constaret. Nunc [2]

diversi niteant cum mille colores,
Transitus ipse tamen spectantia lumina fallit:
Usque adeo quod tangit idem est, tamen
ultima distant.

Videmus in eo aliquid flammei, aliquid lutei, aliquid
caerulei et alia in picturae modum subtilibus lineis
ducta. Ut ait poeta, an dissimiles colores sint, scire
non possis, nisi cum primis extrema contuleris. Nam

[1] *quasi* V.
[2] Gercke places *ut ait poeta* here and removes it from a few
lines below where he adds *ut* before *an dissimiles colores sint.*

sometimes. When he fills his mouth with water and gently sprays it on clothes spread out on stretchers it appears as though the various colours which usually shine in a rainbow are produced in that sprayed air. Undoubtedly the reason for this is in the moisture.[1] 3 For a rainbow never occurs unless there are clouds.

But let us investigate how a rainbow is formed. A number of authorities say that there are some little drops which transmit sunlight and other little drops which are too condensed to be translucent. Brightness is therefore caused by the first group, shadow by the second. A rainbow is caused thus by the intermingling of the two. The part which admits sunlight is bright. The part is dark which shuts out sunlight and casts a shadow over things nearest to it.

Other authorities maintain this is not so. It could 4 seem reasonable if the rainbow had only two colours; that is, if it consisted of light and dark. But as things are:

> Although a thousand different colours gleam,
> Their mere transition escapes the watching eye.
> So alike are adjacent colours.
> Yet far-parted colours are distinct.[2]

In a rainbow we see some red, some yellow, some blue, and other colours, as in a painting, drawn in thin bands. As the poet says, you cannot discern whether the colours are dissimilar until you compare the last with the first. The point of transition is

---

[1] Aristotle 3.4.274b 1-6: a rainbow is produced when someone sprinkles a fine spray in the sunshine, which creates a reflection of the sun in drops of water.

[2] Ovid *Met.* 6.65-67.

commissura decipit, usque eo mira arte naturae:
quod a simillimo coepit, in dissimillimo desinit. Quid
ergo istic duo colores faciunt lucis atque umbrae, cum
innumerabilium ratio reddenda sit?

5 Quidam ita existimant arcum fieri: in ea parte in
qua iam pluit singula stillicidia pluviae cadentis
singula esse specula, a singulis ergo reddi imaginem
solis; deinde multas imagines, immo innumerabiles,
et devexas et in praeceps euntes confundi; itaque
arcum esse multarum solis imaginum confusionem.

6 Hoc sic colligunt. Pelves, inquiunt, mille sereno die
pone, omnes habebunt imagines solis; in singulis
foliis dispone guttas, singulae habebunt imaginem
solis.[1] At contra ingens stagnum non amplius habebit quam [2] unam imaginem. Quare? Quia omnis
circumscripta levitas et circumdata suis finibus
speculum est. Itaque piscinam ingentis magnitudinis insertis [3] parietibus divide, totidem illa habebit
imagines solis quot lacus habuerit; relinque illam sic
ut est diffusa, semel tibi imaginem reddet. Nihil
refert quam exiguus sit umor aut lacus; si determina-
tus est, speculum est. Ergo stillicidia illa infinita quae
imber cadens defert, totidem specula sunt,[4] totidem
solis facies habent. Hae [5] contra intuenti [6] pertur-
batae apparent, nec dispiciuntur intervalla quibus

---

[1] *deinde multas* (above, paragraph 5) ... *imaginem solis*
omitted in HE. [2] *nisi* ABV.
[3] *in plures* ABV (instead of *insertis*).
[4] *totidem specula sunt* omitted in ABV.
[5] *hae* Fortunatus, Oltramare; *haec* HEZB[1]V.
[6] *vi venti* AB[1]; *videnti* B[2].

deceptive, as a result of the marvellous art of nature which starts with the similar and ends with the dissimilar. Therefore, what do the two colours of light and dark do in this case, when an explanation must be given for innumerable colours?

Other authorities theorize that a rainbow is 5 formed as follows: in the region of the sky where it is already raining each little drop of falling rain is an individual mirror; in each mirror, therefore, is reflected an image of the sun. Finally, many, even countless, images both sinking and falling rapidly are mingled together. In this way, they say, a rainbow is a fusion of many images of the sun. They 6 amass the following analogies. Set out a thousand basins of water, they say, on a clear day. All will reflect the sun's image. Put drops of water on separate tree-leaves. Every drop will show a reflection of the sun. However, a large pond will not show more than one image. Why? Because every smooth surface that is circumscribed and surrounded by its own boundaries functions as a mirror. So, divide a large fishpond by installing partitions. It will have the same number of images of the sun as it has compartments. Leave it just as it was, with its surface extended. It will reflect only one image for you. It does not matter how scanty the area of moisture or the body of water is. If it has boundaries, it is a mirror. Accordingly, the countless drops which falling rain carries are so many mirrors, having so many reflections of the sun. To the observer, these reflections appear fused together. The intervals which separate one from the other are not distinguishable since distance prevents close scrutiny. Then,

singulae distant, spatio prohibente discerni; deinde[1]
pro singulis apparet una facies turbida ex omnibus.

7   Aristoteles idem iudicat.[2] Ab omni, inquit,
levitate acies radios suos replicat; nihil autem est
levius aqua et aere; ergo etiam ab aere spisso visus
noster in nos redit. Ubi vero acies hebes et infirma
est, qualislibet aeris ictu deficiet. Quidam itaque
hoc genere valetudinis laborant ut ipsi sibi videantur
occurrere, ut ubique imaginem suam cernant.
Quare? Quia infirma vis oculorum non potest
perrumpere ne sibi quidem proximum aera, sed
8 resilit.[3] Itaque, quod in aliis efficit densus aer, in his
facit omnis; satis enim valet qualiscumque ad imbecillam aciem repellendam. Longe autem magis
visum nobis nostrum remittit aqua,[4] quia crassior
est et pervinci non potest, sed radios luminum nostrorum moratur et eo unde exierunt reflectit.

    Ergo, cum multa stillicidia[5] sint, totidem specula
sunt; sed, quia parva sunt, solis colorem sine figura
exprimunt. Deinde, cum in stillicidiis innumerabili-
bus et sine intervallo cadentibus reddatur idem
color, incipit facies esse non multarum imaginum et
intermissarum, sed unius longae atque continuae.

9   " Quomodo," inquis, " tu mihi multa milia imaginum istic esse dicis ubi ego nullam video? Et quare,
cum solis color unus sit, imaginum diversus est? "

---

[1] *unde* Gercke.
[2] *iudicat* AZ Oltramare instead of *indicat* most MSS.
[3] Gercke, Oltramare; *resistit* MSS.

36

instead of individual drops there appears a single blurred reflection from all the drops.

Aristotle thinks the same way.[1] He says that the 7 eyesight reflects its own rays from every smooth surface. Of course, nothing is smoother than water and air. Thus, even from dense air our gaze is reflected back to us. In fact, when vision is weak and dull it will fail at the slightest stab of air. Some people suffer therefore from this kind of infirmity—they see their own reflection everywhere and seem to be running into themselves. Why? Because their weak vision is not able to penetrate even the air nearest them, but rebounds. Thus, what dense air 8 causes in most cases, all air causes in their case. Any sufficient air at all is able to repel their weak vision. Water reflects our gaze much more because it is dense and cannot be penetrated. Our visual rays are stopped and sent back to where they came from.

Therefore, when there are numerous raindrops they act as so many mirrors, but because they are small they reflect only the sun's colour, not its shape. Eventually, when the same colour is reflected in the innumerable drops that fall without interval, the reflection begins to be not that of many separate images but of a single, long, continuous image.

"How," you ask, "do you assert that there are 9 many thousands of images there where I see none? And, although there is one colour in the sun, why are there many colours in its reflections?" To refute

---

[1] Aristotle 3.4.373b 1–35.

---

[4] Haase, Oltramare; *itaque* MSS.
[5] *multa in pluvia stillicidia* Z.

Ut et haec quae proposuisti refellam et alia quae non minus refellenda sunt, illud dicam oportet, nihil esse acie nostra fallacius non tantum in his a quibus subtiliter pervidendis illam locorum [1] diversitas submovet, sed etiam in his quoque quae ad manum cernit. Remus tenui aqua tegitur et fracti speciem reddit; poma per vitrum aspicientibus multo maiora sunt; columnarum intervalla porticus longior iungit.

10 Ad ipsum solem revertere. Hunc, quem toto terrarum orbe maiorem probat ratio, acies nostra sic contraxit ut sapientes viri pedalem esse contenderent, quem velocissimum omnium scimus, nemo nostrum moveri videt, nec ire crederemus, nisi appareret isse. Mundum ipsum praecipiti velocitate labentem et ortus occasusque intra momentum temporis revolventem nemo nostrum sentit procedere. Quid ergo miraris, so oculi nostri imbrium [2] stillicidia non separant et ex ingenti spatio intuentibus minutarum imaginum discrimen interit?

[1] Gronovius, Oltramare for *colorum* MSS.
[2] *innumerabilia* ABV.

---

[1] Seneca here gives examples of three kinds of optical illusion, one caused by refraction, one by magnification, one by perspective.

these objections you have stated, and other object-
tions which no less demand refutation, I need only say
that nothing is more deceiving than our eyesight, not
only in the case of objects which distance prevents
the eyesight from accurately examining, but also in
the case of objects which the eye perceives close at
hand. An oar is covered with shallow water and
gives the appearance of being broken. Fruits are
much larger when seen through glass. A colonnade,
as it grows longer, merges its columns together without spaces between.[1]

Go back to the sun itself. Although reason proves 10
it is larger than the globe of the earth, our sight has
so contracted it that philosophers have contended that
it is the size of a foot.[2] We know it is the swiftest of
heavenly bodies, but no one of us sees it move. In
fact, we would not believe it moved at all except that
it obviously has changed position.[3] Not one of us
perceives that the universe itself moves, gliding along
at headlong speed, unrolling its risings and settings
within a moment of time. Why are you surprised if
our eyes do not separate the raindrops of a shower,
and if from a great distance an observer fails to dis-
tinguish distances between minute images?

[2] Cicero *De Fin.* 1.30: " Epicurus considers [the sun] perhaps a foot in diameter, for he pronounces it to be exactly as
large as it appears, or a little larger or smaller." Since for the
Epicureans all knowledge is based on what the senses perceive,
they had to maintain that the sun was only as large as it appeared to the senses; for to admit that it was much bigger
would require admitting some source of knowledge other than
sense perception.

[3] Below, Bk. 7.2.3, Seneca mentions a theory that the earth
is moving and we are rising and setting.

11 Illud dubium esse nulli potest quin arcus imago
solis sit roscida et cava nube concepta. Quod ex
hoc tibi appareat: numquam non adversa soli est;
sublimis aut humilis, prout ille se submisit aut
sustulit in contrarium mota, illo enim descendente
altior est, alto depressior. Saepe talis nubes a
latere solis est nec arcum efficit, quia non ex recto
12 imaginem trahit. Varietas autem non ob aliam
causam fit quam quia pars coloris a sole est, pars a
nube illa;[1] umor modo caeruleas lineas, modo virides,
modo purpurae similes et luteas aut igneas ducit,
duobus coloribus hanc varietatem efficientibus,
remisso et intento. Sic enim et purpura eodem
conchylio non in unum modum exit; interest quamdiu
macerata sit, crassius medicamentum an aquatius
traxerit, saepius mersa sit et excocta an semel
13 tincta. Non est ergo mirum si, cum duae res sint,
sol et nubes, id est corpus et speculum, tam multa
genera colorum exprimuntur quam multis generi-
bus possunt ista[2] incitari aut relanguescere; alius
est enim color ex igneo lumine, alius ex obtunso et
leniore.
14 In aliis rebus vaga inquisitio est, ubi non habemus
quod manu tenere possimus et late coniectura
mittenda est; hic apparet duas causas esse arcus,
solem nubemque, quia nec sereno umquam fit, nec

[1] Oltramare adopts Gercke's suggestion of *a sole est, pars a
nube* along with Fortunatus' elimination of *in* before *illa*.
Alexander believes *sole est sparsa, pars nube*; *in illa* is the
original reading.
[2] *ita* JO.

No one can doubt that a rainbow is a reflection of 11
the sun formed in a moist, hollow cloud. This should
be obvious to you from the following: the reflection
is always opposite the sun, moving inversely high or
low just as the sun has sunk or moved upwards.
When the sun is sinking, the rainbow is higher, when
the rainbow is lower, the sun is moving up. Often a
cloud of that type is alongside the sun but does not
produce a rainbow because it does not receive the
image straight on. The multicolour occurs for no 12
other reason than that a part of the colour comes from
the sun, a part from that particular cloud. The
moisture produces now blue bands, now green, now
purple-like, and yellow or fiery red, with the two
colours, dark and bright, creating the variety. For,
purple cloth also dyed from the same shellfish does
not come out the same way. It makes a difference
how long it has been soaked, whether it has assimi-
lated a thick colouring matter or a watery one,
whether it has been dipped and boiled several times or
dyed only once. Since there are two things, the sun 13
and the clouds, that is, the object and the mirror, it is
not surprising, then, that as many kinds of colour are
revealed as can be intensified or greyed in numerous
ways. For one colour comes from a fiery light,
another from a duller and softer light.

In other matters concerning a rainbow research is 14
vague, where we have nothing we can get our hands
on and mere conjectures must be applied extensively.
But here it is obvious that there are two causes of a
rainbow, sun and cloud, because a rainbow never
occurs in a clear sky, nor in a sky so cloudy that it hides
the sun. Therefore, it is certain a rainbow depends

nubilo ita ut sol lateat; ergo utique ex his est
quorum sine altero non est.

1   4. Iam nunc illud accedit quod aeque manifestum
est speculi ratione imaginem reddi, quia numquam
nisi e contrario redditur, id est nisi ex altera parte
stetit quod appareret, ex altera quod ostenderet.[1]
Rationes, quae non persuadent sed cogunt, a geo-
metris afferuntur nec dubium cuiquam relinquitur
quin arcus imago solis sit male expressi ob vitium
figuramque speculi. Nos interim temptemus alias
probationes quae de plano legi possint.

2   Inter argumenta sic nascentis arcus pono quod
celerrime nascitur. Ingens enim variumque corpus
intra momentum subtexitur caelo et aeque celeriter
aboletur. Nihil autem tam cito redditur quam a
speculo imago; non enim facit quicquam sed ostendit.

3   Parianus Artemidorus adicit etiam quale genus
nubis esse debeat quod talem soli imaginem reddit.
Si speculum, inquit, concavum feceris, quod sit

----

[1] Gercke, Oltramare for *ostendere* HPGZABV.

----

[1] Seneca did not know that the rainbow is a dioptric not
a catoptric effect; and so he confuses colour and image. Cf
Aristotle 3.2.372a 17: all atmospheric lights are phenomena
of reflection, different only in the manner of reflection and in
the reflecting surface.
[2] Both Aristotle (3.4.373b 1) and Pliny (2.150) place the
rainbow opposite the sun.
[3] *de plano legi* means "be read on level ground," and not

on both of them and does not exist without both of them.

4. Now take this proof, which is just as obvious: 1 the image is reflected in the manner of a mirror,[1] because it is never reflected except from a position directly opposite;[2] that is, unless on one side there is the object reflected, on the other the mirror reflecting it. The proofs offered by mathematicians are not only persuasive but convincing, and no one is left with any doubt that a rainbow is an image of the sun, imperfectly reflected because of the flawed shape of the mirror. Meanwhile, let us try other proofs, the sort that can be picked up in the open.[3]

Among such proofs about the development thus of 2 a rainbow I propose the fact that it comes into existence very quickly. In less than an instant the huge, multicoloured form is woven in the sky, and just as quickly fades away. Moreover, nothing is rendered so suddenly as an image from a mirror, for a mirror does not create anything, it only reflects it.[4]

Artemidorus of Parium[5] even describes of what 3 type the cloud ought to be which sends such a reflection back to the sun. If you construct a concave mirror, he says, which is like a ball cut in half, and if

read as if posted up on a judicial platform or heard spoken there.

[4] With reference to our convenient English words "reflect" and "reflection," note that classical Latin does use the verb *reflectere* and the noun *reflexio*, but rarely in connection with mirrors or light; and that it does not use a noun *reflectio* at all.

[5] In Bk. 7.13–14 Seneca attacks Artemidorus as a philosopher whose "whole account of the universe is a shameless lie." This Artemidorus is otherwise unknown.

sectae pilae pars, si extra medium constiteris, quicumque iuxta te steterint inversi tibi videbuntur et
4 propiores a te quam a speculo. Idem, inquit, evenit,
cum rotundam et cavam nubem intuemur a latere, ut
solis imago a nube discedat propiorque nobis sit et
in nos magis conversa. Color illi igneus a sole est,
caeruleus a nube, ceteri utriusque mixturae.

1   5. Contra haec illa dicuntur. De speculis duae
opiniones sunt. Alii enim in illis simulacra cerni
putant, id est corporum nostrorum figuras a nostris
corporibus emissas ac separatas; alii non imagines in
speculo sed ipsa aspici corpora retorta oculorum acie
et in se rursus reflexa. Nunc nihil ad rem pertinet
2 quomodo videamus quodcumque videmus; sed
quoquomodo, imago similis [1] reddi debet e speculo.
Quid autem est tam dissimile quam sol et arcus, in
quo neque figura solis neque color neque magnitudo
apparet? Arcus longe amplior est longeque ea
parte qua fulget rubicundior quam sol, ceteris vero
coloribus diversus.

3   Deinde, cum velis speculum inesse aeri, des oportet mihi eandem levitatem corporis, eandem aequalitatem, eundem nitorem. Atqui nullae nubes habent
similitudinem speculi; per medias saepe transimus
nec in illis nos cernimus; qui montium summa con-

---

[1] *sed, quae modo est imago, similis* Oltramare. Alexander
argues convincingly for Schultess' *quoquomodo* written as one
word with a comma after it, making *imago* the subject of *reddi
debet.*

you stand outside its centre, those who stand next to you will seem upside down to you and closer to you than to the mirror. The same thing happens, he says, **4** when we look at a round hollow cloud from the side.[1] The image of the sun separates from the cloud and is closer to us and turned more towards us. Its fiery red colour comes from the sun, its blue from the cloud; the other colours are mixtures of these two.

5. Arguments are stated against these theories. **1** There are two opinions about mirrors. Some think that replicas are seen in mirrors; that is, that the shape of our body has emanated and separated from our body. Others believe that there are no images inside the mirror but that the body itself is seen because eyesight is bent back and reflected on itself again. Well, it does not matter how we see whatever we see. In any case an image similar to the object **2** must be reflected from the mirror. Yet what is so much unlike as the sun and the rainbow, in which neither the shape of the sun, nor its colour, nor its size appears? A rainbow is far larger and, in the part which gleams, much redder than the sun, and different in its other colours, too.

Next, when you state the theory that air serves as **3** a mirror you ought to show me the same smoothness of surface, the same levelness, the same brightness. Yet no clouds have this resemblance to a mirror. Often we pass right through them and do not see ourselves in them. People who climb to the top of a

---

[1] Pliny 2.150: the reflection of the sun from a hollow cloud. Aristotle 3.4.373b 20–25: the sun is mirrored in the cloud but it is the image of the colour not of the shape.

scendunt, despectant nubem nec tamen imaginem
in illa suam aspiciunt.

4 "Singula stillicidia singula specula sunt." Concedo, sed illud nego ex stillicidiis constare nubem.
Habent enim quaedam ex quibus fieri stillicidia
possint, non ipsa. Ne aquam quidem habet nubes
5 sed materiam futurae aquae. Concedamus [1] tibi et
guttas innumerabiles nubibus inesse et illas faciem
reddere, non tamen unam omnes reddunt, sed
singulae singulas. Deinde inter se specula coniunge,
in unam imaginem non coibunt, sed unumquodque [2]
in se similitudinem visae rei claudet. Sunt quaedam
specula ex multis minutisque composita, quibus si
unum ostenderis hominem, populus apparet, una-
quaque particula [3] faciem suam exprimente. Haec,
cum sint coniuncta et simul collocata, nihilominus
seducunt imagines suas et ex uno quidem turbam
efficiunt, ceterum catervam illam non confundunt,[4]
sed diremptam in facies singulas distrahunt. Arcus
autem uno circumscriptus est ductu, una totius est
facies.

6 "Quid ergo?" inquit. "Non et aqua rupta
fistula sparsa et remo excussa habere quiddam simile
his quos videmus in arcu coloribus solet?" Verum
est, sed non ex hac causa ex qua tu videri vis, quia
unaquaeque stilla recipiat imaginem solis. Citius
enim cadunt stillae quam ut concipere imagines

---

[1] *concedam* ABV.   [2] Leo, Oltramare for
unaquaeque HZG; *quaeque particula* ABV.
[3] *parte* ABV.   [4] *contrahunt* V.

mountain look down on a cloud and yet they do not see their own reflection in it.

" Individual drops of water are separate mirrors." 4 I grant that, but I deny that a cloud consists of drops of water. Clouds contain certain elements from which drops can be formed, but they do not contain the drops themselves. A cloud does not even have water but only the material of water to be. Yes, 5 let me grant you that there really are innumerable drops of water in the clouds and that they reflect an object. None the less, all together will not reflect an assembled image. Individual drops give individual reflections. Then, join mirrors together, and they will not unite into a single image but each and every mirror will enclose within itself a likeness of the visible object. Some mirrors are a composite of many tiny mirrors. If you place one man in front of them a whole population appears, and each little part expresses an image of its own. These mirrors, even though joined and set close together, none the less isolate images of their own and make from one man a crowd. Moreover, they do not blend that crowd together but separate and divide it into individual images. On the other hand, a rainbow is confined by only one boundary; it is a single reflection of the whole.

He asks: " What about this? Does not water 6 sprinkled from a burst pipe, or shaken off by an oar, usually have a kind of resemblance to those colours we see in a rainbow? " That is true, but not for the reason you want it to seem: namely, that each drop of water receives a reflection of the sun. Actually, the drops fall too rapidly to be able to form an

possint. Standum est, ut id quod imitantur exci-
piant. Quid ergo fit? Colorem, non imaginem
ducunt. Alioquin, ut ait Nero Caesar disertissime,

Colla Cytheriacae splendent agitata columbae

et variis coloribus pavonum cervix, quotiens aliquo
deflectitur, nitet. Numquid ergo dicemus specula
eiusmodi plumas, quarum omnis inclinatio in colores
novos transit?

7   Non minus nubes diversam naturam speculis
habent quam aves quas rettuli, et chamaeleontes, et
reliqua animalia quorum color aut ex ipsis mutatur,
cum ira vel cupidine incensa cutem suam variant
umore suffuso, aut positione lucis, quam prout rectam

8   vel obliquam receperunt, ita colorantur. Quid enim
simile speculis habent nubes, cum illa non perluceant,
hae transmittant[1] lucem; illa densa et coacta, hae
rarae sint; illa eiusdem materiae tota, hae e diversis
temere compositae et ob hoc discordes nec diu
cohaesurae? Praeterea videmus ortu solis partem
quandam caeli rubere,[2] videmus nubes aliquando

----

[1] *transmutant* KL.
[2] *videmus . . . rubere* omitted in ABV.

----

[1] Opinions vary concerning Nero's ability as a poet. According to Tacitus (*Ann.* 13.3; 14.6) the verses written in his
youth showed a kind of elementary accomplishment but the
poems composed in collaboration with his friends, as a game,
had no inspiration and lacked unity. Nero wrote a poem on
the Trojan War (perhaps the one he performed while Rome
was burning) and planned an epic on Roman history in 400 books
(Dio 62.29). Suetonius (*Nero* 52) claims to possess some of
Nero's well-known verses written in his own hand, even with

image of the sun. They need to be motionless in order to receive what they imitate. What does happen? They depict the colour, not the image. Besides, as Nero Caesar says so elegantly:

> The neck of the dove of Venus
> Glistens in movement.[1]

And the neck of the peacock gleams with many colours whenever it moves one way or another. Are we going to say that feathers of this kind are mirrors, whose every tilting movement changes into new colours?

Clouds have a nature no less different from a 7 mirror than the birds I mentioned, and chameleons, and other animals whose colour changes; either those which alter from within themselves their colour by an infusion of moisture when they are aroused by anger or rut, or those which take on a hue from the position of the light, in so far as they receive it directly or obliquely. Actually, what resemblance do clouds 8 have to mirrors? While mirrors are not even translucent, clouds transmit light; mirrors are dense and solidified, clouds are rarefied; mirrors are entirely of the same material, clouds are made up accidentally from different elements and for that reason are unstable and not likely to stick together long. Furthermore, at sunrise we see certain parts of the sky turn red, and sometimes we see fiery red clouds. In the

deletions and changes. They prove to Suetonius' satisfaction that Nero was not guilty, as rumoured, of publishing other poets' work as his own. The rumour may have been associated with the widely known fact that many of Nero's speeches in the early part of his reign were written by Seneca.

ignei coloris; quid ergo prohibet, quomodo hunc unum colorem accipiunt solis occursu, sic multos ab illis trahi, quamvis non habeant speculi potentiam?

9 " Modo," inquit,[1] " inter argumenta ponebas semper arcum contra solem excitari, quia ne a speculo quidem imago redderetur nisi adverso. Hoc," inquit, " commune nobis est; nam, quemadmodum opponendum est speculo id cuius in se imaginem transferat, sic, ut nubes infici possint, ita sol ad hoc apte ponendus est. Non enim idem facit, undecumque effulsit, et ad hoc opus est radiorum idoneus ictus."

10 Haec dicuntur ab his qui videri volunt nubem colorari. Posidonius et hi qui speculari ratione talem effici iudicant visum hoc respondent: " Si ullus esset in arcu color, permaneret et viseretur eo manifestius quo propius; nunc imago arcus, ex longinquo clara, interit, cum ex vicino ventum est."

11 Huic contradictioni non consentio, cum ipsam sententiam probem. Quare? Dicam: quia coloratur quidem nubes, sed ita ut color eius non undique appareat. Nam ne ipsa quidem undique apparet;

[1] *inquis* E.

---

[1] Posidonius (c. 135–51 B.C.) spent most of his life at Rhodes where he became head of a Stoic school. He was a historian, geographer, ethnographer, astronomer, naturalist, and philosopher who exercised great influence on Roman writers in the

same way that they receive this one colour from their contact with the passing sun, what prevents them from deriving many colours from the sun even though they do not have the properties of a mirror?

" Among the arguments above," he says, " you 9 propose that a rainbow is always produced opposite the sun because an object is not reflected even by a mirror unless it is directly in front of the mirror. This is a theory we have in common," he says, " for just as the object whose image the mirror transfers to itself must be placed opposite the mirror, in the same way the sun must be placed suitably for this effect in order that the clouds can be tinted. For the light does not produce the same effect irrespectively of the direction whence it has shone forth. The angle of the rays as they strike must be appropriate for this."

Such opinions are expressed by those who insist 10 that a cloud merely seems to be coloured. Posidonius [1] and others who conclude that such a phenomenon is produced in the manner of a mirror reply as follows: " If there were any colour in a rainbow it would persist and be seen more clearly the closer it is; whereas the image of the rainbow, distinct at a distance, fades away when you come close to it."

I do not agree with this refutation, even though 11 I do approve of its principle. Why? I will tell you: the cloud is actually coloured but in such a way that the colour is not apparent from all sides. Actually, a cloud itself is not visible from all sides; for no one

first centuries before and after Christ. He visited Rome in 86 B.C. Varro studied under him, Cicero visited him at Rhodes, and Marius and Pompey were among his friends. All his writings have been lost.

nubem enim nemo qui in ipsa est videt. Quid ergo
mirum, si color eius non videtur ab eo a quo ipsa non
visitur? Atqui ipsa, quamvis non videatur, est; ergo
et color. Ita non est argumentum falsi coloris quod
apparere accedentibus desinit. Idem enim in ipsis
evenit nubibus, nec ideo falsae sunt quia non videntur.

12 Praeterea, cum dicitur tibi nubem sole suffectam,
non dicitur tibi colorem illum inustum esse velut duro
corpori et stabili ac manenti, sed ut fluido et vago et
nihil amplius quam brevem speciem recipienti.
Sunt etiam quidam colores qui ex intervallo vim
suam ostendunt: purpuram Tyriam, quo melior est
saturiorque, eo altius oportet teneas ut fulgorem
suum ostendat.[1] Non tamen ideo non habet colorem
illa, quia, quae[2] optimum habet, non quomodocumque
explicatur ostendit.

13 In eadem sententia sum qua Posidonius ut arcum
iudicem fieri nube formata in modum concavi speculi
et rotundi, cui forma sit partis e pila secta. Hoc
probari, nisi geometrae adiuverint, non potest, qui
argumentis nihil dubii relinquentibus docent solis
illam esse effigiem non similem.

---

[1] *ostendat* ABV; *teneat* most MSS., Gercke, Oltramare;
emittat Z; *intendat* Garrod, Alexander.   [2] *quem* Alexander.

---

[1] Oltramare places all of paragraph 12 inside quotation
marks and makes it a continuation of the quotation in para-

who is inside a cloud can see it. Why is it surprising, then, if the cloud's colour is not visible to someone to whom the cloud itself is not visible? And yet, although the cloud is not visible it is there; and so therefore is its colour. Thus, it is no proof that the colour is counterfeit because it ceases to be apparent as you get close to it. For the same thing happens in the case of clouds themselves, and yet they are not unreal simply because they are not discernible. Besides,[1] when you are told that a cloud is tinted by the sun you are not being told that the colour is branded, as it were, into a hard, stable, and enduring body but into a fluid, unstable body which receives nothing more than a brief impression. There are also certain dyes which show their qualities at a distance: for example, Tyrian purple. The better and richer saturated a cloth is, the higher you ought to hold it up so that it may reveal its brilliance. Simply because a cloth which has the best colour does not show it when unfolded in any chance way does not mean that thus it does not have the colour.

I am of the same opinion as Posidonius in that a rainbow presumably is formed from a cloud fashioned like a concave, round mirror, the shape of which is that of a half-section cut out of a ball.[2] This cannot be proved without the help of geometers, who demonstrate with arguments leaving no doubt that the rainbow is a rough representation of the sun, not an exact resemblance.

graph 10 from Posidonius and others. It makes better sense as a part of Seneca's argument.

[2] Above, in Chapter Four, Seneca attributes this theory to Artemidorus.

Neque enim omnia ad verum [1] specula respondent.
14 Sunt quae videre extimescas, tantam deformitatem corrupta facie visentium reddunt, servata similitudine in peius; sunt quae cum videris placere tibi vires tuae possint, in tantum lacerti crescunt et totius corporis super humanam magnitudinem habitus augetur; sunt quae dextras facies ostendant; sunt quae sinistras; sunt quae detorqueant et vertant. Quid ergo mirum est eiusmodi speculum in nube quoque fieri quo solis species vitiosa reddatur?

1 6. Inter cetera argumenta et hoc erit quod numquam maior arcus dimidio circulo apparet et quod eo minor est quo altior sol . . .[2]

2 "Quare tamen, si imago solis est arcus, longe ipso sole maior apparet?" Quia est alcuius speculi natura talis ut maiora multo quae vidit ostendat et in portentuosam magnitudinem augeat formas, alicuius invicem talis ut minuat.

3 Illud mihi dic quare in orbem eat facies, nisi orbi redditur? Dices enim fortasse unde sit illi color varius; unde talis figura sit, non dices, nisi aliquod

---

[1] *adversus* HPE[1]ABV.
[2] Oltramare transfers the following *ut ait Vergilius . . . promittit* to the end of Chapter 8.

Even mirrors do not reproduce everything with fidelity. There are some mirrors you are afraid to 14 look into: they reflect such a deformity from the distorted image of the viewer; the likeness is preserved—but made to look worse than it is. There are other mirrors which can make you pleased with your strength when you look into them. Your arms grow so much larger and the appearance of your whole physique is increased to more than human proportions. Some mirrors show the right side of the face, others the left. Others twist and invert the face. Why is it surprising that a mirror of this sort also occurs in a cloud and reflects a defective image of the sun?

6. Among other arguments there will also be this: 1 a rainbow never appears larger than a half circle; also, the smaller it is, the higher the sun . . .[1]

" But if the rainbow is a reflection of the sun, why 2 does it appear far larger than the sun itself? " Because it is the characteristic of a certain type of mirror to show the objects it sees much larger, and it enlarges shapes to monstrous proportions. On the other hand, it is a characteristic of another type of mirror to reduce objects.

Tell me this: Why is the image circular if it is not 3 reflecting a circle? For perhaps you will tell me from what source it gets its varied colours; you will

[1] Something is missing here or out of place. Seneca discusses theories about the rainbow's half circle below, Chapter 8.1–5. Perhaps in this chapter he dealt with the inverse relationship between the rainbow and the sun (mentioned above, Chapter 3.11; cf. Pliny 2.150) and the section has been lost. The manuscripts jump at this point to the quotation from Virgil which can be found at the end of Chapter 8.

exemplar ad quod formetur ostenderis. Nullum
autem quam solis est, a quo cum tu quoque fatearis
illi colorem dari, sequitur ut et detur forma. Denique
inter me teque convenit colores illos quibus caeli
regio depingitur a sole esse; illud unum inter nos
non convenit: tu dicis illum colorem esse, ego videri.
Qui sive est, sive videtur, a sole est. Tu non expedies
quare color ille subito desinat, cum omnes fulgores
4 paulatim discutiantur.[1] Pro me est et repentina
eius facies et repentinus interitus. Proprium enim
hoc speculi est, in quo non per partes struitur quod
apparet, sed statim totum fit. Aeque cito omnis
imago aboletur in illo quam ponitur; nihil enim
aliud ad ista efficienda vel removenda opus est quam
ostendi et abduci. Non est ergo propria in ista nube
substantia, nec corpus est sed mendacium, sine re
similitudo. Vis scire hoc ita esse? Desinet arcus,
si obtexeris solem. Oppone, inquam, soli alteram
nubem, huius varietas interibit.

5 "At maior aliquanto est arcus quam sol!" Dixi
modo fieri specula quae multiplicent omne corpus
quod imitantur. Illud adiciam omnia per aquam
videntibus longe esse maiora. Litterae quamvis

---

[1] *paulatim appareant et paulatim discutiantur* Gercke.

56

not tell me from what source it gets its particular shape unless you point out some model on which a rainbow may be formed.   But there is no model other than the sun   When *you* also admit that colour is given to a rainbow by the sun it follows that its shape also is given to it by the sun.   In short, you and I agree that these colours, with which the region of the sky is painted, are from the sun.   There is one point we do not agree on: *you* say the colour is real, *I* say it is only apparent.   Whether it actually exists or only seems to exist, it comes from the sun.   You will not explain why this colour disappears suddenly while all other atmospheric lights are dispersed gradually.   Both the rainbow's sudden appearance and its 4 sudden demise are on my side of the argument.   For this is the peculiarity of a mirror: a reflection is not built up in sections but is immediately formed in its entirety.   Every image in a mirror is abolished with as great a speed as it is formed.   For to produce or to remove such an image nothing is needed other than that the object be displayed or withdrawn. Accordingly, there is not an actual substance in that reflecting cloud; there is not a corporeality but only an apparition, a similarity without reality.   Do you want to be quite certain that this is so?   The rainbow will cease to exist if you hide the sun.   I say place another cloud in front of the sun; the multicolours of the rainbow will be gone.

" But the rainbow is considerably larger than the 5 sun! "   I have already said there are mirrors which increase every object they reflect.   I will add that everything is much larger when you look at it through water.   Letters, however tiny and obscure, are seen

minutae et obscurae per vitream pilam aqua plenam
maiores clarioresque cernuntur. Poma formosiora
quam sunt videntur, si innatant vitro. Sidera
ampliora per nubem aspicienti videntur, quia acies
nostra in umido labitur nec apprehendere quod vult
fideliter potest. Quod manifestum fiet, si poculum
impleveris aqua et in id conieceris anulum; nam,
cum in ipso fundo anulus iaceat, facies eius in summa
6 aqua redditur. Quicquid videtur per umorem longe
amplius vero est: quid mirum maiorem reddi imaginem solis, quae in nube umida visitur, cum ex duabus
causis hoc accidat? Quia in nube est aliquid
vitro simile quod potest perlucere; est aliquid et
aquae, quam, etiamsi nondum habet, iam parat,[1] id
est iam eius natura est in quam ex sua vertatur.

1   7. " Quoniam," inquit,[2] " vitri fecisti mentionem
ex hoc ipso argumentum contra te sumam. Virgula
solet fieri vitrea, striata [3] vel pluribus angulis in
modum clavae torosa.[4] Haec, si in transversum
solem accipit, colorem talem qualis in arcu videri
solet reddit, ut scias non imaginem hic solis esse,
sed coloris imitationem [5] ex repercussu."

2   Primum in hoc argumento multa pro me sunt:
quod apparet a sole fieri; quod apparet leve quiddam
esse debere et simile speculo quod solem repercutiat;

---

[1] *apparat* P; *apparet* ABV.   [2] *inquis* ET.
[3] Haase, Gercke, Oltramare to replace *stricta* MSS.
[4] *torsa* λG; *tortuosa* F²ABV; *et orosa* Z.

larger and clearer through a glass ball filled with water. Fruits seem more beautiful than they actually are if they are floating in a glass bowl. Stars appear larger when you see them through a cloud because our vision grows dim in the moisture and is unable to apprehend accurately what it wants to. This will be demonstrated if you fill a cup with water and throw a ring into it. For, although the ring lies on the bottom, its image is reflected on the surface of the water. Anything seen through moisture is 6 far larger than in reality. Why is it so remarkable that the image of the sun is reflected larger when it is seen in a moist cloud, especially since this results from two causes? In a cloud there is something like glass which is able to transmit light; there is also something like water. Even if the cloud does not yet have water it is already forming it; that is, there exists already the property of the water into which the cloud may be changed from its own property.

7. " Since you have mentioned glass," he says, 1 " I will take from glass itself an argument against you. A glass rod is commonly made which is striated, or protruding with many angles like a club. If it receives the sun's rays obliquely it sends back such colour as is usually seen in a rainbow. So you know there is not an image of the sun here but an imitation of its colour, from reflection."

First of all, there are many points on my side in this 2 argument. Obviously, a rainbow is caused by the sun. Obviously there must be something smooth and like a mirror which may reflect the sun. Finally,

---

⁵ *mutationem* HPZ; *immutationem* E.

deinde quod apparet non fieri ullum colorem sed speciem falsi coloris, qualem, ut dixi, columbarum cervix et sumit et ponit, utcumque deflectitur. Hoc autem et in speculo est, cui nullus inditur color, sed
3 simulatio quaedam coloris alieni. Unum hoc tantum mihi solvendum est quod non visitur in ista virgula solis imago. Cuius bene exprimendae[1] capax non est; ita conatur quidem reddere imaginem, quia levis est materia et ad hoc habilis, sed non potest, quia enormiter facta est. Si apta fabricata foret, totidem redderet soles quot habuisset in se toros qui[2] quia discernuntur inter se nec satis in vicem speculi nitent, incohant tantum imagines, nec exprimunt, et ob ipsam viciniam turbant et in speciem coloris unius abducunt.

1 8. At quare arcus non implet orbem, sed pars dimidia eius videtur, cum plurimum porrigitur incurvaturque? Quidam ita opinantur: "Sol, cum sit multo altior nubibus, a superiore illas tantum percutit parte; sequitur ut inferior pars earum non tingatur[3] lumine; ergo, cum ab una parte solem accipiant, unam eius partem imitantur, quae numquam dimidia maior est."

[1] *explicandae* AB.
[2] † *inspectores. Quae* Oltramare. Leo suggested *in se toros*, which gets strong support from Alexander.
[3] Gercke, Oltramare to replace *tangatur* MSS.

it is obvious that no actual colour is formed but only the appearance of a counterfeit colour, the sort that the neck of a pigeon alternately takes on or puts aside whenever it changes position, as I have already said. This also is the case in a mirror, which assumes no colour but only a kind of copy of the colour of something else. I must settle only one thing: the image 3 of the sun is not seen in that glass rod. The rod is incapable of reproducing the image accurately. In fact, it tries to reflect the image because the material is smooth and suitable for this, but it cannot because it is shaped irregularly. If a suitably formed glass rod were made, it would reflect as many suns as it has knobs. Because the knobs are units separated from each other and are not sufficiently shiny to serve as mirrors, they only start images; they do not portray them distinctly. Because of their proximity the images are jumbled together and reduced to the appearance of a single colour.

8. But why does a rainbow not form a complete 1 circle but appears as a half section of a circle even when it is extended and curved out to its greatest length? Some authorities have the following opinion:[1] " Since the sun is much higher than the clouds, it strikes them only on the upper side; it follows that their lower side is not coloured by the light. Therefore, since they receive the sun only on one part, they reproduce only one part of the sun, which is never more than half."

[1] The authorities Seneca refers to are unknown. Aristotle gives a lengthy explanation of why the rainbow can never be a complete circle (3.5.375b 16–377a 28; cf. 3.2.371b 18). Pliny (2.150) merely asserts that the rainbow is always a semicircle.

2 Hoc argumentum parum potens est. Quare? Quia, quamvis sol ex superiore parte sit, totam tamen percutit nubem; ergo et tingit. Quidni?[1] cum radios transmittere soleat et omnem densitatem perrumpere. Deinde contrariam rem proposito suo dicunt. Nam, si superior est sol et ideo superiori tantum parti nubium affunditur, numquam terra tenus descendet arcus; atqui usque in humum demit-

3 titur. Praterea numquam non contra solem arcus est. Nihil autem ad rem pertinet supra infrave sit, quia totum quod contra est latus verberatur. Deinde aliquando arcum et occidens facit. Tum certe ex inferiore parte nubes ferit terris propinquus; atqui et tunc dimidia pars est, quamvis solem nubes ex humili et sordido accipiant.

4 Nostri, qui sic in nube quomodo in speculo lumen[2] volunt reddi, nubem cavam faciunt et sectae pilae partem, quae non potest totum orbem reddere, quia ipsa pars orbis est. Proposito accedo, argumento non consentio. Nam, si in concavo speculo tota facies oppositi orbis exprimitur, et in semiorbe

5 nihil prohibet totam aspici pilam. Etiamnunc diximus circulos apparere soli lunaeque in similitudinem arcus circumdatos; quare ille circulus iungitur, in arcu numquam? Deinde quare semper concavae nubes solem accipiunt, non aliquando planae et tumentes?

---

[1] *quid nunc ergo contingat* B.   [2] *imaginem* Z.

This argument is not very strong. Why? Because, although the sun is on the upper side it none the less strikes the entire cloud and therefore also colours it. And why not? The sun ordinarily sends its rays through and penetrates any density in the clouds. Furthermore, they make a statement contrary to their own proposition. For if the sun is higher and thus pours its light on to the upper side only of the clouds, a rainbow would never descend as far as the earth. And yet it does come down as far as the ground. In addition, a rainbow never exists except opposite the sun. It does not matter whether the sun is higher or lower, because the whole side of the cloud is struck which is opposite the sun. Then, at times, a setting sun also makes a rainbow. Then, surely, when it is near the earth the sun strikes clouds on their lower side. But yet even then the rainbow is a half circle, albeit the clouds receive the sun's rays from a base and impure region.

Our Stoics, who insist that light is reflected in a cloud the same way as in a mirror, make the cloud hollow and a section of a ball cut in half which cannot reflect a complete circle because it itself is only part of a circle. I concede to the proposition but I do not agree with the argument. For, if the entire figure of a circle is reflected in front of a concave mirror, surely nothing prevents an entire ball from being seen in a semicircular mirror. I have already said that circles resembling a rainbow appear placed around the sun and the moon. Why is this circle joined, but never in a rainbow? Then, again, why do concave clouds always receive the sun, not sometimes flat or convex clouds?

6   Aristoteles ait post autumnale aequinoctium qualibet hora diei arcum fieri; aestate non fieri, nisi aut incipiente aut inclinato die. Cuius rei causa manifesta est. Primum, quia media diei parte sol calidissimus nubes evincit nec potest imaginem suam ab his recipere quas scindit. At matutino tempore aut vergens in occasum minus habet virium; ideo [1] 7 a nubibus sustineri et repercuti potest. Deinde, cum arcum facere non soleat nisi adversus his in quibus facit nubibus, cum breviores dies sunt, semper obliquus est; itaque qualibet diei parte, etiam cum altissimus est, habet aliquas nubes quas ex adverso ferire possit. At temporibus aestivis super nostrum verticem fertur; itaque medio die excelsissimus terras rectiore aspicit [2] linea quam ut ullis nubibus possit occurri; omnes enim sub se tunc habet.

8   Ut ait Vergilius noster,

               et bibit ingens arcus,

cum adventat imber. Sed non easdem, undecumque apparuit, minas affert. A meridie ortus magnam vim aquarum vehet; vinci enim non potuerunt valentissimo sole, tantum illis est virium. Si circa occasum refulsit, rorabit [3] et leviter impluet. Si ab ortu circave surrexit, serena promittit.

---

[1] *calidus est et ideo* AV (instead of *habet virium; ideo*).
[2] *accipit* H[1]PV.   [3] *tonabit* ABV.

Aristotle says that after the autumnal equinox a **6**
rainbow occurs at any hour of the day; in the summer
it does not occur except at the beginning or end of the
day.[1] The reason is clear. First, because at midday
the sun is very hot and overcomes the clouds. It is
impossible for the sun's image to be reflected by
clouds which the sun tears apart. But in the morning
or when it sinks to its setting the sun has less strength
and so can be resisted and reflected by the clouds.
Secondly, the sun does not usually produce a rainbow **7**
unless it is opposite the clouds in which it produces
one. When days are shorter the sun's rays are always
oblique; so, at any time of the day, even when the
sun is highest, it has some clouds which it can strike
straight on. But in summertime the sun passes
overhead. Thus, it is very high at midday and looks
down on the earth in too vertical a line to be able to
be met by any clouds. For the sun then has all the
clouds beneath it.

As our Virgil says: **8**

> And the mighty rainbow
> Drinks [2]

when rain is approaching. But it offers different
threats depending on where it appears. When it
rises in the south it will bring a great rainstorm; for
the rains cannot be dispersed by the strongest sun,
so great is their force. If it shines towards the west
there will be dew and a light shower. If the rainbow
rises in the east, or thereabouts, it promises clear
weather.[3]

[1] Aristotle 3.5.377a 11–28.   [2] *Georg.* 1.380.
[3] Pliny 2.150: rainbows do not reliably predict any kind of
weather, rain or fair.

1   9. Nunc de virgis dicendum est, quas non minus pictas variasque aeque pluviarum signa solemus accipere.[1] In quibus non multum operae consumendum est, quia virgae nihil aliud sunt quam imperfecti arcus. Nam facies illis est quidem picta sed nihil curvati habens; in rectum iacent.

2   Fiunt autem iuxta solem fere in nube umida et iam se spargente. Itaque idem est in illis qui in arcu color; tantum figura mutatur, quia nubium quoque in quibus extenduntur alia est.

1   10. Similis varietas in coronis est; sed hoc differunt quod coronae ubique fiunt ubicumque sidus est, arcus non nisi contra solem, virgae non nisi in vicinia solis. Possum et hoc modo differentiam omnium reddere: coronam si diviseris, arcus erit; si direxeris, virga. In omnibus color multiplex, ex caeruleo fulvoque varius. Virgae soli tantum adiacent; arcus solares lunaresque sunt; coronae omnium siderum.

1   11. Aliud quoque virgarum genus apparet, cum radii per angusta foramina nubium tenues et intenti distantesque inter se diriguntur. Et ipsi signa imbrium sunt.

2   Quomodo nunc me hoc loco geram? Quid vocem? Imagines solis?[2] Historici soles vocant et binos ternosque apparuisse memoriae tradunt. Graeci

---

[1] *aspicere* A.
[2] *imagines? soles?* Leo; *solesne an imagines solis* Garrod.

9. At this point mention should be made of Streaks, 1
which, no less varicoloured than a rainbow, we
commonly accept as equally a sign of rain. Not
much effort need be spent on them because Streaks
are merely imperfect rainbows. They have the
painted appearance of a rainbow but have no curve;
they lie in a straight line. Generally, they form near 2
the sun in a moist cloud that has already started to
dissolve. Consequently, there is in them the same
colour which is in a rainbow; only the shape is
changed because the clouds also in which they are
spread out have a different shape.

10. There is a similar multicolour in halos; but 1
they differ in that halos occur anywhere, wherever
there is a celestial body; whereas a rainbow occurs
only opposite the sun and Streaks only in the vicinity
of the sun. I can differentiate between all three of
them in this way: if you bisect a halo there will be a
rainbow; if you straighten it out, a Streak. In all
three there is a multiple colour varying from blue to
orange. Streaks lie only close to the sun. Rainbows
are solar or lunar. Halos belong to all celestial bodies.

11. Another kind of Streak also appears when 1
thin, extended rays that are separated from one
another are sent through narrow openings in the
clouds. They, too, are a sign of rain.

Now, how am I to express myself in this section? 2
What should I call these things? Images of the
sun? Historians call them " suns " and record that
they have appeared two and three at a time.[1] The

---

[1] For example, Livy 28.11 (two suns) and 41.21.12 (three
suns). Pliny (2.150) says no more than three suns have ever
been seen at one time.

parhelia appellant, quia in propinquo fere a sole visuntur aut quia accedunt ad aliquam similitudinem solis. Non enim totum imitantur, sed magnitudinem [1] eius figuramque; ceterum nihil habent ardoris hebetes et languidi. His quod nomen imponimus? An facio quod Vergilius, qui dubitavit de nomine, deinde id de quo dubitaverat posuit?

> Et quo te nomine [2] dicam,
> Rhaetica? Nec cellis ideo contende Falernis.

Nihil ergo prohibet illas parhelia vocari.

3 Sunt autem imagines solis in nube spissa et vicina in modum speculi. Quidam parhelion ita definiunt: nubes rotunda et splendida similisque soli. Sequitur enim illum nec umquam longius relinquitur quam fuit, cum apparuit. Num quis nostrum miratur, si solis effigiem in aliquo fonte aut placido lacu vidit? Non, ut puto. Atqui tam in sublimi facies eius quam inter nos potest reddi, si modo idonea est materia quae reddat.

1 12. Quotiens defectionem solis volumus deprehendere, ponimus pelves quas aut oleo aut pice implemus, quia pinguis umor minus facile turbatur et ideo quas recipit imagines servat; apparere autem imagines

---

[1] *imaginem* ET.   [2] Virgil has *carmine*.

---

[1] Aristotle (3.2.372a 11) gives a short description of parhelia and lists them with ῥάβδοι, " rods."
[2] *Georg.* 2.95–96. Seneca quotes incorrectly, as he often

68

Greeks call them " parhelia," [1] either because they are commonly seen near the sun, that is, alongside it, or because they are near to some resemblance to the sun. They do not resemble the sun entirely, only its size and shape. Moreover, dull and feeble, they have nothing of the sun's heat. What name to give them? Should I do what Virgil did when he hesitated over a term and then wrote down the term about which he was in doubt?

> And you,
> What name shall I call you,
> Rhaetian wine?
> Yet do not, on this account, try
> To compete with Falernian wines. [2]

So, nothing prevents them from being called parhelia.

In fact, images of the sun do exist in thick and 3 nearby clouds as they would in a mirror. Some authorities define a parhelion in this way: it is a round, bright cloud resembling the sun. It follows the sun and is never left farther behind than it was when it first appeared. Is anyone of us surprised if he sees an image of the sun in some fountain or placid lake? As I think, no. Yet the sun's image can be reflected on high just as it is on our earth if only the material is suitable for reflecting it.

12. Whenever we want to watch an eclipse of the 1 sun we set out basins which we fill with oil or pitch, because the heavy liquid is not easily disturbed and so preserves the images which it receives. Moreover,

does, and out of context, misrepresenting Virgil in order to illustrate a point.

non possunt nisi in liquido et immoto. Tunc solemus notare quemadmodum luna soli se opponat et illum tanto maiorem subiecto corpore abscondat, modo ex parte, si ita competit ut in latus eius incurreret, modo totum. Haec dicitur perfecta defectio, quae stellas quoque ostendit et intercipit lucem, tunc scilicet cum uterque orbis sub eodem libramento stetit.

2 Quemadmodum ergo utriusque imago in terris aspici potest, ita in aere, cum sic coactus aer et limpidus constitit ut faciem solis acciperet. Quam et aliae nubes accipiunt, sed transmittunt, si aut mobiles sunt aut rarae aut sordidae. Mobiles enim spargunt illam; rarae emittunt; sordidae turpesque non sentiunt, sicut apud nos imaginem maculosa non reddunt.

1 13. Solent et bina [1] fieri parhelia [2] eadem ratione. Quid enim impedit quominus tot sint quot nubes fuerint aptae ad exhibendam solis effigiem? Quidam in illa sententia sunt, quotiens duo simulacra talia existunt, ut iudicent in illis alteram solis imaginem esse, alteram imaginis. Nam apud nos quoque, cum plura specula disposita sunt ita ut alteri sit con-

---

[1] *in luna* ABV.   [2] *parhelia et plura* Z.

images cannot appear except in motionless liquid. Then we are accustomed to note how the moon places itself in front of the sun. By interposing its mass the moon hides the much larger sun, sometimes totally, sometimes only partially if it happens that the moon meets only one side of the sun. A so-called total eclipse also shuts out the daylight and reveals the stars. It occurs, of course, when the centre of both spheres have come to a balance with the earth's —all on the same straight line.[1]

So, just as the image of both the sun and the moon 2 can be seen reflected on earth, so also it can be seen reflected in the atmosphere, whenever air exists so compressed and clear that it receives an image of the sun. Other clouds, too, receive the image but they throw it off if they are moving or thin or full of impurities. Moving clouds disperse it; thin ones let it go. Clouds contaminated with impurities do not receive impressions, just as on earth soiled surfaces do not reflect an image.

13. Often also two parhelia are formed on the 1 same principle. But what prevents them from being as numerous as there are clouds suitable for showing an image of the sun? Some authorities are of this opinion: they judge that whenever two such copies exist one of them is an image of the sun, the other an image of an image. Even in our own experience, when several mirrors are so arranged that one has a

---

[1] Seneca gives, in *De Beneficiis* 5.6.4, a more detailed description of the eclipse of the sun, including the statement that a total eclipse occurs when the moon, the sun and the earth (the earth omitted in the Latin in the *Natural Questions* passage) are on a straight line.

spectus alterius, omnia implentur, et una imago a
vero est, ceterae imaginum effigies sunt. Nihil
enim refert quid sit quod speculo ostendatur; quicquid videt, reddit. Ita illic[1] quoque in sublimi, si
sic nubes fors aliqua disposuit ut inter se conspiciant,
altera nubes solis imaginem, altera imaginis reddit.

2 Debent autem hae nubes quae hoc praestant densae
esse, leves, splendidae, planae, et naturae solis
similes.[2] Ob hoc omnia eiusmodi simulacra candida
sunt et similia lunaribus circulis, quia ex percussu
oblique accepto sole respondent. Nam, si infra
solem nubes fuerit et propior, ab eo dissipatur.
Longe autem posita radios non remittet nec imaginem efficiet; sic[3] apud nos quoque specula, cum
procul a nobis abducta sunt, faciem non reddunt, quia
acies nostra non habet usque ad nos recursum.

3 Pluviarum autem et hi soles—utar enim historica
lingua—indicia sunt, utique si a parte austri constiterunt, unde maxime nubes ingravescunt. Cum
utrimque solem cinxit talis effigies, tempestas, si
Arato credimus, surgit.

1 14. Tempus est alios quoque ignes percurrere,
quorum diversae figurae sunt. Aliquando emicat

---

1 Haase, Gercke, Oltramare for *illis* HPZG; *illud* ABVT.
2 *et naturae solis similes* Leo; *vice functurae solis* Oltramare;
naturae solis simillimae Alexander; *planae* (*plene* FG) *naturae
solis* MSS.   3 Gercke, Oltramare for *quia* MSS.

view of another they are all filled with images, but one is a reflection of the original object, others are copies of the reflection. For it makes no difference what it is that is shown to a mirror; whatever the mirror sees, it reflects. So, there also in the sky, if some chance has so placed clouds that they are visible to one another, one cloud sends back the image of the sun, another an image of the image. The clouds **2** which show this phenomenon must be dense, smooth, bright, flat, and like the nature of the sun. For this reason all phenomena of this type are white and similar to moon-shaped discs, because they reflect bright light when they are struck obliquely by the sun. If the cloud is below the sun and too near it is dispersed by the sun. Yet placed far away it will not bounce back the sun's rays or reflect its image. So in our experience, mirrors also do not reflect our image when they are removed some distance from us because our vision does not have a way back all the way to us.

In addition, these " suns "—for I will use the **3** historians' term—are a sign of rain, especially if they have occurred in the southern region, where the heaviest rainclouds develop. When such an image surrounds the sun on both sides a storm is coming— if we believe Aratus.[1]

14. It is time to consider, briefly, other atmo- **1** spheric fires, of which there are various forms. At

---

[1] Aratus was born about 315 B.C. in Cilicia and spent part of his life at the court of Macedonia. He wrote a poem, *Phainomena*, dealing with astronomical and meteorological phenomena. Cicero's translation of it is thought to have influenced Lucretius. See *Phain.* 880 ff.

stella, aliquando ardores sunt, hi nonnumquam fixi et
haerentes, nonnumquam volubiles. Horum plura
genera conspiciuntur. Sunt bothyni,[1] cum velut
corona cingente introrsus ingens [2] caeli recessus est
similis effossae in orbem specu; sunt pithiae, cum
magnitudo [3] vasti rotundique ignis dolio similis vel
fertur vel uno loco flagrat; sunt chasmata, cum
aliquod spatium caeli desedit et flammam velut
dehiscens in abdito ostentat.

2 Colores quoque horum omnium plurimi sunt: quidam ruboris acerrimi, quidam evanidae ac levis
flammae, quidam candidae lucis, quidam micantes,
quidam aequaliter et sine eruptionibus aut radiis
fulvi. Videmus ergo

Stellarum [4] longos a tergo albescere tractus.

3 Hae velut stellae exiliunt et transvolant viden-
turque longum ignem porrigere propter immensam
celeritatem, cum acies nostra non discernat transitum
earum,[5] sed, quacumque cucurrerunt, id totum
igneum credat. Tanta est enim velocitas motus ut
partes eius non dispiciantur, summa prendatur;
intellegimus magis qua ierit [6] stella quam qua eat.

---

[1] Casaubon for *ut ei* HPZ; *putei* Gercke.
[2] Fortunatus for *ignes* PABV; *igneus* HFZT; *igne* J².
[3] *in magnitudine* ABV.
[4] Virgil has *flammarum*. Oltramare prints *Flammarum*
with the argument that *Stellarum* is a copyist's error not
Seneca's. See below, Bk. 7.20.1, where Seneca quotes the
same line with an error in word order.

times a star flashes, at times there are glowing
lights. These are sometimes stationary and sticking
to one spot, sometimes whirling past. Many kinds
of them are seen. There are *bothyni*:[1] within a surrounding corona there is a great gap in the sky like a
hole dug in a circle. There are *pithiai*:[2] an enormous
round mass of fire, like a barrel, either darts by or
blazes in one place. There are *chasmata*:[3] some
area of the sky settles and, gaping in hiding—so to
speak—sends out flame.

The colours of all these are also very numerous: 2
some are a very bright red, some a pale and light
flame, some a white light, some flickering, some
uniformly yellow and without outbursts or rays.
Therefore we see:

> Long trails of stars
> Glowing white behind.[4]

These so-called stars leap out and fly across and on 3
account of their great speed seem to trail a long flame.
Our sight does not discern their passing but believes
the entire path is on fire wherever they fly. The
speed of their transit is so great that its stages are
not observable. Only the movement as a whole is
grasped. We understand more where the star has

[1] Aristotle 1.5.342a 34–342b 24:βόθυνοι.
[2] Pliny 2.90: *pitheus doliorum cernitur figura.*
[3] Aristotle 1.4.342a 34:χάσματα.
[4] Virgil *Georg.* 1.367. The same line is given with a change
of word order in Bk. 7.20.1.

---

[5] Haase, Gercke, Oltramare for *eorum* MSS.
[6] Gercke, Oltramare for *perit* HPZF¹; *pereat* F²ABV.

4 Itaque velut igne continuo totum iter signat, quia visus nostri tarditas non subsequitur momenta currentis, sed videt simul et unde exiluerit et quo pervenerit. Quod fit in fulmine. Longus nobis videtur ignis eius, quia cito spatium suum[1] transilit et oculis nostris occurrit universum per quod deiectus est. At ille non est extenti corporis per omne qua venit; neque enim tam longa et extenuata in impetum valent.

5 Quomodo ergo prosiliunt? Attritu aeris ignis incensus vento praeceps impellitur. Non semper tamen vento attrituve fit; nonnumquam et aliqua opportunitate aeris nascitur. Multa enim sunt in sublimi sicca calida terrena, inter quae oritur et pabulum suum subsequens defluit ideoque velociter rapitur.

6 At quare color diversus est? Quia refert quale sit id quod incenditur, quantum et quam vehemens quo incenditur. Ventum autem significant eiusmodi lapsus, et quidem ab ea parte qua erumpunt.

1 15. " Fulgores," inquis, " quomodo fiunt quos Graeci σέλα appellant? " Multis, ut aiunt, modis. Potest illos ventorum vis edere; potest superioris caeli fervor, nam, cum late fusus sit ignis, inferiora aliquando, si sunt idonea accendi, corripit; potest

---

[1] *suum* Z Oltramare; *sursum* HPABV; *suum sursum* K.

gone than where it is. So, it marks the entire route 4
as though by a continuous flame because the slowness
of our vision does not follow the successive instants of
its flight but sees at the same instant where it started
and where it ended. The same thing happens in
lightning. Its fire seems continuous to us because it
quickly leaps along its route, and the space through
which it falls appears a unity to our eyes. But its
shape is not extended through the entire space it
crosses. Such long and thin bodies are too weak for
the effort.

How, then, do they get started? The fire is ignited 5
by the friction of the air and propelled violently by a
wind. Yet it is not always caused by wind or
friction. Sometimes the fire is generated by certain
favourable conditions in the atmosphere. For in the
sky there are many elements, dry, hot, earthy, among
which fire originates and flows down following after
its own type of fuel; consequently, it moves at great
speed.

But why does it have various colours? Because 6
it makes a difference what element it is that is set
ablaze and the quantity and force by which it is set on
fire. Falling lights of this sort indicate wind; and, in
fact, wind from the region where they started burning.[1]

15. You ask: "The lights which the Greeks call 1
sela—how are they produced?" In many ways,
they say. It is possible for the force of the winds
to produce them. The high temperature of the
upper atmosphere can cause them. For since fire is
extended far and wide there, it sometimes seizes
the lower regions if elements there are suitably

[1] Pliny (2.100) says that fierce winds come from that region.

stellarum motus cursu suo excitare ignem et in
subiecta transmittere. Quid porro? Non potest
fieri ut aer vim igneam usque in aethera elidat, ex
qua fulgor ardorve sit vel stellae similis excursus?

2   Ex his fulgoribus quaedam praeceps eunt similia
prosilientibus stellis, quaedam certo loco permanent
et tantum lucis emittunt ut fugent tenebras ac diem
repraesentent, donec consumpto alimento primum
obscuriora sint, deinde flammae modo quae in se
cadit per assiduam deminutionem redigantur ad
nihilum. Ex his quaedam in nubibus apparent,
quaedam supra nubes, cum aer spissus ignem quem
propior terris diu paverat usque in sidera expressit.

3 Horum aliqua non patiuntur moram sed transcurrunt
aut extinguuntur subinde quam reluxerant. Haec
fulgura [1] dicuntur, quia brevis illorum facies et
caduca est nec sine iniuria decidens; saepe enim
fulminum noxas ediderunt. Ab his tacta nos dicimus siderata, id est [2] icta sine fulmine, quae ἀστε-

4 ρόπληκτα Graeci vocant. At quibus longior mora est
et ignis fortior motumque caeli sequens aut etiam
proprios cursus agunt, cometas nostri putant, de
quibus dictum est. Horum genera sunt pogoniae et
cyparissiae [3] et lampades et alia omnia quorum ignis in

---

[1] Schultess, Oltramare for *fulgores* MSS.
[2] *siderata, id est* supplied by Oltramare; *fulgurata, id est*
Gercke.
[3] Fortunatus, Oltramare for *citharissiae* HPV; *cytharissiae*
Z; *cithare* AB.

---

[1] Pliny 2.91: some move like planets, others are stationary.

flammable. The motion of the stars in their flight can kindle fire and transmit it to the regions below. What more? Can it not happen that the air expels all the way to the upper atmosphere the essence of fire, from which there may be a flash, or a glow, or a rushing twinkle like a star?

Some of these flashes pass by abruptly like shooting 2 stars, others remain in a fixed position[1] and emit only enough light to dispel the darkness and give the illusion of daylight until, having consumed their fuel, they first become dimmer; then, in the manner of a fire which collapses upon itself, they steadily diminish and are reduced to nothingness. Some of them appear in the clouds, some above the clouds when the dense air has driven all the way to the stars the fire which it had maintained for a long time closer to the earth. Some of them do not last long. They dart 3 past or they are extinguished as soon as they glow. These are called Flashes, because their appearance is brief and dying. Yet their descent is not without harm, for often they accomplish the damage of lightning-bolts. We call objects hit by them " starstruck," that is, struck but not by an actual lightning bolt. The Greeks have the term *asteroplekta*. But 4 the ones which last a long time, and have a stronger flame, and follow the motion of the sky or even maintain their own course, our Stoics call comets (which have already been discussed).[2] Types of these are: Bearded,[3] Cypress Trees, and Lamps—as well

[2] It is the subject of Book Seven, which was published before Book One.
[3] Pliny 2.89: The Greeks call them *pogoniae* because the lower part spreads a mane like a long beard.

exitu sparsus est. Dubium an inter hos ponantur trabes et pithiae raro visi; multa enim conglobatione ignium indigent, cum ingens illorum orbis aliquantum matutini amplitudinem solis exuperet.

5 Inter haec licet ponas et quod frequenter in historiis legimus caelum ardere visum, cuius nonnumquam tam sublimis ardor est ut inter sidera ipsa videatur, nonnumquam tam humilis ut speciem longinqui [1] incendii praebeat. Sub Tiberio Caesare cohortes in auxilium Ostiensis coloniae cucurrerunt tamquam conflagrantis, cum caeli ardor fuisset per magnam partem noctis parum lucidus crassi fumi-

6 dique ignis. De his nemo dubitat quin habeant flammam quam ostendunt; certa illis substantia est. De prioribus quaeritur—de arcu dico et coronis— decipiant aciem et mendacio constent, an in illis quoque verum sit quod apparet.

7 Nobis non placet in arcu aut corona subesse aliquid corporis certi, sed illam iudicamus speculi [2] esse fallaciam alienum corpus nihil aliud quam mentientis. Non est enim in speculo quod ostenditur. Alioquin non exiret nec alia protinus imagine obduceretur, nec innumerabiles modo interirent modo exciperentur [3]

---

[1] *humilis* ABV.
[2] Gercke, Oltramare for *populis* HPZ; Alexander argues for *populis.*   [3] *eriperentur* HZG.

as all the others which have fire scattered behind them as they go out. It is doubtful whether Boards and the rarely seen Barrels should be placed in this category, for they require a great mass of fire. The immensity of their spheres at times surpasses the size of the morning sun.

Among these you may also include a phenomenon 5 which we read about frequently in history:[1] the sky seems to be on fire. Sometimes its glow is so high it appears to be actually among the stars. Sometimes it is so low that it gives the illusion of a fire some distance away. In the reign of Tiberius Caesar[2] watchmen rushed to the aid of the colony at Ostia just as though it were ablaze, since throughout most of the night there had been a glow in the sky, dull, as of a thick smoky fire. Concerning these pheno- 6 mena no one doubts that they have the flame which they show;[3] there is a definite substance to them. Concerning those I discussed earlier—I mean the rainbow and halos—there is a question whether they deceive our vision and consist of an illusion, or whether what appears in them also is real.

I am not satisfied with the theory that there exists 7 some definite substance in a rainbow or a corona, but I conclude that what occurs is in fact simply the deception of a mirror, which does nothing other than counterfeit an object that is outside itself. What is shown does not really exist in the mirror. Otherwise it would not pass out of it or be covered immediately by another image, and countless shapes would not

[1] For example, Livy 31.12.   [2] A.D. 14–37.
[3] Aristotle 1.7.344b 15–19: a proof that they are fiery is that they are a sign of coming wind and drought.

8 formae. Quid ergo? Simulacra ista sunt et inanis verorum corporum imitatio, quae ipsa a quibusdam ita compositis ut hoc possint detorquentur in pravum. Nam, ut dixi, sunt specula quae faciem prospicientium obliquent; sunt quae in infinitum augeant, ita ut humanum habitum modumque excedant nostrorum corporum.

1 16. Hoc loco volo tibi narrare fabellam, ut intellegas quam nullum instrumentum irritandae voluptatis libido contemnat et ingeniosa sit ad incitandum furorem suum.

Hostius [1] fuit Quadra,[2] obscenitatis in scaenam [3] usque productae. Hunc divitem avarum, sestertii milies servum, divus Augustus indignum vindicta iudicavit, cum a servis occisus esset, et tantum [4] non [5]

2 pronuntiavit iure caesum videri. Non erat ille ab uno tantummodo sexu impurus, sed tam virorum quam feminarum avidus fuit [6] fecitque specula huius notae cuius modo rettuli imagines longe maiores reddentia, in quibus digitus brachii mensuram et crassitudinem [7] excederet. Haec autem ita disponebat ut, cum

---

[1] *Hostis* PBV. [2] *quidam* ABV (instead of *Quadra*).
[3] *cenam* ELO. [4] *tamen* EλAVT. [5] *mox* E.
[6] Haase and Gercke would omit *fuit*. Alexander thinks it possibly represents an original *futuit*.
[7] *longitudinem* ABV.

now fade, now be reflected. What, then? These **8** are illusions and the unsubstantial imitations of real objects which themselves may be perversely distorted in mirrors constructed by someone in such a way that they can do this. For, as I have said, there are mirrors which distort the faces of those who look into them, and mirrors which enlarge them so enormously that they exceed the size of our bodies and even human appearance.

16. At this point I want to tell you a little story so **1** that you may understand how lust scorns no instrument for rousing passion and how ingenious it is for inciting its own aberration.

There was a man named Hostius Quadra, whose obscene acts even became the subject of a theatrical performance.[1] He was rich, greedy, a slave to his millions. The deified Augustus did not consider him worth being avenged when he was murdered by his slaves, and almost proclaimed that he seemed to have been murdered justly. He was vile in relation **2** not to one sex alone but lusted after men as well as women. He had mirrors made of the type I described (the ones that reflect images far larger) in which a finger exceeded the size and thickness of an arm. These, moreover, he so arranged that when he was

---

[1] A popular form of theatrical show at Rome was the mime, a licentious farce which was originally without dialogue, but acquired literary form in the first century B.C. and often dealt with obscene acts. The Roman audience tended to interpret lines even from old plays as having a reference to current events and scandals, and the actors deliberately stressed such lines (cf. Ovid, *Tristia* 2.497–516; Cicero, *Pro Sestio* 55.118–123; *ad Att.* 2.19; Suetonius *Tib.* 45). Seneca may here present a play on words *obsc(a)enitatis in sc(a)enam*.

virum ipse pateretur, aversus omnes admissarii sui
motus in speculo videret ac deinde falsa magnitudine
ipsius membri tamquam vera gaudebat.

3   In omnibus quidem balneis agebat ille dilectum
et aperta mensura legebat viros, sed nihilominus
mendaciis quoque insatiabile malum oblectabat. I
nunc et dic speculum munditiarum causa repertum.
Foeda dictu sunt quae portentum illud ore suo
lancinandum [1] dixerit feceritque, cum illi specula
ab omni parte opponerentur, ut ipse flagitiorum
suorum spectator esset et, quae secreta quoque
conscientiam premunt quaeque sibi quisque [2] fecisse
se negat, non in os tantum sed in oculos suos ingereret.

4 At hercule scelera conspectum sui reformidant. In
perditis quoque et ad omne dedecus expositis
tenerrima est oculorum verecundia. Ille, quasi
parum esset inaudita et incognita pati, oculos suos
ad illa advocavit nec quantum peccabat videre
contentus specula sibi per quae flagitia sua divideret
disponeretque circumdedit; et, quia non tam
diligenter intueri poterat, cum caput merserat
inguinibusque [3] alienis obhaeserat, opus sibi suum per

5 imagines offerebat. Spectabat illam libidinem oris
sui; spectabat admissos sibi pariter in omnia viros;
nonnumquam inter marem et feminam distributus

---

[1] *lacerandum* A²BV; *lenocinandum* Eλ.
[2] *et quae accusatus quisque* ABV.
[3] *cum compressus erat clunibusque* AV instead of *cum caput
. . . inguinibusque.*

offering himself to a man he might see in a mirror all the movements of his stallion behind him and then take delight in the false size of his partner's very member just as though it were really so big.

In all the public baths he would recruit favourites 3 and choose men by their obvious size, but none the less his insatiable evil took delight in misrepresentations. Go on now and say that the mirror was invented for the sake of touching up one's looks! The things that monster said and did (he ought to be torn apart by his own mouth) are detestable to talk about. Mirrors faced him on all sides in order that he might be a spectator of his own shame. Also, secret acts which press upon the conscience and which every man denies that he has done,[1] he not only presented to his mouth but to his eyes as well. But, by Hercules, 4 crimes avoid the sight of themselves! Even among those who are degenerate and inured to every disgrace there is still some modesty, very tenuous, at what the eyes see. As though it were not enough to submit himself to unheard of—even unknown—acts he summoned his eyes to witness them. Not content to see how greatly he sinned he surrounded himself with mirrors by which he separated one by one and assembled his vices. And, because he could not watch so attentively when his head dipped in and clung to his partner's private parts, he displayed his own doings to himself through reflections. He used 5 to look at that obscene lusting of his own mouth. He used to watch men admitted all alike to his person for

[1] Dio (61.10.3–6) reports the gossip that Seneca, in addition to adulterous affairs with women, took delight in older boys and taught this vice to Nero.

et toto corpore patientiae expositus spectabat nefanda. Quidnam homo impurus reliquit quod in tenebris faceret? Non pertimuit diem, sed illos concubitus portentuosos sibi ipse ostendit, sibi ipse approbavit, quem non putes in ipso habitu pingi noluisse.

6 Est aliqua etiam prostitutis modestia et illa corpora publico obiecta ludibrio aliquid quo infelix patientia lateat obtendunt; adeo in quaedam lupanar quoque verecundum est. At illud monstrum obscenitatem suam spectaculum fecerat et ea sibi ostentabat quibus abscondendis nulla satis alta nox est.

7 "Simul," inquit, "et virum et feminam patior. Nihilominus illa quoque supervacua mihi parte alicuius contumelia marem exerceo; omnia membra stupris occupata sunt; oculi quoque in partem libidinis veniant et testes eius exactoresque sint. Etiam ea quae a conspectu corporis nostri positio submovit arte visantur,[1] ne quis me putet nescire quid faciam.

8 Nil egit natura quod humanae libidini ministeria tam maligna dedit, quod aliorum animalium concubitus melius instruxit; inveniam quemadmodum morbo meo et imponam[2] et satisfaciam. Quo nequitiam

---

[1] *ante versentur* AV.
[2] *potiar* A; *patior* V[1]; *potior* V[2].

all the doings. Sometimes shared between a man and a woman, and with his whole body spread in position for submitting to them, he used to watch the unspeakable acts. What did the foul creature leave for performance in darkness? He did not shrink from daylight but even showed himself monstrous coitions, and gave approval of them to himself. You would not suppose that he would not have been willing to have his portrait painted in such a position!

Even among prostitutes there exists some sort of 6 modesty, and those bodies offered for public pleasure draw over some curtain by which their unhappy submission may be hidden. Thus, towards certain things even a brothel shows a sense of shame. But that monster had made a spectacle of his own obscenity and deliberately showed himself acts which no night is deep enough to conceal.

" At the same time," he said, " I submit to both 7 a man and a woman. Nevertheless, also with that part of my body not occupied I perform the role of a male[1] in the violation of another person. All my organs are occupied in the lechery. Let my eyes, too, come into their share of the debauchery and be witnesses and supervisors of it. By means of a device let even those acts be seen which the position of our bodies removes from sight, so that no one may think I do not know what I do. Nature did poorly in pro- 8 viding such scanty accessories to human lust. She better arranged the coition of other animals. I will discover a way to deceive my sick wants and satisfy them. To what purpose my depravity if I sin only to

[1] This is the meaning maintained by Housman rather than "I work on a man."

meam, si ad naturae modum pecco? Id genus
speculorum circumponam mihi quod incredibilem
9 magnitudinem imaginum[1] reddat. Si liceret mihi,
ad verum ista perducerem; quia non licet, mendacio
pascar. Obscenitas mea plus quam capit videat et
patientiam suam ipsa miretur."

Facinus indignum! Hic fortasse cito et antequam
videret occisus est; ad speculum suum immolandus
fuit.

1 17. Derideantur nunc philosophi quod de speculi
natura disserant, quod inquirant quid ita facies
nostra nobis et quidem in nos obversa reddatur, quid
sibi rerum natura voluerit quod, cum vera corpora
edidisset, etiam simulacra eorum aspici voluit,
2 quorsus pertinuerit hanc comparare materiam ex-
cipiendarum imaginum potentem; non in hoc scilicet
ut ad speculum barbam velleremus aut ut faciem
viri poliremus (in nulla re illa luxuriae negotium
concessit).

Sed primum omnium, quia imbecilli oculi ad sus-
tinendum comminus solem ignoraturi erant, formam
eius hebetato lumine[2] ostendit. Quamvis enim
orientem occidentemque eum contemplari liceat,
tamen habitum eius ipsum qui verus est, non rubentis
sed candida luce fulgentis, nesciremus, nisi in aliquo
nobis umore lenior et aspici facilior occurreret.
3 Praeterea duorum siderum occursum, quo interpolari

the limit of nature? I will surround myself with mirrors, the type which renders the size of objects incredible. If it were possible, I would make those 9 sizes real; because it is not possible, I will feast myself on the illusion. Let my lust see more than it consumes and marvel at what it undergoes."

Shameful behaviour! Perhaps he was murdered quickly, even before he saw it; he ought to have been immolated in front of a mirror of his own.

17. Now let philosophers be ridiculed because they 1 rant about the nature of a mirror and because they inquire why our face is thus reproduced for us and even turned towards us. Also, what did nature intend in creating real objects and yet wanting reflections of them to be seen? What did it mean 2 that nature provided material able to receive images? Surely it was not in order that we men may pluck out our whiskers in front of a mirror or make our faces smooth. In no respect has nature made a gift of hard work to luxury.

First of all, nature shows the sun's form with its brightness dimmed in reflection, since our eyes, too weak to endure the sun directly, would be ignorant of it. For although it is possible for the rising and setting sun to be stared at, none the less we would not know its actual appearance—the one which is true, not red but shining with a brilliant white light— if it did not appear to us in some liquid as softer and easier on the eyes. In addition, we would not see 3

---

¹ *incredibili magnitudine imaginem* E.
² *illum lumine* ZAV; *illud lumine* HE.

dies solet, non videremus, nec scire possemus quid
esset, nisi[1] liberius humi solis lunaeque imagines
videremus.

4   Inventa sunt specula ut homo ipse se nosset, multa
ex hoc consecuturus,[2] primum sui notitiam, deinde
ad quaedam consilium : formosus, ut vitaret infamiam ;
deformis, ut sciret redimendum esse virtutibus
quicquid corpori deesset; iuvenis, ut flore aetatis
admoneretur illud tempus esse discendi et fortia
audendi; senex, ut indecora canis deponeret, ut de
morte aliquid cogitaret. Ad haec rerum natura
facultatem nobis dedit nosmet ipsos videndi.

5   Fons cuique perlucidus aut leve saxum imaginem
reddit :

> nuper me in litore vidi
> Cum placidum ventis staret mare.

Qualem fuisse cultum putas ad hoc se speculum
comentium ? Aetas illa simplicior et fortuitis contenta nondum in vitium beneficia[3] detorquebat nec
inventa naturae in libidinem luxumque rapiebat.[4]

6   Primo faciem suam cuique casus ostendit. Deinde,

---

[1] *quid esset quod solem nulla obversante nube subduceret nisi* Z.
[2] Gertz, Gercke, Oltramare for *consequuntur* or *consecuntur*
in most MSS.; *consectantur* AV.
[3] *blandicias* V; *beneficium* E.
[4] *trahebat* AV.

the conjunction of the two heavenly bodies (by which daylight is interrupted, ordinarily) nor would we be able to know what it was if we did not see, rather freely, the images of the sun and the moon on the ground.

Mirrors were invented in order that man may know 4 himself, destined to attain many benefits from this: first, knowledge of himself; next, in certain directions, wisdom.   The handsome man, to avoid infamy. The homely man, to understand that what he lacks in physical appearance must be compensated for by virtue.   The young man, to be reminded by his youth that it is a time of learning and of daring brave deeds. The old man, to set aside actions dishonourable to his grey hair, to think some thoughts about death.   This is why nature has given us the opportunity of seeing ourselves.

A clear fountain or a polished stone returns to each 5 man his image:

> Recently I saw myself
> On the shore
> When the sea stood becalmed
> From the winds.[1]

What sort of refined life do you think those people led who groomed themselves at this kind of mirror? That was a simpler age, content with what chance offered, and it had not yet twisted benefits into vice nor seized upon inventions of nature for the purpose of lust and extravagance.

At first, chance revealed to man his own face. 6

---

[1] Virgil *Ec.* 2.25–26.

cum insitus sui mortalibus amor dulcem aspectum
formae suae faceret, saepius ea despexere in quibus
effigies suas viderant. Postquam deterior populus
ipsas subit terras effossurus obruenda, ferrum
primum [1] in usu fuit—et id impune homines eruerant,
si solum eruissent—tunc deinde alia terrae mala,
quorum levitas aliud agentibus speciem suam obtulit,
quam hic in poculo, ille in aere ad aliquos usus
comparato vidit; et mox huic proprie ministerio
praeparatus [2] est orbis, nondum argenti nitor sed
fragilis vilisque materia.

7   Tunc quoque, cum antiqui illi viri incondite vive-
rent, satis nitidi si squalorem opere collectum adverso
flumine eluerant, cura [3] comere capillum fuit ac
prominentem barbam depectere, et in hac re sibi
quisque, non alteri in vicem, operam dabat. Ne [4]
coniugum quidem manu crinis ille quem effundere
olim mos viris fuit attrectabatur, sed illum sibi ipsi
sine ullo artifice formosi quatiebant, non aliter quam
iubam generosa animalia.

8   Postea, iam rerum potiente luxuria, specula totis
paria corporibus auro argentoque caelata sunt, gemmis
deinde adornata; et pluris [5] unum ex his feminae

---

[1] *subiit in ipsas terras se effusurus ferrum obruendum primum*
AV instead of *ipsas . . . primum.*
[2] *formatus* Z.   [3] *parva cura* Gercke.
[4] *Ne* supplied by Haase, Oltramare.
[5] *populis* PFO; *poculis* AV.

Then, when love of self, innate in mortals, had made the sight of their form pleasing, men looked down oftener into those surfaces where they saw their own images. After a worse people went into the very earth to dig out things that ought to be buried, iron was first in use. Men might have dug it out with impunity if they had just dug up iron.[1] Then came the other evils of the earth. Their smoothness offered a reflected image to people intent upon something else; one man saw his reflection in a cup, another in bronze that was procured for some real use; and next a disc was prepared especially for this function, not yet of the brilliance of silver, but of a material fragile and cheap.

Then, also, those men of ancient times lived in- **7** elegantly. They were refined enough if they washed off in a counter-running stream the grime collected in working. They took care to arrange their hair and to comb their flowing beards, and in this task each man attended to himself, not to another in turn. That hair, which it was the custom of men formerly to let stream down, was not touched by the hand even of a wife; but men shook it out for themselves, handsome without any artifice, just as noble animals shake out a mane.

Later, when luxury had already become supremely **8** powerful, full-length mirrors were carved of gold and silver, then adorned with jewels. One of these

---

[1] Perhaps there is a double meaning—all would have been well (a) if men had dug up iron and no other metal; (b) if men had simply dug up iron and not used it (for weapons). Note that Lucretius (5.1287) says with truth that bronze was used before iron.

constitit quam antiquarum dos fuit illa [1] quae publice
dabatur imperatorum pauperum liberis. An tu
existimas auro inditum habuisse Scipionis filias
9 speculum, cum illis dos fuisset aes grave? O felix
paupertas quae tanto titulo locum fecit! Non cepissent illam [2] dotem, si habuissent. At quisquis ille
erat cui soceri loco senatus fuit intellexit accepisse
se dotem quam fas non esset reddere. Iam liber-
tinorum virgunculis in unum speculum non sufficit
illa dos quam dedit populus Romanus animose.[3]
10 Processit enim paulatim in deterius [4] opibus ipsis
invitata [5] luxuria et incrementum ingens vitia cepe-
runt, adeoque omnia indiscreta sunt diversissimis [6]
artibus ut, quicquid mundus muliebris vocabatur,
sarcinae viriles sint; omnes dico, etiam militares.
Iam speculum ornatus tantum causa adhibetur?
Nulli non vitio necessarium factum est.

---

[1] Pincianus, Oltramare for *fuit non illa* MSS.
[2] *non cepissent illam* Leo, Gercke, Oltramare; *non fecisset*
HPEAV; *illa* in most of the MSS.; *non fecisset illa* Alexander.
[3] *populus Romanus animose* Oltramare; *pro aïo se* (that
is *pro animo se*) HPEG; *pro ammosa* Z; *pro se Scipio* AV.
[4] *molestius paulatim* AV.
[5] *mutata* AV.
[6] *perversissimis* AV.

mirrors cost a woman more than the dowry of ladies of long ago, the dowry which was given at public expense to the children of penniless generals. Do you believe the daughters of Scipio[1] had a mirror set in gold when their dowry was only heavy brass money? Happy the poverty which gave opportunity for such 9 great glory! They would not have received that dowry if they had owned such a mirror. But whoever the man was for whom the Senate took the place of a father-in-law, he realized that he had received a dowry which he would not have the right to render.[2] That dowry which the Roman people proudly bestowed is not enough now for the little daughters of freedmen to buy one mirror.

Luxury, encouraged by sheer opulence, has 10 gradually developed for the worst, and vices have taken on enormous growth. All things are so mixed up by the most various refinements that what used to be called the ornament of a woman is now a man's accoutrement; I mean all men, even soldiers. Is a mirror now used only for the sake of good grooming? There is no vice for which it has not become indispensable.

[1] Valerius Maximus (4.4.10) says this is the uncle of the Scipio who defeated Hannibal. In *Ad Helviam Matrem* (12.6) Seneca tells the same story of the daughters of Scipio and their dowry and makes their father the Scipio who "extracted tribute from Carthage."

[2] If he divorced his wife he would have to return the dowry to the Senate and the Roman people.

BOOK II

LIGHTNINGS AND THUNDERS

LIBER SECUNDUS[1]

DE FULMINIBUS ET TONITRIBUS[2]

1   1. Omnis de universo quaestio in caelestia, sublimia, terrena dividitur.   Prima pars naturam siderum scrutatur et magnitudinem et formam ignium
quibus mundus includitur, solidumne sit caelum ac
firmae concretaeque materiae an ex subtili tenuique
nexum, agatur an agat, et infra sese sidera habeat an
in contextu sui fixa, quemadmodum anni vices servet,
solem retro flectat, cetera deinceps his similia.

2   Secunda pars tractat inter caelum terramque
versantia.   Haec[3] sunt nubila, imbres, nives, venti,
terrae motus, fulgura[4]

et humanas motura tonitrua mentes;

quaecumque aer facit patiturve, haec sublimia
dicimus, quia editiora imis sunt.   Tertia illa pars de
aquis, terris, arbustis, satis quaerit et—ut iuris-
consultorum verbo utar—de omnibus quae solo
continentur.

[1] *Liber sextus* KT; *octavus* GH; *quartus* Gercke; [*Liber
Secundus*] ⟨ *Liber Sextus* ⟩ Oltramare.
[2] Supplied by Gercke, Oltramare.   The MSS. give no title.
[3] Gercke; *hic* most MSS. Oltramare; *hinc* O.
[4] *venti . . . fulgura* supplied by Gercke, Oltramare.

98

BOOK II

LIGHTNINGS AND THUNDERS

1. Any study of the universe is divided into uranology, meteorology, and geography.[1] The first division investigates the nature of the heavenly bodies and the size and shape of the fires which enclose the universe; whether the sky is solid and made up of firm and compact matter or woven together from subtle and thin material; whether it is moved or imparts motion, and whether the stars are beneath it or fixed in its structure; how it maintains the seasons of the year, turns the sun back—and, in short, other investigations like these.

The second division deals with phenomena occurring between the sky and the earth, such as clouds, rain, snow, wind, earthquakes, lightning, and

> Thunder which will move
> The mind of men;[2]

and whatever the atmosphere does or undergoes. Such phenomena we call *sublimia* because they are higher than the low phenomena on earth. The third division investigates water, land, trees, plants, and—to use a legal term—everything contained in the ground.[3]

---

[1] *caelestia* "matters of the sky"; *sublimia* "matters up aloft"; *terrena* "matters of the earth."
[2] Ovid *Met.* 1.55. [3] As opposed to *res mobiles.*

3   " Quomodo," inquis, " de terrarum motu quaestionem eo posuisti loco quo de tonitribus fulguri-
busque [1] dicturus es ? " Quia, cum motus [2] spiritu
fiat, spiritus autem aer sit agitatus, etiamsi subit
terras, non ibi spectandus est; cogitetur in ea sede in
qua illum natura desposuit.

4   Dicam quod magis mirum videbitur: inter caelestia de terra dicendum erit. " Quare ? " inquis.
Quia, cum propria terrae ipsius excutimus suo loco,
utrum lata sit et inaequalis et enormiter proiecta an
tota in formam pilae spectet et in orbem partes suas
cogat, alliget aquas an aquis alligetur, ipsa animal sit
an iners corpus et sine sensu, plenum quidem
spiritus sed alieni, et cetera huiusmodi quotiens in
manus venerint, terram sequentur et in imo [3]

5   collocabuntur; at ubi quaeretur quis terrae situs sit,
qua parte mundi consederit, quomodo adversus
sidera caelumque posita sit, haec quaestio cedet
superioribus et, ut ita dicam, meliorem condicionem
sequetur.

1   2. Quoniam dixi de partibus in quas omnis rerum
naturae materia dividitur, quaedam in commune
dicenda sunt, et hoc primum praesumendum inter ea

2   corpora quibus [4] unitas est aera esse. Quid sit hoc
et quare praecipiendum fuerit, scies, si paulo altius
repetiero et dixero esse aliquid continuum,[5] aliquid

---

[1] *fulgoribusque* EPAVB; *fulminibusque* Z.
[2] *motus terrae* ABV.   [3] *uno* EFGJKT; *imis* ABV.
[4] *corpora a quibus* ABV; *compar a quibus* HPFGZ.
[5] *esse aliquid unum, aliquid continuum* Gercke.

" Why," you ask, " have you put the study of earth- 3
quakes in the section where you will talk about
thunder and lightning?" Because, although an
earthquake is caused by a blast, a blast is none the
less air in motion. Even if the air goes down into
the earth it is not to be studied there. Let it be
considered in the region where nature has placed it.

I will say something which will seem even more 4
surprising: in the section on astronomy it will be
necessary to talk about the earth. " Why? " you
ask. Because when we examine in their own section
the properties of the earth, whether it is flat, un-
symmetrical, and irregularly elongated, or resembles
exactly the shape of a ball and organizes its parts into
a globe; whether it confines the waters or is confined by them, whether it is an animal or an inert
mass without feeling, full of air but not its own
breath; and other questions of this sort, whenever
they come to hand—all belong to geology and will
be placed in the lowest category. But when we 5
investigate what the position of the earth is, in what
part of the universe it has settled, how it is situated
in respect to the stars and the sky—such an inquiry
will belong to the higher phenomena and attain a
better status, so to speak.

2. Since I have talked about the categories into 1
which the whole subject of nature is divided, I must
make some general comments. First, this must be
taken as a premise: atmosphere is among those
substances which have unity. What this means and 2
why it must be grasped to begin with, you will understand if I go back over it a little more deeply and
say that some things are continuous, some are

commissum; et [1] commissura est [2] duorum coniunc-
torum inter se corporum tactus, continuatio est
partium inter se non intermissa coniunctio. Unitas
3 est sine commissura continuatio. Numquid dubium
est quin ex his corporibus quae videmus tractamus-
que, quae aut sentiuntur aut sentiunt, quaedam sint
composita? Illa constant aut nexu aut acervatione
aut compactione,[3] ut puta funis, frumentum, navis—
rursus non composita, ut arbor, lapis. Ergo con-
cedas oportet ex his quoque quae sensum quidem
effugiunt, ceterum ratione prenduntur, esse in
quibusdam unitatem corporum.

4   Vide quomodo auribus tuis parcam. Expedire
me poteram, si philosophorum lingua uti voluissem,
ut dicerem unita corpora. Hoc [4] cum tibi remittam,
tu invicem mihi refer gratiam. Quare istud? Si
quando dixero unum, memineris me non ad numerum
referre, sed ad naturam corporis nulla ope externa
sed unitate sua [5] cohaerentis. Ex hac nota corporum
aer est.

1   3. Omnia quae in notitiam nostram cadunt aut
cadere possunt mundus complectitur. Ex his quaedam partes eius sunt, quaedam materiae loco relicta;
desiderat enim omnis natura materiam, sicut ars
2 omnis quae manu constat. Quid sit hoc, apertius

---

[1] *et enim* Gercke, Oltramare.
[2] *commissura est* supplied here by Gercke, Oltramare.
[3] *aut compactione* supplied by Gercke, Oltramare.

composites.[1] A composite is the contact of two bodies joined to each other. Continuity is the uninterrupted joining of parts to each other. Unity is continuity without the composite feature. There is 3 no doubt that of the substances which we see and handle, which either are perceived or perceive, some are composites. They attain form by assembly, accumulation, or construction (for example, a rope, grain, a ship—whereas a tree or a rock is a noncomposite). Therefore, you ought to concede that also among things that escape the senses, but are apprehended by thought, some have a unity of substance.

See how I spare your ears. I could have saved my- 4 self trouble if I had been willing to use the jargon of philosophers and say " united bodies." Since I grant you this concession, thank me in return. What am I trying to say? Any time I say " one," remember that I am referring not to a number but to the characteristic of a body which is cohesive by its own oneness, not by external help. Atmosphere belongs to this brand of substances.

3. The term " universe " includes all things 1 which are, or can be, within our knowledge. Some of these are " parts " of the universe, others remain in the realm of " material." All nature requires material, just as every art does which involves handiwork. I will explain more clearly what this means. 2

[1] In *Epist.* 102.6 Seneca also discusses continuous bodies (man), composite bodies (ships, houses), and collective bodies (an army, a populace).

---

[4] *Haec* λ.   [5] *sola* λ.

faciam. Pars est nostri oculus, manus, ossa, nervi.
Materia sucus recentis cibi iturus in partes. Rursus
quasi pars est sanguis nostri, qui et tamen est
materia; praeparat enim is alia, [1] et nihilominus in
numero eorum est quibus totum corpus efficitur.

1   4. Sic mundi pars est aer, et quidem necessaria.
Hic est enim qui caelum terramque conectit, qui
ima ac summa sic separat ut tamen iungat. Separat,
quia medius intervenit; iungit, quia utrique per
hunc inter se consensus est; supra se dat quicquid
accepit a terris, rursus vim siderum in terrena trans-
fundit.

2   Quasi partem mundi voco ut animalia et arbusta.
Nam genus animalium arbustorumque pars universi
est, quia in consummationem totius assumptum [2] et
quia non est sine hoc universum. Unum autem
animal et una arbor quasi pars est, quia, quamvis
perierit, tamen id ex quo perit, totum est. Aer
autem, ut dicebam, et caelo et terris cohaeret;
utrique innatus est. Habet autem unitatem quicquid alicuius rei nativa pars est. Nihil enim nascitur
sine unitate.

1   5. Terra et pars est mundi et materia. Pars
quare sit, non puto te interrogaturum, aut aeque
interroga [3] quare caelum pars sit; quia scilicet non

---

[1] *is alia* Oltramare for *id alia* MSS.; *vitalia* Gercke; *idem
alimentum* Garrod; *ad alia* Alexander.

[2] *in consummatione universi acceptum* AV.

[3] *aut aeque interroga* Oltramare, Alexander; *ut aeque interrogas* or *interroges* MSS.; *ut neque interrogas* Kroll, Garrod.

The eye, the hand, bones, sinews—each is a part of us. The material is the juice of recent food which will go to the parts. Again, blood is a part of us, as it were; but it is also the material, for it provides for the other parts. Yet it still belongs to the group of parts which makes up the entire body.

4. Thus, atmosphere is a part of the universe and, in fact, an essential part. This is what connects heaven and earth and separates the lowest from the highest in such a way that it none the less joins them. It separates because it intervenes midway; it joins because through it there is a communication between the two. It transmits to the upper region whatever it receives from the earth. On the other hand, it transfuses to earthly objects the influences of the stars.

I call such things as animals and trees a quasi-part of the universe. Now, the class of animals and trees is a part of the universe because it is considered in the sum of the whole and because there is no universe without such a class; but a single animal or single tree is a quasi-part because even when it is lost nevertheless the whole from which it is lost is still intact. But the atmosphere, as I was saying, is connected both to sky and to earth; it is innate to both. Moreover, whatever is an inborn part of anything has unity. Nothing is born without unity.

5. The earth is both a part and a material of the universe.[1] I do not think you will ask why the earth is a part; otherwise you must equally ask why the sky is a part; because surely the universe can no more

[1] In this section and the next sections several readings in the Latin are most uncertain.

magis sine hoc quam sine illa universum potest esse.
Materia porro mundi propterea est terra [1] quod †cum
his universis [2] est ex quibus alimenta [3] omnibus animalibus, omnibus satis, omnibus stellis dividuntur.

2 Hinc viritim singulis,[4] hinc ipsi mundo tam multa
poscenti subministrantur;[5] hinc profertur quo sus-
tineantur tot sidera tam exercita [6] tam avida per
diem noctemque ut in opere ita in pastu. Omnium
quidem rerum natura, quantum in nutrimentum sui
satis sit, apprehendit; mundus autem, quantum in
aeternum desiderabat, invasit. Pusillum tibi exemplar magnae rei ponam: ova tantum complectuntur
umoris quantum ad effectum animalis exituri sat est.

1 6. Aer continuus terrae est et sic appositus ut
statim ibi [7] futurus sit unde illa discesserit. Pars
totius est mundi; sed tamen, quicquid terra in
alimentum caelestium misit, recipit, ut scilicet
materia, non pars, intellegi debeat; ex hoc omnis
inconstantia eius tumultusque est.

2 Hunc quidam ex distantibus corpusculis, ut pul-
verem, struunt plurimumque a vero recedunt.
Numquam enim nisi contexti per unitatem corpori
nisus est, cum partes consentire ad intentionem de

---

[1] *Materia porro ... est terra* supplied by Oltramare; *aliqu*
terrae materiae loco sunt Gercke; *potest esse, quod cum hi*
Alexander.   [2] *universum* ABV Alexander.
   [3] *ex quibus alimenta* Z; *ex quibus quam alimenta* HPEG; *e*
quibus id est ex illo et alimenta ABV; *ex hac alimenta* Gercke
ex quibus. Quam ob rem materia? quia ex hac aliment
Alexander.   [4] *quicquid est virium* ABV Alexander
   [5] *subministratur* V Alexander.   [6] *exercitata* ZABV
   [7] *sibi* AV.   [8] *discedunt* λ.

be such without the sky than it can without the earth. Furthermore, the earth is, in addition, a material of the universe because the earth includes those universal materials from which is shared out the sustenance for all creatures, all vegetation, all the stars. From 2 this source are provisions supplied for all created things one by one, from this source too provisions for the universe itself, which demands so much. The many stars, which are so active, and so eager day and night, are sustained in their work and in their sustenance by what is provided from this source. All nature takes from the earth as much as is sufficient for its nourishment. But the universe has appropriated as much as it needs for ever. I will give you a tiny illustration of a great phenomenon: eggs contain only as much moisture as they need for the formation of the creature that will be hatched.

6. The atmosphere is in continuous contact with 1 the earth and juxtaposed in such a way that it will immediately occupy the place the earth has just left. The atmosphere is a part of the whole universe. On the other hand, it receives whatever the earth sends for the nourishment of the heavenly bodies, so that it actually ought to be understood as a material not a part. All the atmosphere's instability and disturbance is derived from this earthly element.

Some authorities [1] construe that the atmosphere is 2 made up of separate little bodies, as dust is; but they are greatly mistaken. For effort can never exist in a body unless the body is held together by unity, since the componants need to work in harmony and to

---

[1] Democritus, Epicurus, and Lucretius.

beant et conferre vires. Aer autem, si in atomos inciditur,[1] sparsus est; tendi[2] vero disiecta non possunt.

3   Intentionem aeris ostendent tibi inflata nec ad ictum cedentia; ostendent pondera per magnum spatium ablata gestante vento; ostendent voces, quae remissae claraeque sunt prout aer se concitavit. Quid enim est vox nisi intentio aeris, ut audiatur,
4   linguae formata percussu? Quid? cursus et motus omnis, nonne intenti spiritus opera sunt? Hic facit vim nervis, velocitatem currentibus; hic, cum vehementer concitatus ipse se torsit, arbusta silvasque convolvit et aedificia tota corripiens in altum frangit; hic mare per se languidum et iacens incitat.
5   Ad minora veniamus. Quis sine intentione spiritus cantus est? Cornua et tubae et quae aquarum pressura maiorem sonitum formant quam qui ore reddi potest, nonne aeris intentione partes[3] suas explicant? Consideremus quae ingentem vim per occultum agunt: parvula admodum semina et quorum exilitas in commissura lapidum locum invenit in tantum convalescunt ut ingentia saxa deturbent et monumenta[4] dissolvant; scopulos interim rupesque radices minutissimae ac tenuissimae findunt. Hoc

---

[1] *dividitur* ABV.   [2] Schultess, Oltramare for *teneri* MSS.
[3] *artes* Z.   [4] *detrahant et in momenta* ABV.

assemble their strength for tension. But if the atmosphere is cut up into atoms it is scattered. Moreover, separated bodies cannot be in tension.

Inflated objects, so inflated that they do not 3 yield to a blow, will demonstrate to you the tension of atmosphere. Heavy objects will show it—ones which have been moved over a great distance with only the wind supporting them. Voices will show it, which are faint or clear accordingly as the air vibrates. For what is voice except the tension of air formed by the tongue striking it so as to become audible? Well, what about running and all 4 motion? Are they not the effects of air in tension? This is what gives strength to sinews, speed to runners. When air is violently agitated it twists upon itself, carries off trees and woods, snatches up entire buildings and shatters them. Air stirs up the sea, which is quiet and motionless by itself.

Let us turn to lesser effects. What song can be 5 sung without the tension of air? Horns, and trumpets, and instruments which by water pressure [1] form a sound greater than that which can be produced by the mouth—do they not accomplish their function by tension of the air? Let us examine things which produce great hidden force, such as very tiny seeds whose thinness finds a place in the joints of stones, and grow so powerful that they dislodge huge rocks and demolish monuments; while very thin, minute roots split crags and cliffs.

---

[1] Seneca is probably referring to the hydraulic organ. Nero was fascinated by such water organs and towards the end of his life he vowed that if he retained his power he would give a performance on the water organ (Suet. *Nero* 41 and 54).

quid est aliud quam intentio spiritus, sine qua nihil
validum et contra quam nihil validum est?

6   Esse autem unitatem in aere vel ex hoc intellegi
potest quod corpora nostra inter se cohaerent. Quid
enim est aliud quod teneat illa quam spiritus? Quid
est aliud quo animus noster agitetur? Quis est illi
motus nisi intentio? Quae intentio nisi ex unitate?
Quae unitas, nisi haec esset in aere? Quid autem
aliud producit fruges et segetem imbecillam ac
virentes exigit [1] arbores ac distendit in ramos aut in
altum erigit [2] quam spiritus intentio et unitas?

1   7. Quidam aera discerpunt et in particulas didu-
cunt ita ut illi inane permisceant. Argumentum
autem existimant non pleni corporis sed multum
vacui habentis quod avibus in illo tam facilis motus,
quod maximis minimisque per illum transcursus est.

2 Sed falluntur. Nam aquarum quoque similis facilitas
est, nec de unitate illarum dubium est, quae sic
corpora accipiunt ut semper in contrarium acceptis
refluant; hanc nostri circumstantiam, Graeci ἀντιπερίστασιν [3] appellant. Quae in aere quoque sicut
in aqua fit; circumsistit enim omne corpus a quo
impellitur. Nihil ergo opus erit admixto inani. Sed
haec alias.

[1] *exigit* ZBO Oltramare; *erigit* Gercke.
[2] *aut in altum erigit* ejected by Haase, Gercke.
[3] ἀντιπερίστασιν supplied by Haase, Gercke, Oltramare for
anteperistas HPEZ; *autem peristasin* ABV.

---

[1] Lucretius (1.330–397) gives the Epicurean arguments for

This is nothing but the tension of air, without which nothing is strong and against which nothing is strong.

That there is unity in air can be realized also from 6 the cohesiveness of our bodies. What holds them together? Air. What else is it that puts our soul in motion? What is the air's motion? Tension. What tension can there be except from unity? What unity could this be unless it were the unity in the air? Moreover, what produces leguminous crops and slender standing grain-crops and forces up green trees and spreads out their branches or lifts them on high if it is not tension and unity in air?

7. Some authorities tear the air apart and separate 1 it into particles in such a way that they mix void with air. They regard the easy movement of birds through air as proof that air is not a compact body but one that has numerous voids because there is a passage through it for the largest and smallest birds.[1] But they are mistaken. Water has a similar trait, and yet there is no doubt about the unity of water, which accepts bodies in such a way that it always flows away from the bodies received. Our Stoics call this *circumstantia* [" encirclement "], the Greeks *antiperistasis* [" replacement "]. It occurs in air as well as in water, for air encircles every body by which it is displaced. There is therefore no need of an admixture of void. But this is discussed elsewhere.[2]

the necessary existence of voids in air and water to permit the movement of birds and fish.
[2] Seneca may mean that he planned to discuss this subject in another work.

1 8. Esse quaedam in rerum natura vehementia magnique impetus non sit diu [1] colligendum; nihil autem nisi intentione vehementius est, tam mehercule quam nihil intendi ab alio poterit, nisi aliquid per semet fuerit intentum. Dicimus enim eodem modo non posse quicquam ab alio moveri, nisi aliquid fuerit mobile ex semet. Quid autem est quod magis credatur ex se ipso habere intentionem quam spiritus? Hunc intendi quis negabit, cum viderit iactari terram cum montibus, tecta murosque, magnas cum populis urbes, cum totis maria litoribus?

1 9. Ostendit intentionem spiritus velocitas eius et diductio. Oculi statim per multa milia aciem suam mittunt; vox una totas urbes simul percutit; lumen non paulatim prorepit sed semel universis rebus infunditur.

2 Aqua autem quemadmodum sine spiritu posset intendi? Numquid dubitas quin sparsio illa quae ex fundamentis mediae harenae crescens in summam usque amphitheatri altitudinem pervenit cum intentione aquae fiat? Atqui nec manus nec ullum aliud tormentum aquam potest mittere aut agere quam spiritus; huic se commodat; hoc attollitur inserto et cogente; contra naturam suam multa

3 conatur et ascendit, nata defluere. Quid? Navigia sarcina depressa parum ostendunt non aquam sibi resistere, quo minus mergantur, sed spiritum? Aqua enim cederet nec posset pondera sustinere, nisi ipsa sustineretur. Discus ex loco superiore in pis-

[1] *diu* supplied by Oltramare.

8. It requires no lengthy thought that in nature 1
certain things exist which have violent movement
and enormous force; yet nothing becomes more
violent but by tension; and equally, by Hercules,
nothing can be in tension from another object unless it
has tension in itself. In the same way we say that
nothing can be moved by another object unless there
is the capacity of mobility in it. But what is more
likely to have tension within itself than air? Who
will say that air does not have tension when he sees it
toss about lands and mountains, houses and walls,
great cities and their peoples, seas with their entire
coastlines?

9. The velocity and expansion of air show its ten- 1
sion: the eyes send their sight instantly over many
miles, a single sound at one moment resounds
through entire cities, light does not creep forth
gradually but in an instant pours over all things.

Moreover, how could water be in tension without 2
air? Take the jet of water that grows from the
bottom of the centre of the arena and goes all the
way to the top of the amphitheatre—do you think
this happens without air tension? Yet neither the
hand nor any sort of mechanical device can emit or
force water out the way air can. The water responds
to the air. It is raised up by the air, which is in-
serted in the pipe and forces it up. Although water
naturally flows down, it struggles mightily against
its nature and rises. How about ships laden with 3
cargo? Do they not show that it is the resistance of
air, not of water, that keeps them from sinking?
Water would give way and be unable to maintain the
weight if it were not itself sustained by air. A discus

cinam missus non descendit, sed resilit; quemadmodum, nisi spiritu referente?

4   Vox autem qua ratione per parietum munimenta transmittitur, nisi quod solido quoque aer inest, qui sonum extrinsecus missum et accipit et remittit,[1] scilicet spiritu non aperta tantum intendens, sed etiam abdita et inclusa, quod illi facere expeditum est, quia nusquam divisus est[2] sed per illa ipsa quibus separari videtur coit secum? Interponas licet muros et mediam altitudinem montium, per omnia ista prohibetur nobis esse pervius, non sibi. Id enim intercluditur tantum per quod illum nos non[3] sequi possumus; ipse quidem per ipsum transit quo scinditur, et media non circumfundit tantum et utrimque cingit, sed permeat.

1   10. Ab aethere lucidissimo aer in terram usque diffusus est, agilior quidem tenuiorque et altior terris nec minus aquis, ceterum aethere spissior graviorque, frigidus per se et obscurus. Lumen illi

2 calorque aliunde[4] sunt. Sed non per omne spatium sui similis est; mutatur a proximis. Summa pars eius siccissima calidissimaque et ob hoc etiam tenuissima est propter viciniam aeternorum ignium et illos tot motus siderum assiduumque caeli circumactum; illa pars ima et vicina terris densa et caliginosa est, quia terrenas exhalationes receptat;

---

[1] *accipit et proximo tradit* Z.   [2] *divisum est* HEZLFJ.
[3] I supply *non*.   [4] *alimentum* ABV.

hurled from a higher position into a pond does not sink but bounces back. How could it do this unless it were beaten back by air?

How is a voice transmitted through the barrier of a 4 wall unless air exists in the solid matter also? Air receives the sound sent from outside and passes it on. The energy of air exerts tension not only on exposed matter but also on concealed and enclosed matter. Air can do this easily because it is never divided but maintains continuity with itself even through objects which seem to separate it. Although you interpose walls and obstructing high mountains, through all such barriers a passageway is prevented not for itself but only for us. For, the only block is that through which *we* are not able to follow the air; but air passes through the very obstacle which separates it. It not only pours around and encircles obstacles in its midst but even permeates them.

10. Air is diffused from the bright atmosphere down 1 to earth. It is thinner, more mobile, and more buoyant than earth and water too but thicker and heavier than upper atmosphere. By itself air is cold and dark. Its light and heat are from another source. Air is not the same throughout its entire 2 expanse. It is altered by its surroundings. Its highest region is extremely dry and hot, and for this reason also very thin because of the nearness of the eternal fires, the many movements of the stars, and the continuous revolution of heaven. The lowest region, near the earth, is dense and dark because it receives the terrestial exhalations. The middle region is more temperate (compared to the

media pars temperatior, si summis imisque conferas,
quantum ad siccitatem tenuitatemque pertinet,

3 ceterum utraque parte frigidior. Nam superiora
eius calorem vicinorum siderum sentiunt. Inferiora
quoque tepent; primum terrarum halitu, qui multum
secum calidi affert; deinde quia radii solis replican-
tur et, quousque redire potuerunt, id duplicato
calore benignius fovent. Deinde etiam illo spiritu
qui omnibus animalibus arbustisque ac satis calidus
est; nihil viveret sine calore.

4 Adice nunc ignes, non tantum manu factos [1] et
certos,[2] sed opertos terris, quorum aliqui eruperunt,
innumerabiles in obscuro et condito flagrant semper.
Hae tot partes eius fertiles rerum habent quiddam
teporis, quoniam quidem sterile frigus est, calor
gignit. Media ergo pars aeris ab his summota in
frigore suo manet; natura enim aeris gelida est.

1 11. Qui cum sic divisus sit, ima [3] sui parte maxime
varius et inconstans ac mutabilis [4] est. Circa terras
plurimum audet, plurimum patitur, exagitat et
exagitatur; nec tamen eodem modo totus afficitur,
sed aliter alibi et partibus inquietus ac turbidus est.

2 Causas autem illi mutationis et inconstantiae alias
terra praebet, cuius positiones hoc aut illo versae

---

[1] *manifestos* O Gercke.
[2] *ceteros* λ.

highest and the lowest regions, as far as dryness and thinness goes), but it is colder than both the other regions. The upper regions of air feel the heat of 3 the nearby stars. The lower regions are also warm; first because of the exhalation of the earth, which carries with it a great deal of warmth; second, because the rays of the sun are reflected back and make the air more genially warm with reflected heat as far as they are able to reach. Besides, the lower air is warmed by the breath which comes from all the animals, trees, and plants; for nothing is alive without heat.

Now, add to this the fires, not only the artificial 4 ones we know about but those that are concealed in the earth. Some of them have erupted, but innumerable fires always blaze in the dark and hidden depths. The many parts of the earth which are fertile in life have the element of heat, since cold is sterile, heat is generative. Accordingly, the middle region of the atmosphere, remote from these influences, remains cold; for atmosphere is by nature cold.

11. Since the atmosphere is divided in such a way, 1 it is especially variable, unstable, and changeable in its lowest region. The air near the earth is the most blustering and yet the most exposed to influences since it is both agitating and being agitated. Yet it is not all affected in the same way. It is restless and disturbed in different parts and in different places.

The earth supplies some causes of the atmosphere's 2 change and instability. The earth's position, turned

---

[3] *ima* E²; *iam* most MSS.
[4] *mirabilis* HPZ.

magna ad aeris temperiem momenta sunt, alias
siderum cursus, ex quibus soli plurimum imputes;
illum sequitur annus, ad illius flexum hiemes aestates-
que vertuntur. Lunae proximum ius est. Sed
ceterae quoque stellae non minus terrena quam
incumbentem terris spiritum afficiunt et cursu [1] suo
occursuve contrario modo frigora, modo imbres
aliasque terris turbide [2] iniurias movent.

3   Haec necessarium fuit praeloqui dicturo de tonitru
fulminibusque ac fulgurationibus. Nam cum in
aere fiant, naturam eius explicari oportebat, quo
facilius appareret quid facere aut pati posset.

1   12. Tria sunt quae accidunt, fulgurationes, fulmina,
tonitrua, quae una facta serius audiuntur. Fulguratio ostendit ignem, fulminatio emittit. Illa,
ut ita dicam, comminatio est et conatio sine ictu;
ista iaculatio cum ictu.

2   Quaedam sunt de quibus inter omnes convenit,
quaedam in quibus diversae sententiae sunt. Convenit de illis, omnia ista in nubibus et e nubibus fieri.
Etiamnunc convenit et fulgurationes et fulminationes
aut igneas esse aut ignea specie.

3   Ad illa nunc transeamus in quibus lis est. Quidam

---

[1] *cursu* E[2] Oltramare; *cultu* HPE[1]Z; *ortu* ABV; *circuitu*
Garrod.
[2] *turbine* EB.

in this or that direction, greatly influences the condition of the atmosphere. The movements of the stars, of which you may consider the sun the most influential, supply other causes. The year follows the sun, and winters and summers alternate in accordance with the sun's circling changes. Next in importance is the influence of the moon. But other heavenly bodies also affect the earth and the atmosphere covering the earth. Their course or their concourse cause, in opposite ways, sometimes cold, sometimes rain, and other inclement disturbances on earth.

It has been necessary for me to make these preliminary statements before going on to talk about thunder, lightning bolts, and lightning flashes. Since they occur in the atmosphere I had to explain the nature of the atmosphere in order that it might be more readily apparent what it can do and what influences it is subjected to.

12. There are three phenomena which occur: lightning flashes, lightning bolts, and thunder. Thunder is made simultaneously with the others but is heard later. A lightning flash displays fire; a lightning bolt emits it. A lightning flash is a threat, so to speak, a feint without actually striking; a lightning bolt is an attack with a hit.

There are certain points which are agreed upon by all authorities, others on which opinions vary. It is agreed that all these phenomena occur in the clouds and come from the clouds. It is further agreed that both lightning flashes and lightning bolts are either fiery or have the appearance of fire.

Now let us get to those points on which there is

putant ignem inesse nubibus; quidam ad tempus
fieri nec prius esse quam mitti. Ne inter illos quidem
qui praeparant ignem convenit; alius enim illum
aliunde colligit. Quidam aiunt radios solis intro-
currentis recurrentisque et saepius in se relatos
ignem excitare. Anaxagoras ait illum ex aethere
destillare et ex tanto ardore caeli multa decidere quae
nubes diu inclusa custodiant.

4   Aristoteles multo ante ignem colligi non putat, sed
eodem momento exilire quo fiat. Cuius sententia
talis est. Duae partes mundi in imo iacent, terra et
aqua. Utraque ex se reddit aliquid: terrenus vapor
siccus est et fumo similis, qui ventos, fulmina, tonitrua facit; aquarum halitus umidus est et in imbres et
5   nives cedit. Sed siccus ille terrarum vapor, unde
ventis origo est, cum coacervatus est, coitu nubium
vehementer a latere [1] eliditur; deinde, †ut latius,†[2]
nubes proximas feriet. Haec plaga cum sono in-
cutitur, qualis in nostris ignibus redditur, cum flamma
vitio lignorum virentium [3] crepat. Et illic spiritus
habens aliquid umidi secum conglobatusque rumpitur

---

[1] *a latere* ABV Oltramare; *alterum* HPGZ; *impactarum* ET;
latarum Alexander.
[2] *ubi latius* ET; *vi latus* Gronovius; *violentius* Kroll;
Oltramare proposes *ut exilit latius;* Alexander accepts *ut latius.*
[3] *virentium* GFT; *urentium* most MSS.

---

[1] Aristotle (2.9.369b 12) assigns this theory to Empedocles,
who believes that some of the sun's rays are trapped in clouds.
[2] Aristotle (2.9.369b 15–30) disagrees with both Empedocles
and Anaxagoras.

dispute. Some think that the fire exists in the clouds;[1] others that it is created for the occasion and does not exist before it is emitted. Even among those who propose a preliminary fire there is no agreement; some collect it from one source, others from another. Some say that as the rays of the sun go in and bounce back they are often accumulated and kindle the fire. Anaxagoras says that fire is distilled from the upper atmosphere and that from the great heat of the sky many fiery particles fall which the clouds inclose and retain for a long time.[2]

Aristotle thinks the fire is not collected much **4** beforehand but it bursts out the same instant it is created.[3] His theory is along these lines:[4] two elements, earth and water, lie in the lower region of the universe. Each emanates something from itself. Vapour from the earth is dry and like smoke; it makes winds, lightning bolts, and thunder. The exhalation of water is moist and changes into rain and snow. But when that dry vapour from earth **5** (from which winds have their origin) has accumulated it is violently struck on one side by its collision with clouds. Then as it is more widely expelled it will strike adjacent clouds. The blow is struck with the sort of sound that is produced in our fireplaces when flames crackle because of imperfections in green wood. The air in the wood, having some element of moisture, is accumulated and breaks out in

[3] Aristotle 2.9.369b 20–370a 10.
[4] Aristotle 2.9.369a 14–369b 5. As he often does, Seneca paraphrases much of the passage he refers to in the *Meteorologica* and is not citing Aristotle's work directly but probably from memory.

flamma. Eodem modo spiritus ille, quem paulo ante exprimi collisis nubibus [1] dixi, impactus aliis nec 6 rumpi nec exilire silentio potest. Dissimilis autem crepitus fit ob dissimilitudinem [2] nubium, quarum aliae maiorem sinum [3] habent, aliae minorem. Ceterum illa vis expressi spiritus ignis est qui fulgurationis nomen habet, levi impetu accensus et vanus. Ante autem videmus fulgorem quam sonum audimus, quia oculorum velocior sensus est et multum aures antecedit.

1 13. Falsam opinionem esse eorum qui ignem in nubibus servant per multa colligi potest. Si de caelo cadit, quomodo non cotidie fit, cum tandundem semper illic ardeat? Deinde nullam rationem reddiderunt quare ignis, quem natura sursum vocat, defluat. Alia enim condicio nostrorum ignium est, ex quibus favillae cadunt, quae ponderis aliquid secum habent; ita non descendit ignis, sed praeci- 2 pitatur et deducitur. Huic simile nihil accidit in illo igne purissimo, in quo nihil est quod deprimatur. Aut si ulla pars eius exciderit, in periculo totus est, quia totum potest excidere quod potest carpi. Deinde illud quod cadit leve est an grave? Leve est? Non potest ruere quod cadere levitas prohibet;

[1] *ignibus* ABV λ.
[2] *dissimilem impactionem* ABV.
[3] *sonum* ET; *sonitum* ABV.

flame.   In the same way, the air, which I said a little while ago was pressed out by colliding clouds and hurled against other clouds, cannot be forced out or escape without making a sound.   However, a **6** different crashing noise is made according to differences in clouds,[1] some of which have a larger cavity, others a smaller.   But air that has been forcibly driven out is fire, which has the name of lightning flash, kindled by a slight impact and without force.   We see the flash before we hear the sound because our eyesight is swift and greatly outdistances our hearing.[2]

13. The theory of those who preserve fire in clouds **1** is erroneous, as can be inferred from many speculations.   If the fire falls from the sky why does it not do so daily since it always blazes as much up there?   Then, they give no explanation why fire, which by nature flows down, rises.   The circumstances of our fires on earth from which sparks fall is another matter.   The sparks have some weight in themselves.   Fire does not descend this way; rather it is forced and conducted downward.   Nothing analogous **2** to this happens in the case of pure celestial fire, in which there is nothing that might be pressed down.   Otherwise, if any part of it falls the whole is in danger because whatever can suffer subtraction can collapse as a whole.   But what about that falling fire?   Is it light or heavy?   Is it light?   Then it cannot tumble because its lightness prevents it from

---

[1] Aristotle 2.9.369b 1–3.
[2] Better is Pliny 2.142: thunder and lightning occur simultaneously but the flash is seen before the thunderclap is heard, as light travels more swiftly than sound.

illud suo se [1] in adyto [2] tenet. Grave est? Quomodo illic esse potuit unde caderet?

3   " Quid ergo? Non aliqui ignes in inferiora ferri
solent, sicut haec ipsa de quibus quaerimus fulmina?"
Fateor. Non eunt tamen, sed feruntur; aliqua illos
potentia deprimit. Quae non est in aethere; nihil
enim illic iniuria cogitur, nihil rumpitur, nihil praeter
4   solitum evenit. Ordo rerum est, et expurgatus ignis
in custodia mundi summa sortitus oras [3] operis
pulcherrimi [4] circumit. Hinc [5] descendere non potest,
sed ne ab externo quidem deprimi, quia in aethere
nulli incerto corpori locus est; certa et ordinata non
pugnant.

1   14. " Vos," inquit,[6] " dicitis, cum causas stellarum
transvolantium redditis, posse aliquas aeris partes ad
se trahere ignem ex locis superioribus et sic ardore
accendi." Sed plurimum interest utrum aliquis
dicat ignem ex aethere decidere, quod natura non
patitur, an dicat ex ignea vi calorem in ea quae
subiacent transilire. Non enim illinc ignis cadit,
2   quod non potest fieri, sed hic nascitur. Videmus
certe apud nos late incendio pervagante quasdam

---

[1] *se* supplied by Oltramare.
[2] *adito* HZF; *abdito* JKVT; *addito* GOP; *abscondito* E.
[3] *horas* most MSS.
[4] Madvig, Oltramare for *pulcherrime* MSS.
[5] *hic* HPEZ; *hinc* ABV Gercke.
[6] *inquit* AB Alexander; *inquam* HEFZV Oltramare.

falling; it maintains itself in its own sanctuary. Is it heavy? Then how could it remain in the place from which it might fall?

"What then? Are not some fires commonly 3 carried to lower regions, just as those lightning bolts we are investigating?" I agree. Yet they do not go; they are carried. Some other force presses them downward, a force which is not in the upper atmosphere, for in that place nothing is compelled by violence, nothing is ruptured, nothing occurs beyond the usual. There exists an order in things, and the 4 fire, which is cleansed and assigned in the guardianship of the universe to the highest regions, circles around the borders of an absolutely beautiful creation. From here it cannot descend. It cannot even be pushed down by external force, because no unstable body has a place in the upper atmosphere. Elements that are fixed and ordered are not in conflict.

14. "When" says he, "you give an explanation 1 of shooting stars you say that some parts of the atmosphere can draw fire from the upper regions and thus be kindled by the heat." But it makes a great deal of difference whether someone says fire falls from the upper atmosphere [1]—which nature does not permit—or says that the heat from a fiery glow leaps across to regions which lie below. For the fire does not fall from the upper regions—it cannot happen—but is generated in the lower regions. Certainly, when a conflagration has 2 blazed over a wide area in one of our cities we see

[1] Above, Chapter 12.3, Seneca ascribes this theory to Anaxagoras.

insulas quae diu concaluerunt ex se concipere flammam; itaque verisimile est etiam in aere summo id
quod [1] ignis rapiendi naturam habet accendi calore
aetheris superpositi. Necesse est enim ut et imus
aether habeat aliquid aeri simile et summus aer non
sit dissimilis imo [2] aetheri, quia non fit statim in
diversum ex diverso transitus; paulatim ista in con-
finio vim suam miscent ita ut dubitare possis aer an
hoc iam aether sit.

1   15. Quidam ex nostris existimant aera, cum in
ignem et aquam mutabilis sit, non detrahere aliunde
causas flammarum novas; ipse enim se movendo
accendit et, cum densos compactosque nubium sinus
dissipat, necessario vastum in tam magnorum corporum diruptione reddit sonum. Illa porro nubium
difficulter cedentium pugna aliquid confert ad con-
citandum ignem sic quemadmodum ferro ad secandum
aliquid manus confert, sed secare ferri est.

1   16. Quid ergo inter fulgurationem et fulmen
interest? Dicam. Fulguratio est late ignis ex-
plicitus, fulmen est coactus ignis et in impetum
iactus. Solemus duabus manibus inter se iunctis
aquam concipere et compressa utrimque palma in
modum siponis exprimere. Simile quiddam et
illic fieri puta: nubium inter se compressarum

---

[1] *id quod* Gercke, Oltramare; *in quo* HPFE.
[2] *summo* HPE.

that some blocks of houses which have been growing hot for a long time catch fire spontaneously. It is much the same way in the upper atmosphere also; it is probable that something which has the capacity to attract fire is kindled by the heat of the atmosphere above it. For it needs be that both the lowest ether has something similar to atmosphere and the highest atmosphere is not dissimilar to the lowest ether, because a transition from different to different does not occur immediately. On the confines they mingle their properties so gradually that you cannot tell whether it is atmosphere or already ether.

15. Some Stoics believe that since air can be changed into fire and water it does not draw new causes of fire from an outside source. Fire kindles itself by movement. When it dissipates dense and compact masses of clouds, it necessarily emits a loud noise in the bursting of such large bodies. Furthermore, this conflict of the resisting clouds contributes somewhat to arousing fire. As an analogy, the hand contributes something to the knife in cutting but it is the knife that cuts.

16. What is the difference between a lightning flash and a lightning bolt? I will explain. A lightning flash is fire that has been spread out over a wide area; a lightning bolt is fire that has been compressed and hurled violently. Sometimes we take up water in our two clasped hands and pressing our palms together squirt out the water the way a pump does. Suppose something like this occurs in the clouds. The constricted space of the compressed clouds forces out the air that is between them and by means of this pressure sets the air afire

angustiae medium spiritum eiciunt et hoc ipso in-
flammant ac tormenti modo emittunt; nam ballistae
quoque scorpionesque tela cum sono expellunt.

1 17. Quidam existimant igneum[1] spiritum per
frigida atque umida meantem sonum reddere. Nam
ne ferrum quidem ardens silentio tinguitur, sed, si in
aquam fervens massa descendit, cum multo murmure
extinguitur. Ita, ut Anaximenes ait, spiritus incidens nubibus tonitrua edit et, dum luctatur per
obstantia atque interscissa vadere, ipsa ignem fuga
accendit.

1 18. Anaximandrus omnia ad spiritum rettulit.
Tonitrua, inquit, sunt nubis ictae sonus. Quare
inaequalia sunt? Quia et ipse ictus inaequalis est.
Quare et sereno tonat? Quia tunc quoque per
crassum[2] et scissum aera spiritus prosilit. At quare
aliquando non fulgurat et tonat? Quia spiritus
infirmior non valuit in flammam, in sonum valuit.
Quid est ergo ipsa fulguratio? Aeris diducentis se
corruentisque iactatio languidum ignem nec exiturum[3] pariens.[4] Quid est fulmen? Acrioris den-
siorisque spiritus cursus.

---

[1] *igneum* Z Oltramare; *in eum* HP; *eum* ET; *ipsum* AV;
istum B.
[2] *percussum* B; *per percussum* T; *per quassum* Gronovius,
Haase.
[3] *exiturum* HPZABV Oltramare, Alexander; *exulturum*
Gercke.
[4] *pariens* Oltramare for *aperiens* MSS.

---

[1] The *ballistae* hurled heavy things such as earthen balls,
the *scorpiones* large javelins.

and hurls it the way a catapult does. Actually, the catapults called *ballistae* and *scorpiones* also hurl their missiles with a noise.[1]

17. Some [2] think the fiery air produces the noise 1 as it passes through cold, wet regions. Hot iron even makes a noise when it is tempered, and if the glowing mass plunges into water it is extinguished with a loud sputtering.[3] So, as Anaximenes [4] says, air falling on clouds produces thunder and, while it struggles to pass through obstacles and openings, it catches fire by its very flight.

18. Anaximander [5] related all these phenomena to 1 air. Thunder, he says, is the sound of a cloud being struck. Why do the sounds of thunder vary? Because the blow itself is also variable. Why does it thunder in a cloudless sky? Because even then the air leaps out through thick and lacerated atmosphere. But why is there sometimes no lightning flash and yet it thunders? Because the air was too weak, not strong enough for fire but strong enough for noise. Then, what is the lightning flash itself? A disturbance of the atmosphere dispersing and rushing together, producing a weak fire that will not discharge. What is a lightning bolt? The motion of more active and denser air.

[2] Such as Archelaus and Anaxagoras.
[3] Pliny 2.112: when the fires of stars fall into the clouds a hissing steam is produced, just as when a red hot iron is plunged into water.
[4] Anaximenes, of Miletus, was a pupil of Anaximander, in the second half of the sixth century.
[5] Anaximander was a pupil of Thales, at Miletus in the first half of the sixth century.

1   19. Anaxagoras [1] ait omnia ista sic fieri ut ex aethere aliqua vis in inferiora descendat. Ita ignis impactus nubibus frigidis sonat; at, cum illas interscindit, fulget, et minor vis ignium fulgurationes facit, maior fulmina.

1   20. Diogenes Apolloniates ait quaedam tonitrua igne, quaedam spiritu fieri; illa ignis facit quae ipse antecedit et nuntiat; illa spiritus quae sine splendore crepuerunt.

2   Utrumque sine altero esse [2] aliquando concedo, ita tamen ut non discreta illis potestas sit, sed utrumque ab utroque effici possit. Quis enim negabit spiritum magno impetu latum, cum effecerit sonum, effecturum et ignem? Quis autem non et hoc concedet aliquando ignem quoque irrumpere posse nubes et non exilire, si plurium acervo nubium, cum paucas perscidisset, oppressus est? Ergo et ignis ibit in spiritum perdetque fulgorem, et spiritus, dum 3 secat vi fera viam [3] incendet. Adice nunc quod necesse est impetus fulminis et praemittat spiritus agatque ante se, et a tergo trahat ventum, cum tam vasto ictu aera inciderit. Itaque omnia, antequam

---

[1] *Anaxagoras* Gercke, Oltramare; *Anaxandrus* (*-dros*) HPEZA²BV; *Anaximandros* A¹ Haase.

[2] *altero esse* Z Oltramare; *altero effixa esse* HPF; *altero fier et esse* ABV; *altero efficax esse* Gercke; *altero aliquando fier concedo* Haase.

[3] *secat vi fera viam* Oltramare; *secata infera* Z; *secata infra* HPEFBA; *dum secat aera* Madvig.

19. Anaxagoras says that all these phenomena 1
occur as a result of some force that descends from
the upper atmosphere to the lower regions. So fire
that is struck against by cold clouds makes a sound;
but when it cleaves through them it makes a flash.
A weaker force of fire produces lightning flashes; a
stronger, lightning bolts.

20. Diogenes of Apollonia[1] says that some thun- 1
der comes from fire, some from air. Fire makes the
thunder which it precedes and announces. Air
makes the thunder which produces noise without a
flash.

I agree that sometimes one exists without the 2
other. None the less, they happen in such a way
that their powers are not independent; one can be
produced by the other. Who will maintain that air
carried with great force will not also produce fire
when it produces sound? Moreover, everyone will
agree also that sometimes fire can burst through
clouds and yet not dart from them; for example, if
it has split a few clouds but is buried by a great mass
of them. In such cases the fire will pass into the air
and lose its flash, yet the air will cause fire while it
violently cuts a path inside the clouds. Now add 3
an inevitable consequence: when the blast of the
lightning bolt strikes the atmosphere with such a
great impact it both sends ahead and drives in front
of itself blasts of air, and also pulls wind behind itself.
Thus, before things are struck by lightning they

---

[1] Diogenes of Apollonia, second half of the fifth century,
developed the theories of Anaximenes. He was one of the
teachers of Plato.

feriantur, intremescunt[1] vibrata vento quem ignis ante se pressit.

1   21. Dimissis nunc praeceptoribus nostris incipimus per nos moveri et a confessis transimus ad dubia. Quid in confesso est? Fulmen ignem esse, et aeque fulgurationem, quae nihil aliud est quam flamma, futura fulmen, si plus virium habuisset; non natura
2 ista sed impetu distant. Esse illum ignem color[2] ostendit, qui non est nisi ex eo.[3] Ostendit effectus: magnorum enim saepe incendiorum causa fulmen fuit; silvae illo concrematae et urbium partes; etiam quae non percussa sunt, tamen adusta cernuntur; quaedam vero veluti fuligine colorantur. Quid quod omnibus fulguratis odor sulphuris est?
3 Ergo et utramque rem ignem esse constat et utramque rem inter se meando distare; fulguratio enim est non perlatum usque in terras fulmen, et rursus licet dicas fulmen esse fulgurationem usque in terras perductam.

4   Non ad exercendum verba diutius hoc idem tracto, sed ut cognata esse ista et eiusdem notae ac naturae probem. Fulguratio est paene fulmen. Vertamus istud, fulmen est plus quiddam quam fulguratio.

---

[1] *intremescunt* HPZ Oltramare; *intremiscunt* GABVT.
[2] *calor* AV.
[3] *nisi ex eo* G Oltramare; *nisi ex igne* Z Alexander.

shake, because they are vibrated by the wind which the fire pushes in front of itself.[1]

21. Now let us dismiss our teachers and begin to 1 move on our own as we pass from what is agreed upon to what is doubtful. What is agreed upon? It is generally agreed that a lightning bolt is fire and so is a lightning flash, which is merely fire that would have become a lightning bolt if it had acquired more force. They differ not in their nature but in their force. Its colour shows that a lightning bolt is fire, 2 since such colour is not present except in fire. Its effects prove it. Often a lightning bolt is the cause of great conflagrations. Forests and sections of cities have been reduced to ashes by it. Even the objects which are not struck are seen to be scorched; in fact, some are coloured as though with soot. And, what about the fact that everything struck by lightning has the odour of sulphur? So, it is generally 3 agreed that both a lightning flash and a lightning bolt are fire and that both differ from each other only in their range of movement. A lightning flash is a lightning bolt that is not carried all the way to the earth. Conversely, you could say that a lightning bolt is a lightning flash that is carried all the way to the ground.

I do not drag out this point at length just to play 4 with words, but to prove that these phenomena are related and are of the same category and nature. A lightning flash is almost a lightning bolt. Let us turn it around: a lightning bolt is something more than a lightning flash.

---

[1] This is what Aristotle says (3.1.371b 10).

1   22. Quoniam constat utramque rem ignem esse,
videamus quemadmodum ignis fieri soleat apud nos;
eadem enim ratione et supra fiet. Fit[1] duobus
modis, uno si excitatur sicut e lapide; altero si
attritu invenitur, sicut cum duo ligna inter se diutius
fricta sunt.   Non omnis hoc tibi materia praestabit,
sed idonea eliciendis ignibus, sicut laurus, hederae et
2 alia in hunc usum nota pastoribus. Potest ergo
fieri ut nubes quoque ignem eodem modo vel per-
cussae reddant vel attritae. Videamus quantis
procellae viribus ruant, quanto vertantur impetu
turbines; id quod obvium fuit, dissipatur et rapitur
3 et longe a loco suo proicitur. Quid ergo mirum, si
tanta vis ignem excutit vel aliunde vel sibi? Vides
enim quantum fervorem sensura sint corpora horum
transitu trita, nec hoc in his tantum debet[2] credi ac
siderum†, quorum ingens in confesso potentia est.

1   23. Sed fortasse nubes quoque in nubes incitatae
feriente[3] vento et leviter urgente ignem evocabunt
qui explendescat nec exiliat; minore enim vi ad
fulgurandum opus est quam ad fulminandum.
2 Superioribus[4] collegimus in quantum fervorem
quaedam affricta perducerentur. Cum autem aer
mutabilis in ignem maximis viribus, id est suis, cum
in ventum[5] conversus est, atteratur, verisimile es·
ignem excuti caducum et cito interiturum, quia no·

---

[1] *Fit* supplied by Gercke, Oltramare.
[2] *debet* FABV Alexander; *debere* most MSS. Oltramare. Fo·
ac siderum Madvig proposed *accidere*. Perhaps *sideribus*
E.H.W.
[3] *feriente* Oltramare for *fremente* or *frementes* most MSS.

22. Since it is agreed that the two are fire, let us 1
see how fire usually occurs on earth, for it will occur
above it also on the same principle. It is produced
in two ways: one, by striking it out, as from a stone,
for example; another, it is acquired by friction, as
when two pieces of wood have been rubbed together
for some time. Not every wood will do this for you,
but only wood suitable for eliciting fire, such as laurel,
ivy, and other wood familiar to shepherds for this use.
It can happen, then, that clouds also produce fire the 2
same way, by percussion or by friction. Think of the
great force which drives squalls, the great impetus
which whirls tornadoes. Whatever gets in their way
is scattered, snatched up, and hurled far from its
place. What surprise is it, then, if such a powerful 3
force strikes fire from something else or even from
itself? You see how great a heat bodies would be
likely to experience when they are battered by the
passing of these winds. This should not be assumed
so much in the case of winds as of heavenly bodies
also, whose enormous power is beyond question.

23. Perhaps, also, when the wind makes contact 1
and presses lightly, clouds are pushed against clouds
and will elicit a fire which glows but does not leap
forth. For less force is needed for a lightning flash
than for a lightning bolt. We have considered above 2
what a glow certain woods produce when rubbed
together. When air, which can be changed into
fire, is subjected to friction by a great force (for
example, by its own force when it changes into wind)

---

4 *Superioribus libris* HPEZ.
5 *in ignem* ABV.

ex solida materia oritur nec in qua possit consistere.
Transit itaque tantumque habet morae quantum
itineris et cursus; sine alimento proiectus est.

1   24. " Quomodo," inquit, " cum dicatis ignis hanc
esse naturam ut petat superiora, fulmen terram
petit? Aut falsum est quod de igne dixistis; est
enim illi aeque sursum iter quam deorsum?" Utrumque verum potest esse. Ignis enim natura in
verticem surgit et, si nihil illum prohibet, ascendit,
sicut aqua natura defertur; si tamen aliqua vis
accessit quae illam in contrarium circumageret, illo
2 intenditur unde imbre deiecta est. Fulmen autem
eadem necessitate qua aqua ascendit[1] deicitur.[2]
Idem his ignibus accidit quod arboribus quarum
cacumina trahi possunt ita ut terram spectent, si
tenera sunt, etiam ut attingant; sed cum permiseris,
in locum suum exilient. Itaque non est quod eum
spectes cuiusque rei habitum qui illi non ex voluntate
3 est. Si igni permittes ire quo velit, caelum, id est
levissimi cuiusque sedem, repetet; ubi est aliquid
quod eum feriat et ab impetu suo avertat, id non
natura, sed servitus eius sit.

1   25. " Dicis," inquit,[3] " nubes attritas edere ignem,
cum sint umidae, immo udae; quomodo ergo possunt
gignere ignem, quem non magis verisimile est ex
nube quam ex aqua generari? "[4]

---

[1] *aqua ascendit* supplied by Oltramare.
[2] *qua excutitur deicitur* Gercke.
[3] *inquit* Z; *inquam* G; *inquis* most MSS.
[4] *generari* ABV; *ex aqua nasci* Oltramare; *ex aqua nasci-turum* Gercke; *est fieri ex nube quam ex aqua* ET; *gign*
Alexander.

it is probable that fire is produced, but a short-lived and quickly perishable fire because it does not arise from solid material on which it can stay fuelled. Therefore, it is transitory and has only the duration of its journey and route. It is hurled forth without fuel.

24. Somebody says, " How does a lightning bolt 1 seek the earth when you say that it is the nature of fire to seek higher places ? Or is what you said about fire not true; for its path is up as well as down ? " Both can be true. By nature fire rises and ascends in a straight line if nothing prevents it, just as water naturally moves downward. However, if some force comes along which moves the water around in an opposite direction it rises towards the place from which it was hurled down by a rainstorm. A 2 lightning bolt, then, falls down by the same necessity which forces water to ascend. The same thing happens to celestial fires which happens to trees whose tops can be bent down so that they point to the earth, even touch the earth if they are slender trees. But, when you release them they spring back into their original position. So, there is no reason for you to take notice of anything's behaviour which is not voluntary to it. If you allow fire to go where it wants 3 to, it will go back to the sky, that is, to the dwelling-place of all the lightest bodies. When there is something which strikes it and averts it from its true direction—that is not its nature, but its subjugation.

25. " You say that clouds produce fire by friction 1 when they are moist, even wet," he says. " How, then, can they generate fire, which is no more believably generated from a cloud than from water ? "

1   26. Ex nube nascitur.[1] Primum in nubibus non
aqua est, sed aer spissus, ad gignendam aquam
praeparatus, nondum in illam mutatus, sed iam
pronus et vergens.   Non est quod existimes eam tum
2 colligi, tum effundi; simul fit et cadit.   Deinde, si
concessero umidam esse nubem conceptis aquis
plenam, nihil tamen prohibet ignem ex umido quoque
educi, immo ex ipso, quod magis mireris, umore.
Quidam negaverunt in ignem quicquam posse
mutari, priusquam mutatum esset in aquam.   Potest
ergo nubes, salva quam continet aqua, ignem parte
aliqua sui reddere, ut saepe alia pars ligni ardet,
alia sudat.

3   Nec hoc dico non contraria inter se ista esse et
alterum altero perimi; sed ubi valentior ignis quam
umor est, vincit; rursus, cum copia umoris exuperat,
tunc ignis sine effectu est; itaque non ardent virentia.
Refert ergo quantum aquae sit; exigua enim non
resistet nec vim ignis impediet.

4   Quidni? Maiorum nostrorum memoria, ut Posidonius tradidit, cum insula in Aegaeo mari surgeret,
spumabat interdiu mare et fumus ex alto ferebatur.
Nox [2] demum prodebat ignem, non continuum sed ex
intervallis emicantem fulminum [3] more, quotiens

---

[1] Gercke, Alexander delete *ex nube nascitur*; *Ignis qui
nascitur primum in nubibus* ABV.
[2] *Nox demum* Madvig, Oltramare; *nam demum* most MSS;
non demum Z.   [3] *fluminum* HPZABV.

---

[1] This was Hiera (Paleokaimeni) which appeared in 197 B.C.
in the Santorin group; where another one Thia (it sank again

138

26. Fire is produced from a cloud. First of all, 1
there is no water in clouds, but dense air which is
ready to produce water. The air is not yet changed
into water but is already prepared for and verging on
the change. You should not believe that the water
is first amassed and afterwards poured down. It is
formed and falls simultaneously. In the second 2
place, even though I may concede that a cloud is
moist and filled with secreted water, still nothing
prevents fire from being drawn out of something
moist also, even out of pure moisture—which will
surprise you even more. Some say that nothing can
change into fire before it has changed into water.
Accordingly, a cloud can emit fire from some part of
itself while the water it contains is unaffected, just
as frequently part of a log burns while the other
part exudes moisture.

Yet I do not say that moisture and fire are not 3
contrary to each other or that one is not destroyed by
the other. But when the fire is stronger than the
water, it conquers. On the other hand, when the
quantity of water is abundant, the fire is ineffectual.
Consequently, green wood does not burn. So, it
makes a difference how much water is present. A
scanty amount will neither resist nor impede the
force of fire.

Why not? According to Posidonius, an island arose 4
in the Aegean Sea, in the tradition of our forefathers.[1]
The sea foamed during the day and smoke was
carried up from the depths. Finally night brought
forth fire, not a continuous fire but one that flashed at

later) appeared on 31 Dec. A.D. 46 or 1 Jan. 47. Cf. Bk.
6.21.1; Pliny *NH* 2.202, 4.70. See our vol. 2, p. 189.

ardor infernus iacentis super undae pondus evicerat.

5 Deinde saxa evoluta rupesque partim illaesae, quas spiritus, antequam urerentur, expulerat, partim exesae et in levitatem pumicis versae. Novissime cacumen usti montis emicuit. Postea altitudini adiectum et saxum illud in magnitudinem insulae

6 crevit. Idem nostra memoria Valerio Asiatico consule iterum accidit. Quorsus haec rettuli? Ut appareret nec extinctum ignem mari superfuso, nec impetum eius gravitate ingentis undae prohibitum exire; ducentorum passuum fuisse altitudinem Asclepiodotus, auditor Posidonii, tradidit, per quam diremptis aquis ignis emersit.

7 Quod si immensa aquarum vis flammarum ex imo subeuntem vim non potuit opprimere, quanto minus impedire [1] poterit ignem nubium tenuis umor et roscidus? Adeo res ista non affert ullam moram ut [2] contra causa [3] ignium sit; quos non videmus emicare nisi impendente caelo; serenum sine fulmine est. Non habet istos metus dies purus, ne nox quidem nisi obscura nubibus.

[1] *impedire* ET; *in ea edere* HPGZ; *in ea extinguere* AV; *in aere extinguere* Fortunatus; *includere* Gercke; *intercludere* Castiglioni.
[2] *ut* Z Oltramare; *quae* PABλ Gercke, Alexander; *quod* HT.
[3] Madvig, Gercke, Oltramare for *causas* MSS.

intervals like lightning, as often as the heat below
overcame the weight of water lying above. Then 5
rocks and boulders were hurled up. The air had
expelled some of them before they were burnt, and
so they were undamaged while others were corroded
and changed to light pumice. Finally, the top of a
burned mountain emerged. Afterwards, the rock
gained height and grew to the size of an island. The 6
same thing happened again in our own time during
the second consulship of Valerius Asiaticus.[1] Why
do I mention these curiosities? So it may be clear
that fire is not extinguished even by a sea covering it
and that its force is not prevented from bursting out
even by an enormous mass of water. Asclepiodotus,[2]
the pupil of Posidonius, says that the height of water
through which the fire reached before it had broken
through was two hundred feet. Well, if that enormous amount of water could not suppress the force of
the flames that emerged from below, how much less
can the thin, dewy moisture of the clouds impede fire?
The moisture of the clouds is so far from affording any
obstacle that on the contrary it is a cause of fire.
We do not see lightning unless the sky is overhanging.
A clear sky is without lightning.[3] A bright day
does not hold this threat, nor does a night unless it is
dark with clouds.

---

[1] In A.D. 46.
[2] All we know of this Asclepiodotus is what Seneca tells us
here, that he was a pupil of Posidonius.
[3] This is what Aristotle says (2.9.369b 23), as does Lucretius
(6.400), and others. When there is lightning in a clear sky it
is a bad omen (cf., for example, Lucan 1.534–535; Virgil
Georg. 1.487). Thunder in a clear sky was well known.

8   " Quid ergo? Non aliquando etiam apparentibus
stellis et nocte tranquilla fulgurat?" Sed scias licet
illic nubes esse unde splendor effertur, quas videri
9 a nobis terrarum tumor non sinit. Adice nunc quod
fieri potest ut nubes summissae [1] et humiles attritu
suo ignem reddant; qui in superiora expressus, in
parte caeli sincera puraque visitur, sed fit in sordida.

1   27. Tonitrua distinxere quidam ita ut dicerent
unum esse genus cuius grave sit murmur, quale
terrarum motum antecedit clauso vento et fremente.
2 Hoc quomodo videatur illis fieri dicam. Cum
spiritum intra se clausere nubes, in concavis partibus
earum volutatus aer similem agit mugitibus sonum,
raucum et aequalem et continuum, utique ubi etiam
umida illa regio est et exitum claudit; ideo eiusmodi
3 tonitrua venturi praenuntia imbris sunt. Aliud
genus est acre, quod acerbum magis [2] dixerim quam
sonorum,[3] quale audire solemus, cum super caput
alicuius dirupta vesica est; talia eduntur tonitrua,
cum conglobata nubes dissolvitur et eum quo distenta
fuerat spiritum emittit. Hic proprie fragor dicitur,
subitus et vehemens. Quo edito concidunt homines
et exanimantur; quidam vero vivi stupent et in

[1] Schultess, Oltramare for *summae* MSS.
[2] *magis* ZA; *mage* HPEFGV.
[3] *sonorum* ABV; *sonum* HPEFGZ.

" But well! Does it not sometimes flash lightning, 8 even when the stars are visible and the night is clear? " But you know that clouds do exist in the region from which the flash comes, clouds that the swelling curve of the earth does not permit us to see. Now add something else that can happen: namely, 9 that low clouds close to the earth produce fire by their own friction. When this fire is forced into the upper regions it is seen in a calm and clear part of the sky, but it actually occurred in a dingy region.

27. Some authorities make a distinction between 1 types of thunder. For example, they say that one kind has a deep rumble like the sound which precedes an earthquake when the wind is obstructed and raging. I will explain how the types of thunder occur, as it seems to them.

When the clouds have air shut up inside, it rolls 2 around in the hollow sections and produces a hoarse, regular, and continuous sound similar to bellowing. This is certainly so when the region is moist and closes off any outlet. So, thunder of this sort is a sign of coming rain. Another kind is sharp, which I 3 should call a pop rather than a regular sound, the sort of noise we usually hear when a bladder is burst over somebody's head.[1] Such thunder is produced when a densely packed cloud is broken up and releases the air with which it had been inflated. This sudden, violent sound is appropriately called a crash. When it occurs, people collapse and are frightened to death. Some are dazed, though still alive, and lose

[1] Lucretius (6.130) and Pliny (2.113) make the same comparison between the sound of thunder and that of a bursting bag of air.

totum sibi excidunt, quos vocamus attonitos, quorum
mentem sonus ille caelestis loco pepulit.

4   Hic fieri illo quoque modo potest ut inclusus [1] aer
cava nube et motu ipso extenuatus diffundatur;
deinde, dum maiorem sibi locum quaerit, a quibus
involutus est, sonum patitur. Quid autem? Non,
quemadmodum illisae inter se manus plausum
edunt, sic illisarum inter se nubium sonus potest esse,
magnus quia magna concurrunt?

1   28. " Videmus," inquit, " nubes impingi montibus
nec sonum fieri." Primum omnium non quocumque
modo illisae sunt sonant, sed si apte compositae ad
sonum edendum. Aversas inter se manus collide,
non plaudent; sed palma cum palma collata plausum
facit; et plurimum interest utrum cavae concutiantur
an planae et extentae. Deinde non tantum ire
nubes oportet sed agi magna vi et procellosa.

2   Etiamnunc mons non findit [2] nubem, sed digerit et
primam quamque partem eius solvit. Ne vesica
quidem, quocumque modo spiritum emisit, sonat: si
ferro divisa est, sine ullo aurium sensu exit; rumpi
illam oportet, ut sonet, non secari. Idem de nubibus
dico; nisi multo impetu dissiluere, non resonant.
Adice nunc quod nubes in montem actae non fran-
guntur, sed circumfunduntur et in aliquas partes
montis, in arbores, ramos, frutices, aspera saxa et

[1] *inclusus* ET; *incussus* HZAB; *incursus* PV.
[2] *fundit* E¹L¹; *confundit* ABV.

their senses entirely. We call them " thunder-struck " because that sound in the sky has unbalanced their minds.

The noise can also happen this way: air which is 4 enclosed in a hollow cloud and rarefied by its own motion expands. Then, as it seeks more space for itself it resounds from what envelopes it. But why ? Just as hands clapped together produce applause, so there can be sound from clouds colliding together ; but the sound is loud because large masses collide.

28. " We see clouds struck on mountains," he says, 1 " yet no sound occurs." First of all, clouds do not make a sound when struck just any sort of way but only if suitably arranged for producing sound. Clap the backs of your hands together. They do not make the sound of applauding. But the palms of the hands struck together make the clapping noise. Also, it makes a great difference whether hollow clouds strike together or flat and extended ones. Finally, the clouds should not merely move together but be driven together violently and tempestuously. Besides, a mountain does not split a cloud but 2 merely disperses it and scatters successive front layers. Not even a bladder pops if it releases air just any sort of way. If it is sliced with a knife, the air escapes without any audible evidence. In order to make a popping sound it should be burst, not cut. I maintain it is the same in the clouds. Unless they burst asunder with great force they do not make a noise. Now add that clouds driven against mountains are not broken up but flow around and are so split among the various parts of the mountain, tree-branches, bushes, and rough projecting boulders,

eminentia ita diducuntur ut, si quem habent spiritum, multifariam emittant, qui, nisi universus erumpit, non
3 crepat. Hoc ut scias, ventus qui circa arborem finditur [1] sibilat, non tonat; lato, ut ita dicam, ictu et totum globum semel dissipante opus est, ut sonitus erumpat qualis auditur, cum tonat.

1 29. Praeter haec natura aptus est aer ad voces. Quidni, cum vox nihil aliud sit quam ictus aer? Debent ergo nubes utrimque conseri [2] et cavae et intentae. Vides enim quanto vocaliora sint vacua quam plena, quanto intenta quam remissa. Item tympana et cymbala sonant, quia illa repugnantem ex ulteriore parte spiritum pulsant, haec et ipso aere [3] non nisi cavo tinniunt.

1 30. Quidam, inter quos Asclepiodotus est, iudicant sic quorundam quoque corporum concursu tonitrum et fulmina excuti posse. Aetna aliquando multo igne abundavit, ingentem vim harenae urentis effudit, involutus est dies pulvere, populosque subita nox terruit. Aiunt tunc plurima fuisse fulmina et tonitrua quae concursu aridorum corporum facta sunt, non nubium, quas verisimile est in tanto fervore aeris
2 nullas fuisse. Aliquando Cambyses ad Ammonem misit exercitum, quem harena austro mota et more

---

[1] *funditur* PABV.
[2] Gercke, Oltramare for *inseri* HPEZ; *dissecari* ABV.
[3] *et ipso aere* Oltramare; *et ipsa aere* HPZ; *et illa aere* ET; *ad ipsum* ABV.

that they release through numerous gaps whatever air they may have. Yet the air does not make a sound unless it all bursts out at once. Here is an **3** understandable example: the wind which is parted around a tree only whispers; it does not make the sound of thunder. A broad blow, so to speak, is needed, a blow that shatters the entire mass at once, to erupt the sound heard when there is thunder.

29. Besides, air is by nature suited for sounds. **1** And why not, since sound is only air which has been struck? Accordingly, the clouds ought to be sealed on all sides and be hollow and taut. You know how hollow vessels are more resonant than full ones, taut things are more resonant than loose things. Tambourines and cymbals likewise produce sound because tambourines make the air on the other side vibrate as it resists, and cymbals ring only when in fact their bronze is concave in shape.

30. Some authorities, among them Asclepiodotus, **1** suppose that thunder and lightning can be produced also by the collision of certain solid bodies. Once Etna was blazing with fire and poured out huge quantities of burning sand.[1] The daylight was wrapped in dust, and sudden darkness terrified people. They say that at the time there was much thunder and lightning caused by the collision, not of clouds, which probably did not exist in such heated air, but of dry bodies. Cambyses once sent an army to Ammon.[2] **2** The sand stirred up by the south wind fell on them

---

[1] Cicero (*Nat. Deorum* 2.96) reports an eruption of Etna that caused darkness over the neighbouring districts for two days. He makes no mention of the sand or thunder and lightning. [2] In 525 B.C. Herodotus 3.26.

nivis incidens texit, deinde obruit; tunc quoque verisimile est fuisse tonitrum fulminaque attritu harenae sese affricantis.

3 Non repugnat proposito nostro ista opinio. Diximus enim utriusque naturae corpora efflare terras et sicci aliquid et umidi in toto aere vagari; itaque si quid tale intervenit, nubem fecit solidiorem et crassiorem quam si tantum simplici spiritu texeretur. Illa frangi potest et edere sonum.

4 Ista quae dixi, sive incendiis vaporantibus aera repleverunt, sive ventis terras verrentibus,[1] necesse est nubem faciant ante quam sonum. Nubem autem tam arida quam umida conserunt; est enim, ut diximus, nubes spissitudo aeris crassi.

1 31. Ceterum mira fulminis, si intueri velis, opera sunt nec quicquam dubii relinquentia quin divina sit illius ac subtilis potentia. Loculis integris et illaesis conflatur argentum; manente vagina gladius ipse liquescit et inviolato ligno circa pila ferrum omne destillat; stat fracto dolio vinum nec ultra triduum

2 ille rigor durat. Illud aeque inter adnotanda ponas licet quod et hominum et ceterorum animalium quae icta sunt caput spectat ad exitum fulminis, quod

---

[1] *verrentibus* HPZ; *urentibus* λ; *uerentibus* EL[1].

---

[1] Above, Chapter 12.4, Seneca ascribes this theory to Aristotle.

[2] Oltramare believes that Seneca is referring to a lost section of Book Four-B.

like snow, covered them, then buried them. Probably at the time there was also thunder and lightning caused by the mutual friction of the sand particles.

Such a guess is not opposed to my own theory. **3** For I have said [1] that the earth exhales two kinds of substances, dry and moist, some of which wander about the whole atmosphere. If a substance of this sort comes along it makes a thicker and more solid cloud than one composed only of pure air. It can burst and make a noise.

Whether those elements I mentioned have filled **4** the atmosphere with smoking fires or with earth-sweeping winds they need to form a cloud before they produce noise. Moreover, dry elements as well as moist make up a cloud. For, as I have said, a cloud is a condensation of thick air. [2]

31. Moreover, the effects of lightning are marvellous, [3] if you are willing to open your eyes to them, and they leave no doubt that there is a subtle and divine power in lightning. Silver coins are fused in intact and undamaged boxes. A sword is melted while the sheath remains. The iron of a javelin is fused while the wood around it is unharmed. A jar is broken and the wine stands congealed stiff for three days, no more. You may also put this among **2** the notable effects of lightning: the heads of men and other animals that have been struck by lightning point in the direction the lightning passed. [4] All

[3] Pliny (2.137) gives a much shorter list of remarkable effects of lightning, as does Lucretius (6.225–235).

[4] Pliny 2.145: all things fall in the opposite direction. A man does not die unless the force of the blow turns him right around.

omnium percussarum arborum contra fulmina astulae surgunt. Quid quod malarum serpentium et aliorum animalium quibus mortifera vis inest, cum fulmine icta sunt, venenum omne consumitur? " Unde," inquit, " scis? " In venenatis corporibus vermis non nascitur; fulmine icta intra paucos dies verminant.

1   32. Quid quod futura portendunt, nec unius tantum aut alterius rei signa dant, sed saepe longum [1] fatorum sequentium ordinem nuntiant, et quidem notis [2] evidentibus longeque clarioribus quam si scriberentur?

2   Hoc inter nos et Tuscos, quibus summa est fulgurum persequendorum scientia, interest: nos putamus, quia nubes collisae sunt, fulmina emitti; ipsi existimant nubes collidi ut fulmina emittantur; nam, cum omnia ad deum referent, in ea opinione sunt tamquam non, quia facta sunt, significent, sed quia significatura sunt, fiant. Eadem tamen ratione fiunt, sive illis significare propositum, sive consequens est.

3   " Quomodo ergo significant, nisi ideo [3] mittuntur?" Quomodo aves non in hoc motae ut nobis occurrerent dextrum auspicium sinistrumque fecerunt. " Et illas," inquit, " deus movit." Nimis illum otiosum et

---

[1] *totum* ABV.
[2] *quidem notis* ZT; *qui ei de totis* H; *qui eidem totis* P; *quidem decretis* AV.   [3] *a deo* ABV.

the splinters of trees that have been struck stand up opposite to the direction of the lightning. Moreover, all the poison of venomous snakes and other animals in which there is a death-dealing power is consumed when they are struck by lightning. "How do you know?" he asks. Worms are not produced in poisoned bodies; such bodies struck by lightning become wormy within a few days.

32. What about the fact that lightning foretells **1** future events and gives signs not only of one or two events but often announces a long series of successive fates, actually with far more obvious and clearer marks of evidence than if these were in writing?

This is the difference between us and the Etruscans, **2** who have consummate skill in interpreting lightning: we think that because clouds collide lightning is emitted; they believe that clouds collide in order that lightning may be emitted. Since they attribute everything to divine agency they are of the opinion that things do not reveal the future because they have occurred, but that they occur because they are meant to reveal the future. Whether it is displaying their purpose or their consequences they none the less occur on the same principle.[1]

"But how do things indicate future events unless **3** they are sent to do so?" In the same way as birds provide favourable or unfavourable auspices even though they are not, in this respect, moved in order to appear to us. "But god moved them," he says. You make god too unoccupied and the administrator

---

[1] Pliny 2.97: misfortunes do not happen because the marvellous occurrences took place but these took place because the misfortunes were going to occur.

pusillae rei ministrum facis, si aliis somnia,[1] aliis exta
4 disponit. Ista nihilominus divina ope gerunter, si
non a deo pennae avium reguntur nec pecudum
viscera sub ipsa securi formantur. Alia ratione
fatorum series explicatur indicia venturi ubique
praemittens, ex quibus quaedam nobis familiaria,
quaedam ignota sunt. Quicquid fit, alicuius rei
futurae signum est. Fortuita et sine ratione vaga
divinationem non recipiunt; cuius rei ordo est, etiam
praedictio est.

5   " Cur ergo aquilae hic honor datus est ut magnarum
rerum faceret auspicia, aut corvo et paucissimis avibus, ceterarum sine praesagio vox est?" Quia
quaedam nondum in artem redacta sunt, quaedam
vero ne redigi quidem possunt ob nimium remotam
conversationem; ceterum nullum animal est quod
non motu et occursu suo praedicat aliquid. Non
omnia scilicet, quaedam notantur.

6   Auspicium observantis est; ad eum itaque pertinet
qui in ea direxit animum. Ceterum fiunt et illa quae
7 pereunt. Quinque stellarum potestates Chaldaeo-
rum observatio excepit. Quid, tu tot illa milia
siderum iudicas otiosa lucere? Quid est porro

---

[1] *omina* Gronovius, Alexander for *somnia*.

---

[1] Pliny 11.186: the heart was missing from a sacrificial
animal, which gave rise to much debate as to whether the
victim had been able to live without the heart or had lost it at
the time.

of trivia if he arranges dreams for some people, entrails for others. None the less, such things are **4** carried out by divine agency, even if the wings of birds are not actually guided by god nor the viscera of cattle shaped under the very axe.[1] The roll of fate is unfolded on a different principle, sending ahead everywhere indications of what is to come, some familiar to us, others unknown. Whatever happens, it is a sign of something that will happen. Chance and random occurrences, and without a principle, do not permit divination. Whatever has a series of occurrences is also predictable.

" But why is this privilege to give auspices of im- **5** portant events assigned to a very few birds, an eagle, or a raven, while the cries of the other birds are without prophetic meaning? " Because some animals have not yet been included in the science of augury. Some, in fact, cannot even be included because acquaintance with them is too remote. However, there is no animal which does not predict something by its movements and by its meeting with us. Of course, not all animals are observable, only some.

An auspice is the observer's auspice.[2] Thus, it **6** pertains to the man who directs his attention towards these signs. Yet signs also occur which pass unnoticed. The observation of the Chaldaeans is re- **7** stricted to the powers of five planets.[3] Well! Do you think that those many thousands of stars shine uselessly? Furthermore, what else is there

---

[2] Pliny 28.17: the power of omens is really in our control, and their influence is conditional upon the way we receive them.

[3] Mercury, Venus, Mars, Jupiter, and Saturn.

aliud quod errorem maximum incutiat peritis
natalium quam quod paucis nos sideribus assignant,
cum omnia quae supra nos sunt partem nostri sibi
vindicent? Summissiora forsitan propius in nos vim
suam dirigunt et ea quae frequentius mota aliter nos
8 aliterque prospiciunt. Ceterum et illa quae aut
immota sunt aut propter velocitatem universo parem
immotis similia non extra ius dominiumque nostri
sunt. Alium aliud aspicit;[1] distributis rem officiis[2]
tractant;[3] non magis autem facile est scire quid
possint, quam dubitare[4] an possint.

1   33. Nunc ad fulmina revertamur. Quorum ars in
haec tria dividitur: quemadmodum exploremus,
quemadmodum interpretemur; quemadmodum expiemus.[5] Prima pars ad formulam pertinet, secunda
ad divinationem, tertia ad propitiandos deos, quos
bono fulmine rogare oportet, malo deprecari; rogare,
ut promissa firment; deprecari, ut remittant minas.

1   34. Summam esse vim fulminis iudicant, quia,
quicquid alia portendunt, interventus fulminis tollit;
quicquid ab hoc portenditur, fixum est nec alterius
ostenti significatione mutatur; quicquid exta, quicquid aves minabuntur, secundo fulmine abolebitur;

---

[1] *Alium aliud aspicit* Madvig, Oltramare for *aliud aspice et* MSS.
[2] Faber, Oltramare, Alexander for *efficis* most MSS; *effectis* G.
[3] Madvig, Oltramare for *tractas* most MSS.; *tracta* T.

which causes the greatest error on the part of horo-
scope experts than the fact that they assign us to
only a few stars while all the stars above us claim a
share of us for themselves? Perhaps the lower
stars, and those which look upon us sometimes one
way sometimes another because they change position
more frequently, influence us more directly. But 8
even those stars which are motionless, or like motionless stars because their speed is equal to that of the
universe, are not without power and control over us.
One star influences one person, another star influences
another. They carry on their work in duties that
have been distributed among them. However, it is
more difficult to know what power they have than to
doubt whether they have power.

33. Now let us return to lightning. The study of 1
lightning is divided into these three areas: how we
investigate it, how we interpret it, how we charm it
away. The first area pertains to classification, the
second to divination, the third to propitiating the
gods; it is fitting to ask when lightning is good,
to pray against it when it is bad; to ask that the
gods fulfil their promises, to pray that they set aside
their threats.

34. People conclude that the power of lightning 1
is supreme because the intervention of lightning
annuls whatever other omens portend; whatever is
foretold by lightning is unalterable and unchanged
by the indication of another sign. The threats of
entrails or of birds will be cancelled by a favourable

---

⁴ *dubitare* V Oltramare; *dubitari* most MSS.
⁵ *expiemus* Z; *exoremus* ABV; *exploremus* HPEF.

quicquid fulmine denuntiatum est, nec extis nec ave contraria refellitur.

2   In quo mihi falli videntur. Quare? Quia vero verius nihil est. Si aves futura cecinerunt, non potest hoc auspicium fulmine irritum fieri, aut non futura cecinerunt. Non enim nunc avem comparo et fulmen, sed duo veri signa, quae, si verum significant, paria sunt. Itaque, quae fulminis interventus submovet extorum vel augurii indicia, male inspecta exta, male servata auguria sunt. Non enim refert utrius rei species maior sit vel natura potentior; si utraque res veri attulit signa, quantum ad hoc, par

3   est. Si dicas flammae maiorem vim esse quam fumi, non mentieris; sed, ad indicandum ignem, idem valet flamma quod fumus. Itaque si hoc dicunt: " Quotiens aliud exta significabunt, aliud fulmina, fulminum erit auctoritas maior," fortasse consentiam. Si hoc dicunt: " Quamvis altera res verum praedixisset, fulminis ictus priora delevit et ad se fidem traxit," falsum est. Quare? Quia nihil interest quam multa auspicia sint. Fatum unum est; quod si bene primo

4   auspicio intellectum est, secundo non interit. Ita dico, non refert an aliud sit per quod quidem quaerimus quoniam de quo quaeritur idem est. Fatum fulmine mutari non potest. Quidni? Nam fulmen ipsum fati pars est.

lightning stroke. Any warning given by lightning is not refuted by contradictory entrails or birds.

On this point they seem to me to be mistaken. 2 Why? Because nothing is truer than the truth. If birds have foretold the future such an auspice cannot be nullified by lightning—or they foretold what was not the future. I am not now comparing a bird with lightning but two revelations of the truth which, if they do foretell the truth, are the same. So, if the intervention of lightning negates the revelations of the entrails or of augury the entrails have been improperly examined, the augury improperly observed. For it does not matter whether the appearance of one or the other omen is larger or more powerful by nature; if both have given indications of the truth they are equal as far as it pertains to the truth. If 3 you say the power of flame is stronger than the power of smoke, you are quite right. But flame has no more power than smoke has to indicate fire. So if people say this: " Whenever entrails indicate one thing, lightning another, the authority of lightning will be greater," I will perhaps agree. If they say this: " Although another omen has foretold the truth a stroke of lightning has nullified prior omens and claimed belief only in itself," it is untrue. Why? Because it makes no difference how many omens there might be. Fate is single. If fate is correctly understood from the first omen it does not become destroyed by the second omen. So I say it does not 4 matter whether we seek the truth by one means or another since the truth which is sought is the same. Fate cannot be altered by a lightning stroke. Why not? For lightning itself is a part of fate.

1 35. " Quid ergo? Expiationes procurationesque
quo pertinent, si immutabilia sunt fata? " Permitte
mihi illam rigidam sectam tueri eorum qui risu[1]
excipiunt ista et nihil esse aliud quam aegrae mentis
2 solacia existimant. Fata aliter[2] ius suum peragunt
nec ulla commoventur prece. Non misericordia
flecti,[3] non gratia sciunt. Cursum irrevocabilem
ingressa[4] ex destinato fluunt. Quemadmodum rapi-
dorum aqua torrentium in se non recurrit, ne
moratur quidem, quia priorem superveniens praeci-
pitat, sic ordinem fati rerum aeterna series rotat,
cuius haec prima lex est, stare decreto.[5]

1 36. Quid enim intellegis fatum? Existimo neces-
sitatem rerum omnium actionumque, quam nulla vis
rumpat. Hanc si sacrificiis aut capite niveae agnae
exorari iudicas, divina non nosti. Sapientis quoque
viri sententiam negatis posse mutari; quanto magis
dei, cum sapiens quid sit optimum in praesentia
sciat, illius divinitati omne praesens sit?

1 37. Agere nunc causam eorum volo qui procuranda
existimant fulmina, et expiationes non dubitant
prodesse aliquando ad summovenda pericula, ali-
2 quando ad levanda, aliquando ad differenda. Quid
sit quod sequatur, paulo post persequar; interim hoc
habent commune nobiscum quod nos quoque existi-
mamus vota proficere salva vi ac potestate fatorum.

---

[1] *risu* supplied by Oltramare.
[2] *aliter* HPZGA; *aequaliter* Gercke; *irrevocabiliter* E.
[3] Haase, Gercke, Oltramare for *flectit* MSS.
[4] Haase, Gercke, Oltramare for *ingesta* MSS.
[5] *de cetero* AV; *de certo* B.

35. " Well, then, what use are expiations and pre- 1
cautions if the fates are immutable? " Permit me
to support that rigid sect of philosophers who accept
such practices with a smile and consider them only a
solace for a troubled mind. The fates perform their 2
function otherwise and are not moved by any prayer.
The fates do not know how to be turned by pity or by
favour. Once started upon an irrevocable course they
flow on in accordance with an unalterable plan. Just
as the water of a rushing torrent does not flow back
upon itself and does not even pause since the flood
coming from behind pushes ahead the water that
passed before, so the eternal sequence of events
causes the order of fate to roll on. And this is its
first law; to stand by its decrees.

36. What do you understand as fate? I consider 1
it the necessity of all events and actions which no
force may break. If you think this is averted by
sacrifices or by the head of a snow-white lamb, you
do not understand the divine. It is your saying that
the decision of a wise man cannot be changed. How
much more true this is in the case of a god! A wise
man knows what is best in the present. For god's
divinity everything is the present.

37. Now I want to support the views of those who 1
believe that lightning can be conjured away and have
no doubt that expiations are useful, sometimes to remove the danger, sometimes to mitigate it, sometimes to postpone it. What considerations follow I 2
will take up after a little while. Meanwhile, they
have this in common with us: namely, that we also
believe vows are useful if they do not impair the
force and power of fate. For, some things have been

Quaedam enim a diis immortalibus ita suspensa
relicta sunt ut in bonum vertant, si admotae diis
preces fuerint, si vota suscepta; ita non est hoc
3 contra fatum, sed ipsum quoque in fato est. " Aut
futurum," inquit, " est aut non; si futurum est, fiet,
etiamsi vota non suscipis; si non est futurum, etiamsi
susceperis vota, non fiet." Falsa est ista interrogatio,
quia illam mediam inter ista exceptionem praeteris:
futurum hoc est, sed si vota suscepta fuerint.

1   38. " Hoc quoque," inquit, " ipsum necesse est
fato comprehensum sit ut aut suscipias vota aut
non." Puta me tibi manus dare et fateri hoc quoque
fato esse comprehensum ut utique fiant vota; ideo
2 fient. Fatum est ut hic disertus sit, sed si litteras
didicerit; at eodem fato continetur ut litteras discat;
ideo docendus est. Hic dives erit, sed si navigaverit;
at, in illo fati ordine quo patrimonium illi grande
promittitur, hoc quoque protinus adfatum est ut etiam
naviget; ideo navigabit. Idem tibi de expiationibus
dico: effugiet pericula, si expiaverit praedictas
divinitus minas; at hoc quoque in fato est, ut expiet;
ideo expiabit.

3   Ista nobis opponi solent, ut probetur nihil volun-
tati nostrae relictum et omne ius faciendi fato [1]
traditum. Cum de ista re agetur, dicam quemadmodum manente fato aliquid sit in hominis arbitrio;

left so in suspense by the immortal gods that they turn to our advantage if prayers are directed to the gods, if vows are undertaken. As a result this is not opposed to fate but is itself also in fate. A person 3 says: " Either it is to be or is not to be. If it is to be it will happen even though you make no vows. If it is not to be it will not happen even though you do make vows." Such a dilemma is not valid because you omit an alternative between the two: this is to be, but only if vows are made.

38. " This also," he says, " needs to be included in 1 fate: either that you make vows or you do not." Suppose I yield to you and agree that it is also in-included in fate that vows are surely to be made. So for this reason they will be made. It is fate that 2 so-and-so will become eloquent but only if he has learned literature. But by the same fate it is required that he learn. So, he must become learned. Another man will become rich but only if he has gone to sea. But in that order of fate wherein a great for-tune is promised him it at once is also decreed that he go to sea. So, he will go to sea. I maintain the same principle in regard to expiation. A man will escape danger if he has expiated the threats foretold by divinity. But this also is in fate: that he expiate. Therefore, he will expiate.

Such reasoning is usually presented to us in order 3 to prove that nothing is left to our free will and that all control of action is handed over to fate. When this matter will be discussed I will tell how some-thing may exist in man's choice while fate remains

---

¹ *fato* added by Leo.

nunc vero id de quo agitur explicui, quomodo, si fati
certus est ordo, expiationes procurationesque [1] pro-
digiorum pericula avertant, quia non cum fato pugnant, sed et ipsae [2] in lege fati sunt.[3]

4   "Quid ergo," inquis, "aruspex mihi prodest?
Utique enim expiare mihi etiam non suadente illo
necesse est." Hoc prodest quod fati minister est.
Sic cum sanitas debeatur [4] fato, debetur et medico,
quia ad nos beneficium fati per huius manus venit.

1   39. Genera fulgurum tria esse ait Caecina, consiliarium, auctoritatis et quod status dicitur. Consiliarium ante rem fit sed post cogitationem, cum
aliquid in animo versantibus [5] aut suadetur fulminis
ictu aut dissuadetur. Auctoritatis est ubi post rem
factam venit, quam bono futuram malove significat.

2 Status est ubi quietis nec agentibus quicquam nec
cogitantibus quidem fulmen intervenit et aut minatur
aut promittit aut monet. Hoc monitorium vocat,
sed nescio quare non idem sit quod consiliarium, nam

3 et qui monet consilium dat. Sed habeat aliquam

---

[1] *propitiationesque* AV.
[2] *et ipsae* Z Oltramare, Alexander; *ipsa* most MSS.
[3] *in lege fati sunt* Oltramare, Alexander; *in fati lege fiunt* E;
dati HZP; *data* most MSS.; *in lege data sunt* Gercke.
[4] *debeatur* E[2] Haase, Oltramare; *videatur* HPEZ; *videatur
esse* AV; *videatur fato deberi* Castiglioni, Alexander.
[5] *cogitantibus* ABV.

---

[1] Oltramare believes that Seneca implies here his intention
to discuss this point in the *Natural Questions*, which he never
does.
[2] The Latin text is doubtful.

undiminished.[1] But for the moment, regarding the point being treated, I have explained how, even if the order of fate is unalterable, expiations and preventations may avert the dangers of omens because they are not in conflict with fate but also themselves exist in the law of fate.[2]

"Well, then," you say, "what benefit is a sooth- 4 sayer to me? In any case it is necessary for me to offer expiation even though he does not advise me to." He provides *this* benefit: the fact that he is a minister of fate. Thus, although the recovery of good health is owed to fate it is also owed to the doctor because the benefit of fate came to us through his hands.

39. Caecina[3] says that there are three kinds of 1 lightning, the advising, the confirming, and that which is called the conditional. The advising one happens before the event but after a thought has been conceived, when people who are planning something in their minds are either persuaded or dissuaded by a stroke of lightning. The confirming lightning comes after action has been done, indicating whether it will be either for bad or for good. The 2 conditional lightning comes to people who are quiet, doing nothing, not even thinking, and it either threatens, promises, or warns. This last kind Caecina calls monitory, but I do not know why it is not the same as the advising kind, for to warn is also to give advice. But it has another distinction and for this 3

---

[3] A. Caecina was the son of the Caecina of Cicero's *Pro A. Caecina*, delivered in 69 B.C. He became the great authority at Rome on divination and lightning and his work on the Etruscan lore known as *Etrusca disciplina* was used by many, including Pliny.

distinctionem et ob hoc separetur a consiliario, quia
illud suadet dissuadetque, hoc solam evitationem
impendentis periculi continet, ut cum timemus ignem,
4 fraudem a proximis, insidias a servis. Etiamnunc
tamen aliam distinctionem utriusque video: consiliarium est quod cogitanti factum est, monitorium
quod nihil cogitanti; habet autem utraque res suam
proprietatem: suadetur deliberantibus; ultro monen-
tur.

1   40. Primo omnium non sunt fulminum genera sed
significationum. Nam fulminum genera sunt illa,
quod terebrat, quod discutit, quod urit. Quod
terebrat subtile est et flammeum, cui per angustis-
simum fuga est ob sinceram et puram flammae tenuita-
2 tem. Quod dissipat conglobatum est et habet
admixtam vim spiritus coacti ac procellosi. Itaque
illud fulmen per id foramen quod ingressum est
redit et evadit; huius late sparsa vis rumpit icta, non
3 perforat. Tertium illud genus, quod urit, multum
terreni habet et igneum magis est quam flammeum;
itaque relinquit magnas ignium notas, quae percussis inhaereant. Nullum quidem sine igne fulmen
venit, sed tamen hoc proprie igneum dicimus quod
manifesta ardoris vestigia imprimit, quod aut urit
4 aut fuscat. Tribus modis urit: aut afflat et levi

---

[1] Pliny 2.137: there are several types of lightning: one
kind, the dry flash, causes no fire but an explosion; another,

reason is separated from the advising, because the advising persuades and dissuades; the monitory is restricted to the sole avoidance of impending danger, as when we fear fire, fraud from associates, treachery from slaves. Besides, now I also see another distinc- 4 tion between the two: the advising is the one made to somebody who is forming plans, the warning to somebody not planning anything. Moreover, either circumstance has its distinctive characteristic: advice is for people who are making plans; people are warned before they make plans.

40. First of all, they are not types of lightning but 1 of interpretation. Types of lightning are as follows: the type that bores, the type that scatters, and the type that burns.[1] The one that bores is subtle and flaming. Because of the unmixed, pure thinness of its flame it finds escape through the narrowest openings. The type that scatters is a mass and has a 2 great amount of condensed and stormy air mixed in it. Thus, the first type escapes by returning through that hole by which it entered. The second scatters its effects widely and breaks through whatever it strikes instead of perforating it. The third type, the 3 one that burns, has a great deal of earthy element and is more fire than flame. And so it leaves great scars of fire which cling to the things struck. Actually, no lightning comes without fire, but we none the less properly call this type fiery because it imprints obvious traces of heat, because it burns or blackens. It burns in three ways: it either scorches 4

the smoky, does not burn but blackens; the third is called 'bright' and produces marvellous effects. Aristotle 3.1.371a 19–20) gives two types: gleaming and smoky.

iniuria laedit, aut comburit, aut accendit. Omnia
ista urunt sed genere et modo differunt: quodcumque combustum est, utique et ustum est; at
5 quod ustum est, non utique combustum est. Item
quod accensum est (potest enim illud ipso transitu
ignis ussisse)—quis nescit uri quidem nec ardere,
nihil autem ardere quod non et uratur? Unum hoc
adiciam: potest aliquid esse combustum nec accensum, potest accensum esse nec combustum.

6 Nunc ad id transeo genus fulminis quo icta fus-
cantur; hoc aut decolorat aut colorat. Utrique
distinctionem suam reddam: decoloratur id cuius
color vitiatur, non mutatur; coloratur id cuius alia fit
quam fuit facies, tamquam caerulea vel nigra vel
pallida.

1 41. Haec adhuc Etruscis philosophisque com-
munia sunt. In illo dissentiunt quod fulmina a
Iove [1] dicunt mitti et tres illi manubias dant. Prima,
ut aiunt, monet et placata est et ipsius Iovis consilio

----

[1] *a Iove* EABV; *novem* HPZG.

---

[1] The manuscripts of the *Grandinem* family give a different
reading: " the Etruscans say nine lightning bolts are hurled
and they assign three *manubiae* (weapons in an arsenal) to
Jupiter." Gellius, *Noctes Atticae* 13–25, discusses the mys-
terious word *manubiae* and explains it as a sort of synonym for
praeda—booty taken *manu* " by hand." In Ammianus Marcellinus 17.7.3 *fatales manubias* are " deadly lightning bolts."
Cp. Serv. *ad Aen.* 11.259 and 8.429. Pliny 2.138: in the litera-

and damages with light marring, or burns up, or sets afire. All these cause burning but they differ in type and degree. Whatever is burned up is, of course, also burnt, but what is burnt is not completely burned up. Likewise, whatever is ignited (for something can be burned by the mere passing of fire)— well, everyone knows that something can be burnt and yet not glow but that nothing glows which is not also burnt. I will add this one point: something can be burned up but not set on fire and something can be set on fire but not burned up. **5**

Now I pass on to the type of lightning which blackens the objects it strikes. This lightning either colours objects or discolours them. To each process I will grant the difference due to it. Something is discoloured when its colour is blemished, not changed. Something is coloured when its appearance becomes other than it was, blue, for example, or black, or whitish. **6**

41. The views up to this point are common to both Etruscans and philosophers. They disagree on this: namely, that the Etruscans say lightning is sent by Jupiter and they assign to him three types of equipment.[1] The first type, so they say, gives a gentle warning and is sent by a decision of Jupiter himself. **1**

cure of the Etruscans nine gods send eleven kinds of *fulmina*, of which three kinds are sent by Jupiter. Only two of these deities, Pliny says, are retained by the Romans, who attribute *fulmina* in the daytime to Jupiter, *fulmina* at night to Summanus. Pliny also says (2.82) that lightning bolts are fires falling to earth from the three upper planets, which are those of Jupiter; thus the origin of the myth that lightning bolts are javelins hurled by Jupiter.

mittitur. Secundam mittit quidem Iupiter, sed ex
consilii sententia, duodecim enim deos advocat; hoc
fulmen boni aliquid aliquando facit, sed tunc quoque
non aliter quam ut noceat; ne prodest quidem
2 impune. Tertiam manubiam idem Iupiter mittit,
sed adhibitis in consilium diis quos superiores et
involutos vocant, quia vastat in quae incidit et utique
mutat statum privatum et publicum quem invenit;
ignis enim nihil esse quod fuit patitur.

1 42. In his[1] prima specie, si intueri velis, errat
antiquitas. Quid enim tam imperitum est quam
credere fulmina e nubibus Iovem mittere, columnas,
arbores, nonnumquam statuas suas petere, uti,
impunitis sacrilegis percussoribus incendiariis,[2] pecu-
des innoxias feriat, et adsumi in consilium a Iove[3]
deos, quasi in ipso parum consilii sit; illa laeta esse
et placata fulmina quae solus excutiat, perniciosa
quibus mittendis maior turba numinum intersit?

2 Si a me quaeris quid sentiam, non existimo tam
hebetes fuisse ut crederent Iovem iniquae volun-
tatis aut certe minus peritiae.[4] Utrum enim tunc
cum emisit ignes quibus innoxia capita percuteret,
scelerata transiret, noluit[5] iustius mittere an non

---

[1] *his* omitted in E.

[2] Schultess, Gercke, Oltramare for *percussis ovibus, incensis aris* MSS.

[3] *adsumi in consilium a Iove* Castiglioni, Oltramare; *ad suum sumi consilium a Iove* Z; *ad suum a Iove* HF; *ad suum consilium vocari* G; *ad suum consilium advocari* ABV.

[4] Oltramare for *certe minus paratum* MSS. Alexander suggests *certe minis imparatum*; Warmington *certe minoris peritiae*.

[5] *aut voluit* B; *an voluit* AV.

Jupiter also sends the second type but in accordance with the advice of his council, for he summons the twelve gods. This lightning occasionally brings about some good, but even then it causes some harm. It does not confer benefits without causing damage. Jupiter also sends the third type of lightning but he 2 summons into council the gods whom the Etruscans call the Superior, or Veiled, Gods, because the lightning destroys whatever it strikes and, particularly, alters the state of private or public affairs that it finds existing. For fire does not permit anything to remain as it was.

42. At first glance,[1] if you are willing to examine 1 the matter closely, antiquity is in error about these things. What is more ignorant than to believe that Jupiter sends lightning bolts from the clouds to strike columns, trees, sometimes his own statues; or to believe that he strikes innocent cattle while the sacrilegious, assassins, and incendiaries are unharmed? It is also ignorant to believe that the gods are called into council by Jupiter as though he lacks the ability to make decisions for himself, and that the lightning bolts which he alone hurls are beneficial and clement, whereas a great crowd of deities is involved in aiming the lightning bolts which cause destruction.

If you ask me what I think, I do not presume the 2 ancients were so dull that they believed Jupiter had ill-will or at least unreliable skill. On the occasions when he has hurled fire which struck innocent heads, when he passed by the wicked, was he unwilling to send

[1] A different MS. reading suggests "in the case of the first kind (of lightning)."

3 successit? Quid ergo secuti sunt, cum haec dicerent?
Ad coercendos imperitorum animos sapientissimi viri
iudicaverunt inevitabilem metum,[1] ut aliquid supra
nos timeremus.   Utile erat in tanta audacia scelerum
esse adversus quod nemo sibi satis potens videretur;
ad conterrendos itaque eos quibus innocentia nisi
metu non placet posuerunt supra caput vindicem, et
quidem armatum.

1   43. Quare ergo id fulmen quod solus Iupiter
mittit placabile est, perniciosum id de quo deliberavit
et quod aliis quoque diis auctoribus misit? Quia
Iovem, id est regem, prodesse etiam solum oportet,
2 nocere non nisi cum pluribus visum est.   Discant hi,
quicumque magnam inter homines adepti sunt
potentiam,[2] sine consilio ne fulmen quidem mitti;
advocent, considerent multorum sententias, noci-
turum [3] temperent, hoc sibi proponant, ubi aliquid
percuti debet, ne Iovi quidem suum satis esse consilium.

1   44. In hoc quoque tam imperiti non fuerunt ut
Iovem existimarent tela mutare.   Poeticam istud
licentiam decet:

Est aliud levius fulmen, cui dextra Cyclopum
Saevitiae flammaeque minus, minus addidit irae;
Tela secunda vocant superi.

[1] *motum* HPE.
[2] *potestatem* Z; *sapientiam* HPA.
[3] *placita* ABV; *nocituri* Garrod; *nocituram sententiam suam*
Alexander.

[1] Ovid *Met.* 3.305–307.

the fire more justly, or did he miss? What, then, were 3
they getting at when they said these things? Being
very wise they decided that fear was necessary for
coercing the minds of the ignorant, so that we might
fear something above ourselves. It was useful, in
times of such insolent crime, that there exist something against which no one might consider himself
powerful enough. And so to terrify men who find
nothing attractive in good behaviour unless it is
backed up by fear, they placed an avenger overhead,
and an armed avenger at that.

43. Why, then, is clement lightning the lightning 1
Jupiter sends by himself but destructive lightning is
something to which he has given much thought and
has sent only in consultation with the other gods?
Because it is right for Jupiter, that is, for a king, to
confer benefits when acting alone even, it seemed
best not to do harm except in company with others. 2
Let those who have attained great power among men
learn that not even lightning is sent without delibera-
tion. Let them summon advisers, let them consider
the opinions of many, let them moderate a decision
that may cause hurt, and whenever something has to
be struck down let them keep in mind that not even
Jupiter's judgment is sufficient for himself.

44. Another point: the ancient sages were not so 1
ignorant that they supposed Jupiter changed his
weapons. This idea is suited only to poetic license:

> There is another, gentler lightning bolt
> To which the hands of the Cyclopes
> Have given less severity and flame, less anger;
> The Upper Gods call them
> The secondary weapons.[1]

2   Illos vero altissimos viros error iste non tenuit, ut existimarent Iovem modo gravioribus, modo[1] levioribus fulminibus et lusoriis uti. Sed voluerunt admonere eos quibus adversus peccata hominum fulminandum est non eodem modo omnia esse percutienda; quaedam stringi debere, quaedam effligi[2] ac distringi,[3] quaedam admoneri.

1   45. Ne hoc quidem crediderunt Iovem, qualem in Capitolio et in ceteris aedibus colimus,[4] mittere manu sua fulmina, sed eundem quem nos Iovem intellegunt, rectorem custodemque universi, animum ac spiritum mundi, operis huius dominum et artificem,

2   cui nomen omne convenit. Vis illum fatum vocare, non errabis; hic est ex quo suspensa sunt omnia, causa causarum. Vis illum providentiam dicere, recte dices; est enim cuius consilio huic mundo providetur, ut inoffensus[5] exeat et actus suos explicet. Vis illum naturam vocare, non peccabis; hic est ex quo nata sunt omnia, cuius spiritu vivimus.

3   Vis illum vocare mundum, non falleris; ipse enim est hoc quod vides totum, partibus suis inditus, et se sustinens et sua. Idem Etruscis quoque visum est, et ideo fulmina mitti dixerunt a Iove quia sine illo nihil geritur.

1   46. " At quare Iupiter aut ferienda transit aut innoxia ferit ? " In maiorem me quaestionem vocas,

---

[1] *gravioribus, modo* supplied by Fickert.
[2] Leo, Oltramare for *eligi* HPEFGABV; *elidi* Curio, Haase.
[3] *distringi* EP; *distingui* HFGABV.

No, those erudite men did not fall into the error 2
of supposing that Jupiter sometimes used heavier,
sometimes lighter lightning bolts, like weapons in a
training school. But they wanted to advise those
who are to hurl punishment at the sins of men that
not all sins are to be struck down in the same way:
some sins need to be restrained, others destroyed and
torn to pieces, others only rebuked.

45. The ancient sages did not even believe that 1
Jupiter, the sort we worship in the Capitol and in
other temples, sent lightning by his own hand.
They recognized the same Jupiter we do, the con-
troller and guardian of the universe, the mind and
spirit of the world, the lord and artificer of this
creation. Any name for him is suitable. You wish 2
to call him Fate? You will not be wrong. It is he
on whom all things depend, the cause of causes. You
wish to call him Providence? You will still be right.
It is by his planning that provision is made for this
universe so that it may proceed without stumbling
and fulfil its appropriate functions. You wish to
call him Nature? You will not be mistaken. It is
he from whom all things are naturally born, and we
have life from his breath. You wish to call him the 3
Universe? You will not be wrong. He himself is
all that you see, infused throughout all his parts,
sustaining both himself and his own. The Etruscans
had the same concept, and so they said lightning was
sent by Jupiter because nothing is done without him.

46. " But why does Jupiter either pass by those 1
who ought to be struck down or he strikes the

---

⁴ *videmus* ABV.   ⁵ *inconfusus* ABV.

cui suus dies, suus locus dandus est. Interim hoc
dico: fulmina non mitti a Iove, sed sic omnia esse
disposita ut etiam quae ab illo non fiunt tamen sine
ratione non fiant, quae illius est. Nam etiamsi
Iupiter illa nunc non facit, Iupiter fecit ut fierent.
Singulis non adest ad omne, sed signum[1] et vim et
causam omnibus dedit.

1   47. Huic illorum divisioni non accedo. Aiunt
aut perpetua esse fulmina, aut finita, aut prorogativa.
Perpetua, quorum significatio in totam pertinet
vitam nec unam rem denuntiat sed contextum rerum
per omnem deinceps aetatem futurarum complectitur; haec sunt fulmina quae prima accepto patri-
monio et in novo hominis aut urbis[2] statu fiunt.
Finita ad diem utique respondent. Prorogativa
sunt quorum minae differri possunt, averti tollique
non possunt.

1   48. Dicam quid sit quare huic divisioni non consentiam. Nam et quod perpetuum vocant fulmen
finitum est, aeque enim ad diem respondet nec ideo
minus finitum est quia multa significat. Et quod
prorogativum videtur finitum est, nam illorum
quoque confessione certum est quousque impetretur
dilatio; privata enim fulgura negant ultra decimum

---

[1] *sed signum* ABV; *sed manum* λ Oltramare; *et manum*
most MSS.
[2] Fortunatus for *orbis* MSS.

innocent?" You involve me in too big a question. I will have to answer it in its own time, its own place.[1] Meanwhile I say this: lightning bolts are not sent by Jupiter but all things are so arranged that even those things which are not done by him none the less do not happen without a plan, and the plan is his. For, although Jupiter does not do these things now, it is Jupiter who brought it about that they happen. He is not present at every event for every person but he gives the signal, the force, the cause, to all.

47. I do not agree with this Etruscan classification: they say that lightning bolts are "perpetual," "limited," or "deferred." The prognostication of the perpetual ones pertains to the entire life; it does not give notice of a single event but embraces the chain of events which will happen throughout the whole subsequent lifetime. These are the lightning bolts which first occur when someone has received an inheritance or a new phase begins for a man or a city. Limited ones correspond exactly to a date. Deferred are those whose threats can be postponed but cannot be averted and cancelled.

48. I will state why it is I do not agree with this classification. The lightning bolt which they call perpetual is also limited, for it, too, corresponds to a date and is thus no less limited just because it signifies multiple events. The one which is supposedly deferred is also limited, for, even by their admission, how long a deferment may be procured is a definite period. They say that private lightning bolts

---

[1] This is the subject of Seneca's *De Providentia*, which—as Oltramare points out—must have been written after the *Natural Questions.*

SENECA

annum, publica ultra tricesimum posse differri. Hoc
modo et ista finita sunt, quia ultra quod non proro-
gentur inclusum est. Omnium ergo fulminum et
omnis eventus dies stata sit; non potest enim ulla
incerti esse comprehensio.

2   Quae inspicienda sint in fulgure, passim et vage
dicunt, cum possint sic dividere quemadmodum ab
Attalo philosopho, qui se huic disciplinae dediderat,
divisa sunt, ut inspiciant ubi factum sit, quando, cui,
in quare, quale, quantum. Haec si digerere in partes
suas voluero, quid postea faciam? In immensa
procedam.

1   49. Nunc nomina fulgurum quae a Caecina
ponuntur perstringam[1] et quid de eis sentiam exponam. Ait esse postulatoria, quibus sacrificia
intermissa aut non rite facta repetuntur; monitoria,
quibus docetur quid cavendum sit; pestifera, quae
mortem exiliumque portendunt; fallacia, quae per
speciem alicuius boni nocent (dant consulatum
malo futurum gerentibus et hereditatem cuius com-
pendium magno luendum sit incommodo); dentanea,[2] quae speciem periculi sine periculo afferunt.

---

[1] Gercke, Oltramare for *aperte stringam* HPABV; *aperte distinguam* E.
[2] *ostentanea* Gercke. Oltramare and Alexander argue that although the MSS. *dentanea* is an unusual word it refers to specific portents in the little understood vocabulary of augury and should not be changed.

---

[1] As a young man Seneca was much influenced by the lectures of Attalus, the Stoic, on "sin, error, and the evils of life,"
as well as on moderation in diet. Seneca says that he often

cannot be deferred beyond ten years, public ones beyond thirty years. In this way they, too, are limited because there is included a " beyond which " they may not be deferred. Therefore, let there be an established limited period for all lightning bolts and for each result. For, there cannot be any knowledge of the unlimited.

The Etruscans speak in general terms and vaguely 2 about what really ought to be noted in lightning. They could have set up classifications as was done by the philosopher Attalus,[1] who had devoted himself to this study, so that they might investigate where the lightning occurred, when, to whom, in what circumstances, what sort, and what amount. If I were willing to arrange lightning bolts into their categories I would not have time for anything else. I would be getting into an enormous task.

49. Now I will briefly give the names proposed for 1 lightning flashes by Caecina and explain what I think about them. He says that there are the " demanding " ones, which demand that sacrifices be redone if interrupted or not performed properly; the " admonitory," which indicate what must be guarded against; the " deadly," which portend death and exile; the " deceptive," which do harm under the guise of some good; for example, they give consulships which will be disastrous for the men in office, or bestow inheritance of which the profit must be compensated for by great trouble; the " threatening," which bear the appearance of danger without danger.

wanted to leave those lectures a poor man and that as a result of Attalus' teaching he gave up oysters and mushrooms for ever (*Epist.* 108.13–16; 110.14–20).

2 Peremptalia,[1] quibus tolluntur priorum fulminum
minae; attestata, quae prioribus consentiunt; atter-
ranea, quae in cluso fiunt; obruta, quibus iam prius
percussa nec procurata feriuntur; regalia, cum
forum [2] tangitur vel comitium vel principalia urbis
liberae loca, quorum significatio regnum civitati
3 minatur. Inferna, cum e terra exilivit ignis; hos-
pitalia, quae sacrificiis ad nos Iovem arcessunt et, ut
verbo eorum molliore utar, invitant. Sed non
irasceretur [3] invitatus; [4] nunc venire eum [5] magno
invitantium [6] periculo affirmant. Auxiliaria, quae
invocata sed advocantium bono veniunt.

1   50. Quanto simplicior divisio est qua utebatur
Attalus noster, vir egregius, qui Etruscorum disci-
plinam Graeca subtilitate [7] miscuerat: ex fulminibus
quaedam sunt quae significant id quod ad nos pertinet, quaedam aut nihil significant aut id cuius
2 intellectus ad nos non pervenit.   Ex his quae significant quaedam sunt laeta, quaedam adversa, quaedam mixta, [8] quaedam nec adversa nec laeta.

---

[1] *peremitalia* HPGZF
[2] Haase, Gercke, Oltramare for *eorum* HPEZG.
[3] *irasceretur* g Gercke, Oltramare; *nasceretur* HPGZAV; *arcesseretur* E.
[4] *imitatus* AV; *invitus* Eg.
[5] *cum* ZGAV.
[6] *insultantium* HPEZG; *consultantium* Haase.
[7] *utilitate* ABV.
[8] *quaedam mixta* supplied by Gronovius, Haase, Gercke, Oltramare.

The " cancelling " lightning flashes cancel the 2
threats of prior lightning. The " confirming " agree
with prior lightning flashes. The " earthy " occur in
a closed place. The " overwhelming " strike things
already previously struck but not expiated. The
" royal " smite the forum or the assembly ground or the
government quarters of a free city, and their meaning for a state is the threat of monarchy. The " in- 3
fernal " cause fire to leap out of the ground.[1] The
" hospitable " summon, or to use their gentler term,
" invite " Jupiter to our company at sacrifices. But
he would not be angry if " invited; " as it is, they
say he comes with great danger to those " inviters." [2]
The " helping " lightning flashes are " called on " but
they come for the good of the " callers." [3]

50. How much simpler is the division which our 1
Attalus used, an outstanding man who had mixed the
skill of the Etruscans with Greek accuracy. Some
lightning bolts signify what pertains to us, others
either signify nothing or they signify something the
understanding of which does not concern us. Some 2
of the lightning bolts which signify something are
favourable, some unfavourable, some mixed, others
neither unfavourable nor favourable. These are the

---

[1] Pliny 2.138: the Etruscans believe that some lightning
bursts out of the ground. It is called *inferum* and is especially
direful in winter.

[2] Pliny (2.140), citing *Annals I* of Lucius Piso, tells the
story of Tullus Hostilius struck by lightning when he incorrectly copied the ritual practiced by Numa (cf. Livy 1.31.8).

[3] [The text is doubtful. *Sed non irasceretur. . . affirmant*
could be a comment intruded into Seneca's words, or an in-
terjection by that imaginary person of whom Seneca often
says *inquis* or *inquit*.—E.H.W.]

Adversorum hae species sunt: aut inevitabilia mala
portendunt, aut evitabilia, aut quae minui possunt,
aut quae prorogari. Laeta aut mansura significant,
3 aut caduca. Mixta aut partem habent boni, partem
mali, aut mala in bonum, bona in malum vertunt.
Nec adversa nec laeta sunt quae aliquam nobis
actionem significant qua nec terreri nec laetari
debemus, ut peregrinationem in qua nec metus
quicquam nec spei sit.

1 51. Revertor ad ea fulmina quae significant quidem
aliquid sed quod ad nos non pertineat, tamquam
iterum eodem anno idem[1] futurum fulmen quod
factum est. Nihil significant fulmina aut id cuius
notitia nos effugit, ut illa quae in vastum mare
sparguntur aut in desertas solitudines; quorum
significatio vel nulla est vel perit.

1 52. Pauca adhuc adiciam ad enarrandam vim
fulminis. Quae non eodem modo omnem materiam[2]
vexat. Valentiora, quia resistunt, vehementius dissipat; cedentia nonnumquam sine iniuria transit:
cum lapide ferroque et durissimis quibusque con-
fligit, quia viam necesse est per illa impetu quaerat,
itaque facit[3] qua effugiat; at teneris et rarioribus
parcit, quamquam flammis opportuna videantur, quia
transitu patente minus saevit.[4] Loculis itaque

---

[1] *idem* ABV; *idem hominum* HPZ; *idem ominans* Garrod.
[2] *naturam* λ. [3] *facit viam* BV.
[4] *saevit* Erasmus, Gercke, Oltramare for *venit* most MSS.;
obstaculum invenit E.

forms of the unfavourable ones: they portend either unavoidable evils, or avoidable ones, or those which can be mitigated, or those which can be deferred. The favourable ones signify benefits which will either likely remain or pass away. The mixed ones 3 either have part good, part evil, or they convert bad to good, good to bad. Neither unfavourable nor favourable are the lightning bolts which indicate for us some enterprise wherein we ought not to be terrified or made happy, as a trip abroad, for example, in which there is neither any element of fear nor of hope.

51. I return to the lightning bolts which do signify 1 something but it does not pertain to us: for example, that the same lightning bolt which has already occurred will occur again in the same year. Some lightning bolts mean nothing; as also that of which the very occurrence escapes our awareness, such as the bolts scattered throughout the vast sea or in desert solitudes. Their significance is either nil or is lost.

52. At this point I will add a few words to describe 1 the force of lightning. It does not affect every material in the same way. It shatters the stronger materials rather violently because they resist. Sometimes it passes through yielding materials without causing damage. With stone and iron and all extremely hard substances it is in conflict because it must find a way through them by sheer drive; and so it makes a path by which it may escape. On the other hand, it spares thin and fairly porous substances, although they might seem suitably inflammable, because when a way through is open the lightning is less destructive. And so while boxes

integris, ut dixi, pecunia quae in his fuit conflata
reperitur, quia ignis tenuissimus per foramina occulta
transcurrit, quicquid autem in tigno solidum invenit
2 et contumax vincit. Non uno autem, ut dixi, modo
saevit, sed quid quaeque vis fecerit, ex ipso genere
iniuriae intellegis et fulmen opere cognosces.
Interdum in eadem materia multa diversa eiusdem
fulminis vis facit, sicut in arbore quod aridissimum
urit, quod durissimum et solidissimum est terebrat
et frangit, summos cortices dissipat, interiores libros
rumpit ac scindit, folia pertundit ac stringit. Vinum[1]
gelat, ferrum et aes fundit.

1   53. Illud est mirum quod vinum fulmine gelatum,
cum ad priorem habitum redit, potum aut exanimat
aut dementes facit. Quare id accidat quaerenti
mihi illud occurrit. Inest vis fulmini pestifera; ex
hoc aliquem remanere spiritum in eo umore quem
coegit congelavitque simile veri est; nec enim
alligari potuisset, nisi aliquod illi esset additum
2 vinculum. Praeterea olei quoque et omnis unguenti
taeter post fulmen odor est; ex quo apparet inesse
quandam subtilissimo igni et contra naturam suam
acto pestilentem potentiam, qua non icta tantum
cadunt sed et afflata. Praeterea quocumque decidit
fulmen, ibi odorem esse sulphuris certum est, qui,
quia natura gravis est, saepius haustus alienat.

[1] *humum* GKABV.

---

[1] Above, Chapter 31.1.

are undamaged, as I said,[1] the money which was in
them is discovered fused because the extremely thin
fire runs through invisible openings but overcomes
whatever it finds solid and resistant inside the wood.
However, as I said, it is not destructive in one way 2
only, but you can understand what each force has
done from the very type of damage.   You can recog-
nize the lightning by its effect.   Sometimes the force
of the same lightning bolt causes many different
effects in the same material; for example, in a tree it
burns through the driest part, bores through and
splinters the very hard and very solid material,
scatters the outer bark, bursts and splits the inner
layers, lashes and strips the leaves.   It congeals wine,
fuses iron and copper.

53. It is strange that wine congealed by lightning 1
either kills or causes insanity when drunk after it returns to its former state.   If anyone asks me why
this happens, this occurs to me: there is a sickness-
bearing power in lightning.   It is probable that
some trace of it remains in liquid which lightning
has condensed and congealed.   The liquid could not
have been solidified unless some cohesive element had
been added to it.   Besides, after lightning there is 2
also a disagreeable odour in oil and in all unguents.
It is clear from this that some sickening power exists
in the subtle fire that has been hurled down contrary to its nature.   Not only does the fire destroy the
things it strikes but even the things it has breathed
upon.   In addition, wherever lightning has struck
there is sure to be an odour of sulphur in the area,
which disturbs the reason if inhaled too much because
it is by nature unwholesome.

3   Sed ad haec vacui revertemur. Fortasse enim libebit ostendere quam omnia ista a philosophia parente artium fluxerint. Illa primum et quaesivit causas rerum et observavit effectus et, quod in fulminis inspectione longe melius est, initiis rerum exitus contulit.

1   54. Nunc ad opinionem Posidonii revertar. E terra terrenisque omnibus pars umida efflatur, pars sicca et fumida; haec fulminibus alimentum est, illa imbribus. Quicquid in aera sicci fumosique pervenit, id includi se nubibus non fert sed rumpit claudentia; inde est sonus quem nos tonitrum vocamus.

2   In ipso quoque aere quicquid extenuatur, simul siccatur et calefit; hoc quoque, si inclusum est, aeque fugam quaerit et cum sono evadit, ac modo universam eruptionem facit eoque vehementius intonat, modo
3   per partes et minutatim. Ergo tonitrua hic spiritus exprimit, dum aut rumpit nubes, aut pervolat; volutatio autem spiritus in nube conclusi valentissimum est atterendi genus. Tonitrua nihil aliud sunt quam citi aeris sonitus, qui fieri, nisi dum aut terit aut rumpitur, non potest.

1   55. "Etsi colliduntur inter se," inquit, "nubes, fit is quem desideras ictus." Sed non universus, neque enim tota totis concurrunt, sed partibus partes;

But we will return to these matters when at leisure. 3
Perhaps it will be good to show how all these investigations have stemmed from philosophy, the parent of the arts. Philosophy first examined the causes of things and observed their effects, and compared the outcome of events with the beginning—which is a far superior method in the investigation of lightning.

54. Now I will return to the theory of Posidonius.[1] From the earth and all terrestial things are exhaled 1 certain elements, some humid, some dry and smoky. The dry and smoky elements are the nutriment for lightning bolts, the humid for rain. Any dry and smoky element that reaches the atmosphere does not permit itself to be enclosed by clouds but breaks through the enclosures; hence comes the sound which we call thunder.

In the atmosphere itself anything that is rarefied 2 immediately dries up and becomes hot. If inclosed, this, too, seeks an outlet and escapes with a noise. Sometimes it makes a total eruption and thunders all the more vehemently; at other times it escapes in parts, little by little. Therefore, this air produces 3 thunder either while it bursts clouds or flies through them. Moreover, the turbulence of the air in an enclosed cloud is the most powerful type of friction. Thunder is nothing other than the sound of disturbed air, which cannot occur except where either the air causes friction or is burst apart.

55. "But if clouds collide with each other," he says, 1 "this is the only blow that you need." But not completely, for entire clouds do not run into entire

[1] Above, Chapter 12.4, Seneca ascribes this theory to Aristotle.

nec sonant mollia, nisi illisa duris sint, itaque non auditur fluctus, nisi impactus est.

2   "Ignis," inquit, "demissus in aquam sonat, dum extinguitur." Puta ita esse, pro me est; non enim ignis tunc sonum efficit sed spiritus per extinguentia effugiens. Ut dem tibi et fieri ignem in nube et extingui, spiritu nascitur et attritu.

3   "Quid ergo," inquit, "non potest aliqua ex his transcurrentibus stellis incidere in nubem et extingui?" Existimemus posse aliquando et hoc fieri; nunc naturalem causam quaerimus et assiduam, non raram fortuitamque. Puta enim me confiteri verum esse quod dicis, aliquando post tonitrua emicare ignes stellis transversis et cadentibus similes, non ob hoc tonitrua facta sunt, sed, cum hoc fieret, tonitrua facta sunt.

4   Clidemos ait fulgurationem speciem inanem esse, non ignem; sic enim per noctem splendorem motu [1] remorum † remorari.[2] Dissimile est exemplum. Illic enim splendor intra ipsam aquam apparet; qui fit in aere erumpit et exilit.

1   56. Heraclitus [3] existimat fulgurationem esse velut apud nos incipientium ignium conatum et primam flammam incertam, modo intereuntem, modo resurgentem; haec antiqui fulgetra dicebant. Tonitrua

---

[1] *motu* Gercke, Oltramare for *motum* HPEFZ.

[2] *remorum remorari* Oltramare for *remorari* Z; *remorare* HPG; *memorare* F; *rememorare* T; *revocare* E; *remorum videri* AV[2]. Perhaps simply *remorum morari*.

[3] *Herodotus* ABV.

clouds, but only parts into parts. Nor do soft substances make a sound unless they collide with hard ones. Thus, a wave is not audible unless it is dashed against an obstacle.

" When fire is plunged into water it makes a sound 2 while it is being extinguished," he says. Suppose this is so; it supports my argument. For the fire does not make the sound but the air which is escaping through the extinguishing water. I grant you that fire is both produced and extinguished in a cloud; but it is born from air and friction.

" Well, then," he says, " is it not possible that 3 some of those shooting stars fall into a cloud and are extinguished? " Let us suppose that this, too, can happen sometimes. But we are now seeking the natural and usual cause, not the rare and accidental. Consider that I admit what you say is true, that sometimes after thunder fires gleam like shooting and falling stars. Thunder was not caused on this account, but when this happened thunder occurred.

Clidemus [1] says that lightning is an empty apparition, not a fire; just as at night a gleam lingers during the movement of oars in water. The parallel is incorrect. Such a gleam appears in the water itself. The one which occurs in the atmosphere bursts and leaps out of its element.

56. Heraclitus estimates that a lightning flash is 1 like the attempts of a fire to ignite on our earth: the first flames are uncertain, at times dying down, at times shooting up. The ancients used to call this

---

[1] Aristotle (2.9.370a 11–21) says that Clidemus had no acquaintance with the theories of reflection, which is generally recognized as the cause of the gleam made by oars in water.

nos pluraliter dicimus; antiqui autem tonitrum dixerunt aut tonum. Hoc apud Caecinam invenio, facundum virum et qui habuisset aliquando in eloquentia nomen, nisi illum Ciceronis umbra pressis-

2 set. Etiamnunc illo verbo utebantur antiqui correpto,[1] quo nos producta una syllaba utimur; dicimus enim, ut splendēre, sic fulgēre; at illis ad significandam hanc e nubibus subitae lucis eruptionem mos erat correpta media syllaba uti, ut dicerent fulgĕre.

1 57. Quid ipse existimem quaeris; adhuc enim alienis opinionibus commodavi manum. Dicam. Fulgurat, cum repentinum late lumen emicuit; id evenit ubi in ignem aer extenuatis nubibus vertitur,

2 nec vires quibus longius prosiliret invenit. Non miraris, puto, si aera aut motus extenuat aut extenuatio incendit; sic liquescit excussa glans funda et attritu aeris velut igne destillat. Ideo plurima aestate sunt fulmina quia plurimum calidi est; facilius autem attritu calidorum ignis existit.

3 Eodem autem modo fit fulgur, quod tantum splendet, et fulmen, quod mittitur.[2] Sed illi levior vis alimentique minus est et, ut breviter dicam quod sentio, fulmen est fulgur intentum. Ergo ubi

---

[1] *correpto* ABV Haase; omitted by Oltramare.
[2] *emittitur* T; *mentitur* PZFλ; *intenditur* E.

---

[1] Lucretius uses *fulgĕre* to describe a lightning flash (see, for example, 5.1095).

[2] A theme favoured by poets—Lucretius 6.178, 306; Lucan 7.513; Ovid *Met.* 2.728; 14.825; Virg. *Aen.* 9.588.

[3] Pliny 2.135–136: lightning is rare in winter and in summer, more frequent in spring and autumn; but frequent in Italy

" heat lightning." We speak of thunderings in the plural. The ancients said *tonitrus* a thunder or *tonus* a thunderpeal. I find this statement in Caecina, a talented man who would have had at one time a name in eloquence, had not the shadow of Cicero suppressed him. Also, the ancients used to use a 2 short syllable in that verb *fulgere* which *we* use with one of the syllables long; for we say *fulgēre* just as we say *splendēre*. But to designate the eruption of sudden light from the clouds it was their habit to use a shortened middle syllable, so that they said *fulgĕre*.[1]

57. You ask what I think. Up to this point I have 1 lent a hand to the opinions of others. I will tell you. There is a heat-flash when a light shines suddenly and over a wide area. This happens when the atmosphere is changed to fire by the rarefication of clouds and does not find the strength to leap out over a rather considerable distance. You are not sur- 2 prised, I presume, if motion rarefies the atmosphere or the rarefication sets it afire in the same way that a ball of lead hurled from a sling liquifies [2] and lets fall drops from the friction of the air as though from fire. Thus, there are more lightning bolts in the summer because there is more heat.[3] Moreover, fire starts more easily from the friction of warm things.

A lightning flash, which only shines, and a lightning 3 bolt, which is discharged, occur in the same way. But a lightning flash has less force and less fuel and—to say briefly what I think—a lightning bolt is a lightning flash intensified. So, when the substance of

where the climate is always somewhat vernal and autumnal. In Rome and Campania lightning occurs in winter and in summer, which does not happen elsewhere.

calidi fumidique natura emissa terris in nubes incidit
et diu in illarum sinu volutata est, novissime erumpit
4 et, quia vires non habet, splendor est. At ubi illa
fulgura plus habuere materiae et maiore impetu
arserunt, non apparent tantum, sed decidunt.
Quaedam existimant utique fulmen reverti, quidam
subsidere ubi alimenta praegravaverunt et fulmen
ictu languidiore delatum est.

1   58. At quare fulmen subitum apparet nec con-
tinuatur assiduus ignis? Quia celere [1] mirique motus
simul et nubes rumpit et aera incendit, deinde desinit flamma motu quiescente. Non enim assiduus
est spiritus cursus, ut ignis possit extendi. Sed
quotiens fortius ipsa iactatione se accendit, fugiendi
impetum capit; deinde, cum evasit et pugna desinit,
ex eadem causa modo usque ad terram profertur,
modo ante dissolvitur, si minore vi pressus est.

2   Quare oblique fertur? Quia spiritu constat
(spiritus autem obliquus est flexuosusque), et quia
natura ignem sursum vocat, iniuria deorsum premit;
incipit autem obliquum esse iter, dum [2] neutra vis
alteri cedit et ignis in superiora nititur, in inferiora
deprimitur.

3   Quare frequenter cacumina montium feriuntur?

---

[1] Gercke, Oltramare for *celer est* PλA²; *celerrimum* A¹;
celerum est HFZLV; *celer ignis undique* ET (instead of *celere
mirique*).

[2] *interdum* P; *interdum dum* λ; *interdum autem* AV (instead
of *iter dum*).

heat and smoke emitted from the earth meets the clouds and is rolled about in their hollows for a long time it finally bursts forth and, because it has no strength, is only a flash. But when those flashes 4 have more matter and burn with greater force they do not merely become visible, they fall to earth. Some think that the lightning bolt returns to the clouds, others that it settles on the ground when the fuel has weighed it down and the bolt has been carried down by a rather feeble blow.

58. But why does lightning make a sudden appear- 1 ance and is not prolonged as a continuous fire? Because being swift and indeed having amazing speed, it breaks through the clouds and sets fire to the atmosphere at the same time; then the flame stops with the cessation of motion. The passage of the air is not continuous enough so that the fire can be extended. But when the air sets itself vigorously afire by its own violent agitation it undertakes the impetus of flight. Then when it has escaped and the conflict is ended it is, for the same reason, sometimes carried as far as the earth; and sometimes, if pressed down by an insufficient force, it is dissipated beforehand.

Why does lightning move obliquely? Because it 2 consists of moving air (the air is oblique and twisting), and, because nature summons fire upward, violence pushes it downwards. Moreover, the path tends to become zigzag when neither force yields to the other and the fire struggles towards the upper regions but is depressed towards the lower.

Why are the tops of mountains frequently struck 3 by lightning? Because they are exposed to the

Quia opposita sunt nubibus et e caelo cadentibus per haec transeundum est.

1   59. Intellego quid dudum desideres, quid efflagites. " Malo," inquis, " fulmina non timere quam nosse; itaque alios doce quemadmodum fiant; ego mihi metum illorum excuti volo, non naturam indicari."

2   Sequor quo vocas. Omnibus enim rebus omnibusque sermonibus aliquid salutare miscendum est. Cum imus per occulta naturae, cum divina tractamus, vindicandus est a malis suis animus ac subinde firmandus, quod etiam eruditis et hoc unum agentibus necessarium est, non ut effugiamus ictus rerum—undique enim in nos tela iaciuntur—sed ut fortiter

3   constanterque patiamur. Invicti esse possumus, inconcussi non possumus. Quamquam interim spes subit, inconcussos quoque esse nos posse. " Quemadmodum? " inquis. Contemne mortem, et omnia quae ad mortem ducunt contempta sunt, sive illa bella sunt, sive naufragia, seu morsus ferarum, seu

4   ruinarum subito lapsu procidentium pondera. Numquid facere amplius possunt quam ut corpus ab animo resolvant? Hoc nulla diligentia evitat, nulla felicitas donat, nulla potentia evincit. Talia fors[1] varia formidine disponit; mors omnes aeque vocat;

5   iratis diis propitiisque moriendum est. Animus ex ipsa desperatione sumatur. Ignavissima animalia, quae natura ad fugam genuit, ubi exitus non patet,

---

[1] *fors* supplied by Oltramare; *fortitudine* PHFZAV; *formidine* ECB. Alexander suggests *alia varie fortuna disponit.*

clouds and anything falling from the sky must pass through them.

59. I know what you have wanted for a long time, 1 and what you keenly ask. You say, " I should rather I did not fear lightning than know about it. So, teach others how lightning bolts occur. *I* want to shake off the fear of them, not have their nature explained to me."

I follow your call. Some moral ought to be mixed 2 in all things and all conversation. When we go into the secrets of nature, when we treat the divine, the soul ought to be delivered from its ills and occasionally strengthened, which is necessary even for learned men, especially those who deal with this study exclusively, not in order that we may escape the blows of things—for weapons are hurled at us from all sides—but in order that we may endure them bravely and firmly. We can be unconquered but 3 we cannot be unshaken. And yet the hope occasionally arises that we also can be unshaken. " How? " you ask. Despise death, and all the things which lead to death have thus been despised, whether they are wars, shipwrecks, or the jaws of wild beasts, or the weight of ruins falling down with a sudden slip. Are they able to do more than 4 separate the body from the soul? This no diligence avoids, no felicity grants, no power overcomes. Fortune assigns such things with varying terrors. Death summons all impartially. Whether the gods are angry or propitious, it is necessary to die. Take 5 courage from this very lack of hope. The most cowardly animals which nature has born only for flight, when no way is open, try to fight with their

temptant pugnam [1] corpore imbelli. Nullus per-
niciosior hostis est quam quem audacem angustiae
faciunt, longeque violentius semper ex necessitate
quam ex virtute confligitur,[2] aut certe paria conantur
animus magnus ac perditus.

6   Cogitemus nos quantum ad mortem perditos esse.
Et sumus. Ita est, Lucili; omnes reservamur ad
mortem. Totum hunc quem vides populum, totum-
que quem usquam cogitas esse, cito natura revocabit
et condet, nec de re sed de die quaeritur; eodem
7 citius tardius veniendum est. Quid ergo? Non
tibi timidissimus omnium videtur et insipientissimus
qui magno ambitu rogat moram mortis? Nonne
contemneres eum qui, inter perituros constitutus,
beneficii loco peteret ut ultimus cervicem praeberet?
Idem facimus; magno aestimamus mori tardius.

8   In omnes constitutum est capitale supplicium, et
quidem constitutione iustissima, quod maximum solet
esse solacium extrema passuris; quorum enim causa,
sors eadem est. Sequeremur traditi a iudice aut
magistratu et carnifici nostro praestaremus obse-
quium; quid interest utrum ad mortem iussi eamus
9 an nati? O te dementem et oblitum fragilitatis tuae
si tunc mortem times cum tonat! Itane? In hoc
salus tua vertitur? Vives si fulmen effugeris?
Petet te gladius, petet lapis, petet bilis; non maximum ex periculis tuis sed speciosissimum fulmen est.
10 Male scilicet actum erit tecum, si sensum morti-

---

[1] Gronovius, Haase, Oltramare for *fugam* HPEAV; *pugnant* ?
[2] Gercke for *corrigitur* most MSS.; *corruitur* E.

weak bodies. No enemy is more deadly than the one whom cornering has made bold. Combat is always offered far more violently by necessity than by courage. Or to put it another way: certainly the great spirit and the desperate strive equally.

Let us consider that we are lost, as far as death is 6 concerned. And we are. This is so, Lucilius; we are all reserved for death. This entire populace which you see, and all you imagine to exist anywhere, nature will summon swiftly and bury. There is no question about the event, only about the day. Sooner or later we must all go to the same place. What then? Does he not appear to you the most 7 fearful and foolish of all men who, by great entreaty, asks for a delay of death? Would you not despise a man who, assigned to those about to die, seeks as a favour to be the last to offer his neck? We do the same thing. We think it important to die a little later.

Capital punishment is the sentence for all mankind, 8 and indeed by a very just constitution because it is usually the greatest solace for those about to suffer the end of life: their cause, their fate, is the same. We should be acquiescent when handed over by a judge or magistrate and be obedient to our executioner. What does it matter whether we go to death by order or by birth? You are demented and 9 forgetful of your frailty if then you fear death when it thunders! So? Does your safety depend on this? Will you live if you escape a lightning bolt? A sword will threaten you, a stone will threaten you, the bile will threaten you. Lightning is not the greatest of your dangers, only the most conspicuous. Surely 10

tuae celeritas infinita praeveniet, si mors tua pro-
curatur, si ne [1] tunc quidem, cum expiras, super-
vacuus sed alicuius magnae rei signum es. Male
11 scilicet tecum agitur, si cum fulmine conderis.[2] Sed
pavescis ad caeli fragorem et ad inane nubilum
trepidas et, quotiens aliquid effulsit, expiras. Quid
ergo? Honestius putas deiectione [3] perire quam
fulmine? Eo itaque fortior adversus caeli minas
surge et, cum undique mundus exarserit, cogita
12 nihil habere te tanta morte perdendum. Quodsi
tibi parari credis illam caeli confusionem, illam tem-
pestatum discordiam, si propter te ingestae illisaeque
nubes strepunt, si in tuum exitium tanta vis ignium
excutitur, at tu solacii loco numera tanti esse mortem
13 tuam. Sed non erit huic cogitationi locus; casus iste
donat [4] metum et inter cetera hoc quoque commodum
eius quod expectationem suam [5] antecedit. Nemo
umquam timuit fulmen, nisi quod effugit.

[1] Gercke, Oltramare for *sine te* HPEZ; *si tu* ABV.
[2] *cecideris* ABV.
[3] *deiectione* BVT; *deiectione animae* V; *deiectione animi* B;
dilectione HFZ.
[4] *demat* AV; *demit* BC.
[5] *tuam* ABV; *sui* Z.

it will not be so bad for you if infinite swiftness fore-
stalls your sensation of dying, if your death is followed
by sacrificial ceremonies, if you are not unessential
even when you die but a sign of some great event.
Surely it is not a terrible fate for you if you are buried
with lightning.   But you shake at a crash in the sky, 11
you tremble at a hollow cloud, and whenever there is
any flash, you expire.   Then why?   Do you think it
more glorious to die from diarrhoea [1] than from a
lightning bolt?   So, rise up all the more bravely
against the threats of heaven, and when the universe
burns on all sides think that you have nothing to lose
in so glorious a death.   But if you believe that dis- 12
turbance in heaven, that discord of tempests, is
being prepared against *you*; if clouds pile up, collide,
and roar on *your* account; if such a great fiery force
is being scattered around for *your* destruction, then
reckon it a comfort that your death is valued at so
much.   But there will be no time for this thought. 13
An accident of this sort bypasses fear and among other
things presents this advantage: it comes before it is
expected.   No one has ever feared any lightning
except that which he has escaped.

---

[1] Also in *Epist.* 120.16 Seneca uses *deiectio*, " downthrow,"
to mean diarrhoea.

BOOK III
TERRESTRIAL WATERS

LIBER TERTIUS [1]

DE AQUIS TERRESTRIBUS [2]

PRAEFATIO 1. Non praeterit me, Lucili virorum
optime, quam magnarum [3] rerum fundamenta ponam
senex, qui mundum circuire constitui et causas
secretaque eius eruere atqui aliis noscenda prodere.
Quando tam multa consequar, tam sparsa colligam,
tam occulta perspiciam? 2. Remittat [4] ergo senectus
et obiciat annos inter vana studia consumptos.
Tanto magis urgeamus et damna aetatis male
exemptae labor sarciat; nox ad diem accedat,
occupationes recidantur, patrimonii longe a domino
iacentis cura solvatur, sibi totus animus vacet et ad
contemplationem sui saltem in ipso fine respiciat. 3.
Faciet ac sibi instabit et cotidie brevitatem temporis
metietur. Quicquid amissum est, id diligenti usu
praesentis vitae recolliget; fidelissimus est ad honesta

---

[1] *Explicit lib. III^us, Incipit VIII^us* G; *expl. lib. II^us, lib.
III^us de Nat. Quaest.* V; *expl. lib. VIII incipit IX* H;
[Liber Tertius] ⟨Liber Septimus⟩ Oltramare.
[2] *De aquis* E; *terrestribus* supplied by Gercke, Oltramare.
[3] *magna* V.

BOOK III

TERRESTRIAL WATERS

PREFACE 1. Lucilius, best of men, I realize how I, an old man,[1] am starting the groundwork for a vast project, once I have decided to survey the universe, to uncover its causes and secrets, and to pass them on to the knowledge of others. When will I catch up with so much material, gather together such scattered fields of study, gain insight into such mysteries? 2. My old age should exempt me from this task and rebuke me with the years spent in idle pursuits. But let me strive all the more and let hard work make up for the omissions of a misspent life. Add night to day and cut other activities short, abandon concern for property that lies far from its owner. The mind should be entirely free for itself. Towards the very end, at least, it should look backward in contemplation of itself. 3. It will do so, and will urge itself on, and daily measure the shortness of time. Whatever has been lost the mind will recover by the diligent use of the life remaining. The most dependable change towards integrity comes from repentance.

---

[1] Seneca is a little older than Lucilius (*Epist.* 26.7) although there is not much difference in their ages (*Epist.* 35.2.) and Lucilius is already advanced in years (*Epist.* 96.3).

---

[4] Oltramare for *premittat* MSS.

ex paenitentia transitus. Libet igitur mihi ex-
clamare illum poetae incliti versum:

Tollimus ingentes animos et maxima parvo [1]
Tempore molimur.

Hoc dicerem, si puer iuvenisque molirer. Nullum
enim non tam magnis rebus tempus angustum est.
Nunc vero ad rem seriam, gravem, immensam post
meridianas horas accessimus. 4. Faciamus quod in
itinere fieri solet: qui tardius exierunt, velocitate
pensant moram. Festinemus et opus nescio an
superabile, magnum certe, sine aetatis excusatione
tractemus. Crescit animus, quotiens coepti magnitudinem attendit [2] et cogitat quantum proposito, non
quantum sibi supersit.

5. Consumpsere se quidam, dum acta regum
externorum componunt quaeque passi invicem
ausique sunt populi. Quanto satius est sua mala
extinguere quam aliena posteris tradere? Quanto
potius deorum opera celebrare quam Philippi aut
Alexandri latrocinia ceterorumque qui exitio gentium
clari non minores fuere pestes mortalium quam
inundatio qua planum omne perfusum est, quam
conflagratio qua magna pars animantium exaruit?
6. Quemadmodum Hannibal Alpes superiecerit scri-

---

[1] *facta* ABV.
[2] *attendit* Oltramare; *ostendit* most MSS.; *aspexit* Z; *ostendis*
Gercke; *quotiens sibi coepti magnitudinem ostendit* Garrod;
quotiens quis coepti magnitudinem ostendit Alexander.

Let me recite these well-known lines of the famous poet: [1]

> We arouse our minds to greatness
> And we strive for grand accomplishments
> In the little time left.

I should make the same statement even if I were undertaking this task in boyhood or young manhood. Any time is too short for such a vast study. But now after middle hours of age's day I have started a work that is serious, difficult, immense. 4. Let me do what is often done on a journey. Those who start late make up for the delay by speed. Let me hurry and, without excusing my old age, treat a subject that is perhaps surmountable but clearly grand. When my mind considers the magnitude of the undertaking it expands and contemplates how much there remains for it to do, not how much remains for it to live.

5. Some writers have exhausted themselves narrating the actions of foreign kings and the misfortunes nations have suffered or inflicted on others in turn. Surely it is better to eliminate one's own ills than to report to posterity the ills of others. It is much better to celebrate the works of the gods than the robberies of a Philip,[2] or of an Alexander, or of others who were no less famous for the destruction of the human race than a flood that inundated every plain or a conflagration that burned up the majority of living creatures. 6. They write how Hannibal

---

[1] Perhaps Seneca is referring to Lucilius, whose verses he quotes in the following chapter, after Ovid and Virgil.
[2] Philip II of Macedon, 382–336 B.C., father of Alexander the Great.

bunt; quemadmodum confirmatum Hispaniae cladibus bellum Italiae inopinatus intulerit fractisque rebus, etiam post Carthaginem pertinax, reges pererraverit contra Romanos ducem promittens, exercitum petens;[1] quemadmodum non desierit omnibus angulis bellum senex quaerere; adeo sine patria pati poterat, sine hoste non poterat.

7. Quanto satius est quid faciendum sit quam quid factum quaerere, ac docere eos qui sua permisere fortunae nihil stabile ab illa datum esse, eius omnia aura fluere mobilius! Nescit enim quiescere; gaudet laetis tristia substituere,[2] utique miscere. Itaque secundis nemo confidat, adversis nemo deficiat: alternae sunt vices rerum. 8. Quid exultas? Ista quibus eveheris in summum nescis ubi te relictura sint; habebunt suum, non tuum finem. Quid iaces? Ad imum delatus es, nunc locus est resurgendi. In melius adversa, in deterius optata flectuntur. 9. Ita

---

[1] *etiam sine exercitu* ABV.
[2] *sustinere et utraque* ABV.

---

[1] Hannibal crossed the Alps in 218 B.C., thus ushering in the Second Punic War, and for over fourteen years marched through Italy with his heterogeneous army of mercenaries, supported in part by revenue from his previous conquests in Spain. After the final defeat of Carthage in 202 B.C. (*post Carthaginem*, as Seneca puts it) by the Romans, Hannibal lived

crossed the Alps, how he unexpectedly carried to Italy a war supported by disasters in Spain; and how even when his fortunes were dashed to pieces after Carthage he was still obstinate and wandered among kings begging for an army and promising to be a general against the Romans; and how as an old man he did not stop searching for war in every corner of the world. So, he could endure being without a country, but he could not stand being without an enemy.[1]

7. It is far better to investigate what ought to be done rather than what has been done, and to teach those who have entrusted their affairs to fortune that nothing given by fortune is stable, and all her gifts flow away more fleetingly than air. For fortune does not know how to be inactive; she enjoys substituting sorrow for happiness, or at least mixing the two. So, no one should be confident in times of success, nor give up in times of adversity. The changes of fortune alternate. 8. Why do you rejoice? Those very circumstances which have carried you to the heights will abandon you, you know not where. They will have *their* end, not yours. Why are you despondent? You have been carried down to a low point, but now is the time to rise again. Failure changes for the better, success for the worse. 9. So, changes must

for another twenty years, plotting against the Romans and trying to escape from their expansion. He fled to the court of King Antiochus III of Syria, who decided to attack the Romans partly on Hannibal's advice. After the defeat and death of Antiochus, Hannibal fled to King Prusias of Bithynia; but upon the arrival of a committee from Rome demanding his surrender, Hannibal took his own life, his only way of escaping the Romans, in 182 B.C.

concipienda est animo varietas non privatarum tantum domuum, quas levis casus impellit, sed publicarum: regna ex infimo coorta supra imperantes constiterunt, vetera imperia in ipso flore ceciderunt. Iniri[1] non potest numerus quam multa ab aliis fracta sint. Nunc cum maxime deus extruit[2] alia, alia submittit, nec molliter ponit, sed ex fastigio suo nullas habitura reliquias iactat.

10. Magna ista, quia parvi sumus, credimus; multis rebus non ex natura sua sed ex humilitate nostra magnitudo est. Quid praecipuum in rebus humanis est? Non classibus maria complesse nec in Rubri maris litore signa fixisse nec, deficiente ad iniurias terra, errasse in oceano ignota quaerentem, sed animo omne vidisse et, qua maior nulla victoria est, vitia domuisse. Innumerabiles sunt qui populos, qui urbes habuerunt in potestate; paucissimi qui se.

11. Quid est praecipuum? Erigere animum supra minas et promissa fortunae; nihil dignum putare quod spcres. Quid enim habet quod concupiscas? Qui a divinorum conversatione quotiens ad humana

___

[1] *inire* Z Oltramare; *inveniri* most MSS.
[2] *exaltat* ABV.

___

[1] *Rubrum mare* could include the Red Sea, the Arabian Sea, and the Persian Gulf. Seneca may have been thinking of Alexander's conquests, and the voyage of his admiral Nearchus

be grasped by your mind not only in private families, which a slight misfortune destroys but also in ruling families. Dynasties have risen from the lowest level of society and become established above the ruling classes; ancient empires have fallen at the very peak of their power. It is impossible to count how many kingdoms have been overthrown by other kingdoms. The divinity now especially exalts some, overthrows others, and does not set them down gently but hurls them from their very pinnacle; and they are not likely to have anything remaining.

10. We believe these affairs of ours are great because we are small. In many instances, size is derived from our own littleness, not from the actual reality. What is important in human existence? Not to have filled the seas with ships, nor to have fixed a flag on the shore of the Red Sea,[1] nor to have wandered over the ocean seeking the unknown when known land has been exhausted for wrongdoing. Rather to have seen the universe in your mind and to have subdued your vices—no victory is greater than this. Innumerable are those who have had peoples and cities under their control; very few have had themselves under control.

11. What is important? To raise your mind above the threats and promises of fortune, to consider nothing worth hoping for. What does fortune have that you should be covetous of? Whenever you withdraw from an association with divine things and turn

from Indus to Euphrates. But as a Roman it is more probable that he had in mind the military expedition of Aelius Gallus in 25 B.C. down the east side of the Red Sea against the Sabaeans of south-west Arabia. Pliny 6.159–162; *Mon. Ancyr.* 26.

recideris, non aliter caligabis quam quorum oculi in densam umbram ex claro sole redierunt.

12. Quid est praecipuum? Posse laeto animo adversa tolerare; quicquid acciderit, sic ferre, quasi tibi volueris accidere. Debuisses enim velle, si scisses omnia ex decreto dei fieri: flere, queri et gemere desciscere est.

13. Quid est praecipuum? Animus contra calamitates fortis et contumax, luxuriae non aversus tantum sed infestus, nec avidus periculi nec fugax, qui sciat fortunam non expectare sed facere et adversus utramque intrepidus inconfususque prodire, nec illius tumultu nec huius fulgore percussus.

14. Quid est praecipuum? Non admittere in animo mala consilia, puras ad caelum manus tollere, nullum bonum petere quod, ut ad te transeat, aliquis dare debet aliquis amittere, optare, quod sine adversario optatur, bonam mentem; cetera magno aestimata mortalibus, etiamsi quis domum casus attulerit, sic intueri quasi exitura qua venerint.

15. Quid est praecipuum? Altos supra fortuita[1] spiritus tollere, hominis meminisse, ut, sive felix eris, scias hoc non futurum diu, sive infelix, scias hoc te non esse, si non putes.[2]

16. Quid est praecipuum? In primis labris

---

[1] *fortunam* ABV.
[2] *nisi cum putes* ABV.

to human affairs you will be blinded, like the eyes of those who turn from bright sunlight to dark shade.

12. What is important? To be able to endure adversity with a cheerful mind. To bear whatever happens just as though you wanted it to happen to you. For you would have been quite right to want it, if you had known that all things happen in accordance with a decree of god. To weep, to complain, to groan is to rebel.

13. What is important? A mind bold and confident against calamity, not only averse to luxury but even an enemy of it, neither eager for danger nor fleeing from it. A mind that knows how to make its fortune, not merely wait for it; how to meet either good or bad fortune unafraid and unconfused; and is not disconcerted either by the tumult of the one or the attractions of the other.

14. What is important? Not to admit evil plans into your thinking, to raise pure hands to heaven, to seek no good which, in order that it may pass over to you, someone must give, someone must lose; to long for goodness of heart, which may be hoped for without an opponent. As for other things judged precious by mortals, even if some chance brings them into your home, regard them as though they are about to leave by the way they came in.

15. What is important? To lift your spirits high above chance occurrences, to be mindful of being a man so that if you are fortunate you understand that it will not likely last long; or if you are unfortunate you know that you are not so, if you do not think you are.

16. What is important? To have your breath on

animam habere; haec res efficit non e iure Quiritium
liberum sed e iure naturae. Liber est autem qui
servitutem suam effugit; haec est assidua et in-
eluctabilis et per diem ac noctem aequaliter premens,
sine intervallo, sine commeatu. 17. Sibi servire
gravissima est servitus. Quam discutere facile est,
si desieris multa te poscere, si desieris tibi referre
mercedem, si ante oculos et naturam tuam posueris
et aetatem, licet prima sit, ac tibi ipse dixeris:
" Quid insanio? Quid anhelo? Quid sudo? Quid
terram, quid forum verso? Nec multo opus est, nec
diu."

18. Ad hoc proderit nobis inspicere rerum naturam.
Primo discedemus a sordidis. Deinde animum
ipsum, quo sano[1] magnoque opus est, seducemus a
corpore. Deinde in occultis exercitata subtilitas
non erit in aperta deterior; nihil est autem apertius
his salutaribus quae contra nequitiam nostram
furoremque discuntur, quae damnamus nec ponimus.

1   1. Quaeramus ergo de terrestribus[2] aquis aut et
investigemus qua ratione fiant, sive, ut ait Ovidius:

Fons erat illimis nitidis argenteus undis

[1] *sano* Z Oltramare; *summo* most MSS.
[2] *terrestribus* Schultess, Gercke, Oltramare for *terris quibus*
HPZG; *aquis* ABV; *terris de quibus* T; *de quibus rebus* E.

---

[1] As if formally freed by a master (Gaius 4.15.)

your very lips; this makes a man free not by right[1] of Roman citizenship but by right of nature. A man is free who has escaped slavery to himself. Such slavery is continuous, ineluctable, pressing constantly day and night without pause, without interruption, without leave of absence. 17. To be a slave to one's self is the most grievous kind of slavery. It is easy to shake off if you cease demanding so much of yourself, if you stop searching for personal profit, if you keep before your eyes your nature and time of life—even if you are still young—and say to yourself: "Why am I a fool? Why do I pant, sweat, upset the earth and the forum? I do not need much, and only for a short time."

18. On this point it will help us to study nature. In the first place we will get away from sordid matters. Second, we will free the mind—and we need one that is sound and great—from the body. Third, the subtlety of thought exercised on the mysteries of nature will be no less successful in dealing with plain problems. Moreover, nothing is plainer than those salutary lessons we are taught against our own iniquities and follies which we condemn but do not renounce.

1. Let us, then, study the waters of the earth or 1 investigate also the causes that produce them, whether, as Ovid says:

> There was a fountain
> Silvery clear
> With shining waters [2]

---

[2] Ovid, *Met.* 3.407.

sive, ut ait Vergilius:

Unde per ora novem vasto cum murmure montis

It mare praeruptum [1] et pelago premit arva sonanti

sive, ut apud te, Iunior carissime, invenio:

Elius [2] Siculis de fontibus exilit amnis

si qua ratio aquas subministrat, quomodo tot flumina ingentia per diem noctemque decurrant; quare alia hibernis aquis intumescant, alia in defectu ceterorum

2 amnium crescant. Nilum interim seponemus a turba, propriae naturae ac singularis, et illi suum diem dabimus. Nunc vulgares aquas persequamur, tam frigidas quam calentes. In quibus calentibus quaerendum erit utrum calidae nascantur an fiant. De ceteris quoque disseremus, quas insignes aut sapor aut aliqua reddit utilitas. Quaedam enim oculos, quaedam nervos iuvant; quaedam inveterata et desperata a medicis vitia percurant; quaedam medentur ulceribus; quaedam interiora potu fovent et pulmonis ac viscerum querelas levant; quaedam supprimunt sanguinem. Tam varius singulis usus quam gustus est.

[1] *praeruptum* HPZABV; *proruptum* most Virg. MSS., although *praeruptum* was known to Servius.
[2] *Elius* Gercke, Oltramare for *elisus* HEZT; *elisius* PFAVλ; *eleus* B.

---

[1] Virgil *Aen.* 1.245–246. The Timavus now enters the Gulf of Trieste gently with 3 mouths.

or, as Virgil says:

> Whence through nine mouths
> With a mighty roar from the mountain
> A sea goes bursting forward
> And presses down the fields
> With its resounding expanse.[1]

or, as I find in your poem, dear Junior; [2]

> A stream of Elis
> Leaps
> From Sicilian springs—

whether any principle supplies the water, how so many great rivers roll down day and night; why some are swollen by winter rains, and some streams grow larger while others subside. For the moment, let us 2 separate the Nile from ordinary rivers; it is unique and exceptional, and we will give it its turn.[3] At present, let us study common waters, both hot and cold. In studying hot waters it must be determined whether they are produced hot or become hot. We will also discuss other waters, those which a flavour or some special usefulness makes remarkable. For example, some cure the eyes, some the sinews; some completely cure ailments that are chronic and given up by doctors. Some heal sores; some on being drunk relieve internal pain and alleviate complaints of the lungs and bowels. Some check bleeding. Their individual uses are as varied as their taste.

[2] Lucilius Junior wrote a poem on Sicily (cf. Seneca *Epist.* 79) which, in its first part, included the legend of the river Alpheus in Elis and the Sicilian spring of Arethusa, as Seneca remarks below, Chapter 26.6.

[3] The Nile is the subject of Book Four-A.

1 2. Aut stant omnes aquae, aut eunt, aut colligun-
tur, aut varias habent venas. Aliae dulces sunt,
aliae varie asperae. Quippe interveniunt salsae
amaraeque aut medicatae, ex quibus sulphuratas
dicimus, ferratas, aluminosas; indicat vim sapor.
2 Habent praeterea multa discrimina, primum tactus:
frigidae calidaeque sunt; deinde ponderis: leves et
graves sunt; deinde coloris: purae sunt, turbidae,
caeruleae, luridae;[1] deinde salubritatis: sunt enim
utiles, sunt mortiferae, sunt quae cogantur in lapidem; quaedam tenues, quaedam pingues; quaedam
alunt, quaedam sine ulla bibentis ope transeunt;
quaedam haustae fecunditatem afferunt.
1 3. Ut stet aqua aut fluat, loci positio efficit: in
devexo fluit, in plano et supino continetur et stagnat.
Aliquando in adversum spiritu impellitur; tunc
cogitur, non fluit. Colligitur ex imbribus. Ex suo
fonte nativa est. Nihil tamen prohibet eodem loco
aquam colligi et nasci. Quod in Fucino[2] videmus, in
quem montes circumiecti quicquid fudit pluvia[3]
derivant, sed et magnae in ipso latentesque venae[4]
sunt; itaque, etiam cum hiberni defluxere torrentes,
faciem suam servat.

---

[1] *luridae* Oltramare for *lucidae* most MSS.; *lividae* E².
[2] *Fuscino* EZABVCOT.
[3] *fluvia* HPZ; *fluvii* ABV.
[4] *venae* Z; *undae* HKJABV; *vel venae unde* P.

2. All waters are still, or running, or collected, or 1
occupy various subterranean channels. Some are
sweet, others have flavours that are disagreeable in
different ways; among them are the salty, the bitter,
and the medicinal. In the last category I mean sulphur, iron, and alum waters. The taste indicates 2
the properties. They have many other distinctive
qualities in addition. First, there is touch: they
are hot or cold. Then weight: they are light
or heavy. Then colour: they are clear, muddy, blue,
yellowish. Then their effect on health: for some are
wholesome, others are deadly. There are certain
waters which thicken into rock, others are thin or fat.
Some give nourishment, some pass through without
any benefit to the drinker; and some waters, when
drunk, stimulate fecundity.[1]

3. The topography of the land causes water either 1
to stand or to flow. On a slope, it flows down. On a
flat, level area it is retained and becomes stagnant.
Sometimes it is forced backwards by the wind; then
it does not flow but is driven. It is collected water
when it comes from the rain. It is native when it
comes from its own spring. However, there is
nothing to prevent water from being both collected
and native in the same place. We see this at Lake
Fucinus, into which the surrounding heights direct
whatever water the rain pours down. But the lake
also has great sources hidden in its depths; thus it
retains its usual appearance even when the winter
torrents have ceased to flow.

---

[1] Below, Chapter 25.11, Seneca says he regards the fecundity
benefits of certain waters as unfounded rumours.

1   4. Primum ergo quaeramus quomodo ad continuandos fluminum cursus terra sufficiat, unde tantum aquarum exeat. Miramur quod accessionem fluminum maria non sentiant; aeque mirandum est quod detrimentum exeuntium terra non sentit. Quid est quod illam aut sic impleverit ut praebere tantum ex recondito possit, aut subinde sic suppleat? Quamcumque rationem reddiderimus de flumine, eadem erit rivorum ac fontium.

1   5. Quidam iudicant terram quicquid aquarum emisit rursus accipere, et ob hoc maria non crescere quia quod influxit non in suum vertunt sed protinus reddunt. Occulto enim itinere subit terras, et palam venit, secreto revertitur. Colaturque in transitu mare, quod per multiplices terrarum anfractus verberatum amaritudinem ponit et pravitatem: in tanta soli varietate saporem exuit et in sinceram aquam transit.

1   6. Quidam existimant, quicquid ex imbribus terra concipit, id illam[1] rursus emittere,[2] et hoc argumenti loco ponunt quod paucissima flumina in his sunt locis

[1] *ad illam* PZK; *ad ima trahi et ad illam* ET; *in flumina* ABV.
[2] *emitti* EABVT.

---

[1] This is an old problem. Aristotle 2.2.255b 20–25: The old question why so great an amount of water disappears (for the sea becomes no larger even though innumerable rivers of immense size are flowing into it every day) is quite a natural one to ask. Pliny believes (2.166) that the theory of veins carrying waters inside the earth explains why seas do not increase with the daily accession of so many rivers.

4. First then, let us investigate how the earth 1
supplies the continuous flow of rivers, and where
such great quantities of water come from. We are
surprised that the seas are not affected by the
addition of the rivers; it is equally surprising that the
earth is not affected by the loss of the waters leaving
it.[1] What is it that has filled the earth up in such a
way that it can either furnish great quantities from
its hidden recesses or make good, as it does repeatedly,
what it has lost? Whatever explanation we give of
a river, the same will be so of streams and springs.

5. Some think[2] that the earth receives back 1
whatever water it has emitted; and for this reason
the oceans do not grow larger because they do not
assimilate the water which flows into them but immediately return it to the land. For, the water enters
the land by hidden routes—openly it comes to the
sea; secretly does it return. Sea water is filtered
in transit[3] because it is battered by the many cir-
cuitous passages in the earth and sets aside its
salinity and impurities. In the many different types
of soil it sheds its disagreeable taste and changes into
fresh water.

6. Some suppose that whatever water the earth 1
receives from rain this it sends out again, and as proof
they point out that there are very few rivers in those

[2] Aristotle (2.2.345b 2–23) presents and refutes the theories
that rivers get their water from the sea. Lucretius (6.631–
638; 5.261–272) states that water flows from the land into the
sea and returns to the land both by surface evaporation and
by distribution under the earth, with all the salt drained out.
[3] Both Aristotle (2.2.354b 19) and Lucretius (2.471–476)
assert that the sea water is filtered and becomes drinkable by
passing through the earth.

2 quibus rarus est imber. Ideo siccas aiunt Aethiopiae
solitudines esse paucosque inveniri in interiore Africa
fontes, quia fervida natura caeli sit et paene semper
aestiva; squalidae itaque sine arbore, sine cultore
harenae iacent raris imbribus sparsae, quos statim
combibunt. At contra constat Germaniam Galliam-
que et proxime ab illis Italiam abundare rivis et
fluminibus, quia caelo umido utuntur et ne aestas
quidem imbribus caret.

1 7. Adversus hoc multa posse dici vides. Primum
ego tibi vinearum diligens fossor affirmo nullam
pluviam esse tam magnam quae terram ultra decem
in altitudinem pedes madefaciat: omnis umor intra
primam crustam consumitur nec in inferiora descen-
2 dit. Quomodo ergo imber suggerere potest amnibus
vires, qui summam humum tinguit? Pars maior
eius per fluminum alveos in mare aufertur; exiguum
est quod sorbeat terra. Nec id servat. Aut enim
arida est et absumit in se quicquid infusum est, aut
satiata, si quid supra desiderium cecidit, excludit, et
ideo primis imbribus non augentur amnes quia totos
in se terra sitiens trahit.

3 Quid quod quaedam flumina erumpunt saxis et
montibus? His quid conferent pluviae, quae per
nudas rupes deferuntur nec habent terram cui
insidant? Adice quod siccissimis locis putei in
altum acti ultra ducentorum aut trecentorum pedum
spatium inveniunt aquarum uberes venas in ea alti-
tudine in quam pluvia [1] non penetrat, ut scias illic
non caelestem esse nec collecticium umorem sed,

1 *pluvia* Z Oltramare; *aqua* HPEABV.

localities where rain is scarce. Thus, they explain 2
that the deserts of Ethiopia are dry and that very
few springs are found in the interior of Africa because the condition of the climate is hot and almost
always summer; and so the sands lie barren without
trees, without cultivation, sprinkled by infrequent
rains which they immediately drink up. On the other
hand, it is well known that Germany and Gaul, and
the parts of Italy next to them, abound in streams
and rivers because they have a moist climate and not
even their summers lack rainfall.

7. It is obvious that much can be said against this 1
theory. First of all, as a diligent vine-gardener myself I assure you that no rainfall is so heavy it wets
the ground to a depth beyond ten feet. All the
moisture is absorbed in the outer surface and does not
get down to the lower levels. How, then, is rain 2
able to supply an abundance to rivers since it only
dampens the surface soil? The greater part of rain
is carried off to sea through river-beds. The amount
which the earth absorbs is scanty, and the earth does
not retain that. For the ground is either dry and
uses up what is poured into it or it is saturated and
will pour off any excess that has fallen into it. For
this reason rivers do not rise with the first rainfall
because the thirsty ground absorbs all the water.

What about the fact that some rivers burst out of 3
rocks and mountains? What will rains contribute to
these rivers, rains which pour down over bare rock
and have no ground in which to settle? Besides, in
very dry localities wells are driven down to a depth
beyond a distance of two hundred or three hundred
feet and find copious veins of water at a level where

4 quod dici solet, vivam aquam. Illo quoque argumento haec opinio refellitur quod quidam fontes in
summo montis cacumine redundant; apparet illos
sursum agi aut ibi concipi, cum omnis pluvialis aqua
decurrat.

1 8. Quidam existimant, quemadmodum in exteriore
parte terrarum vastae paludes iacent magnique et
navigabiles lacus, quemadmodum ingenti spatio
maria porrecta sunt infusa vallibus, sic interiora
terrarum abundare aquis dulcibus nec minus illas late
stagnare quam apud nos oceanum et sinus eius, immo
eo latius quia plus terra in altum patet. Ergo ex
illa profunda copia isti amnes egeruntur. Quos quid
miraris si terra detractos non sentit, cum adiectos
maria non sentiant?

1 9. Quibusdam haec placet causa: aiunt habere
terram intra se recessus cavos et multum spiritus.
Qui necessario frigescit umbra gravi pressus; deinde
piger et immotus in aquam, cum se desiit ferre,
convertitur; quemadmodum supra nos mutatio
aeris imbrem facit, ita infra terras flumen aut rivum.

2 Supra nos non potest stare segnis diu et gravis.
Aliquando enim sole tenuatur, aliquando ventis
expanditur, itaque intervalla magna imbribus sunt.
Sub terra vero, quicquid est quod illum in aquam
convertat, idem semper est, umbra perpetua, frigus

---

[1] Seneca appears to be thinking of deep inlets of the sea into
the land such as the sea-lochs of Scotland and the bays of
S.W. Ireland.

rainwater does not penetrate. So you know that no 4
water from the sky exists there nor any collection of
moisture, but what is commonly called living water.
The theory that all water comes from rain is dis-
proved by another argument: the fact that certain
springs well up on the high tops of mountains. It is
obvious that they are forced up or are formed on the
spot, since all rainwater runs down.

8. Some suppose that just as on the outer surface of 1
the earth lie great marshes and huge navigable lakes;
and just as seas pour into vast spaces of the earth and
form long extended waters in valleys,[1] so, they suppose,
the interior of the earth abounds in fresh waters that
extend no less widely than do our ocean and its gulfs,
indeed all the more widely because the earth extends
farther down. Therefore, the rivers we are talking
about rise from that abundance of water deep down.
Why should you be surprised if the earth does not feel
that those rivers have withdrawn, since the seas do not
feel that they have been added?

9. Others favour this explanation: they say the 1
earth has within itself deep cavities and a great quantity of air which is of course cold because compressed
by the thick darkness; then the inert and uncirculat-
ing air ceases to maintain itself and changes into
water. Just as above the earth a change in the
atmosphere makes rain, so beneath the earth it makes
a river or a stream. The air above us cannot remain 2
inactive and heavy very long. At times it is rarefied
by the sun, at times expanded by the wind, and so
there are long intervals between rainfalls. But
under the earth the conditions, whatever they are,
that change air into water are always constant:

aeternum, inexercitata densitas; semper ergo prae-
3 bebit fonti aut flumini causas. Placet nobis terram
esse mutabilem. Haec quoque quicquid efflavit,
quia non libero aere concipitur, crassescit protinus
et in umorem convertitur. Habes primam aquarum
sub terra nascentium causam.

1   10. Adicias etiam licet quod fiunt omnia ex
omnibus, ex aqua aer, ex aere aqua, ignis ex aere, ex
igne aer; quare ergo non ex terra fiat aqua? Quae
si[1] in alia mutabilis, est etiam in aquam. Immo
maxime in hanc; utraque enim cognata res est,
utraque gravis, utraque densa, utraque in extremum
mundi compulsa. Ex aqua terra fit; cur non aqua
fiat e terra?

2   "At magna flumina sunt!" Cum videris quanta
sint, rursus ex quanto prodeant adspice. Miraris,
cum labantur assidue, quaedam vero concitata
rapiantur, quod praesto sit illis aqua semper nova.
Quid si mireris quod, cum venti totum aera impellant,
non deficit spiritus, sed per dies noctesque aequaliter
fluit? Nec, ut flumina, certo alveo fertur, sed per
vastum caeli spatium lato impetu vadit. Quid si
ullam undam superesse mireris quae superveniat tot
fluctibus fractis?

3   Nihil deficit quod[2] in se redit. Omnium ele-

---

[1] *quasi* ABV (instead of *quae si*).
[2] *quod* B Fortunatus, Oltramare for *quia* most MSS.

perpetual darkness, everlasting cold, inert density. Therefore they will always provide the causes of a spring or a river. We Stoics are satisfied that the 3 earth is susceptible to change. All that the earth exhales, since it is not conceived in a free atmosphere, immediately thickens and is changed into moisture. Here you have the primary cause of water coming into existence underground.

10. You may add, also, the principle that all 1 elements come from all others: air from water, water from air, fire from air, air from fire. So why not water from earth? If the earth is capable of changing into other elements, it is also capable of changing into water. In fact, most especially into water, for the two are related. Both are heavy, both are dense, both are driven to the very extremity of the universe. The earth is formed out of water. Why not water out of the earth?

" But rivers are enormous!" When you consider 2 how large they are, look again at what they come from. Are you surprised because there is always new water available for them while they flow continuously, some even carried off at high speed? You might as well be surprised that when the winds put the entire atmosphere in motion the air does not become deficient but flows on steadily day and night. And the air is not carried in a definite bed, as rivers are, but wanders through the vast expanse of heaven in a broad sweep. You might as well be surprised too that any wave remains to come up after so many waves have broken past.

Nothing becomes deficient which returns to 3 itself. There are reciprocal exchanges on the part

mentorum alterni recursus sunt; quicquid alteri
perit, in alterum transit; et natura partes suas velut
in ponderibus constitutas examinat, ne portionum
4 aequitate turbata mundus praeponderet. Omnia in
omnibus sunt. Non tantum aer in ignem transit, sed
numquam sine igne est; detrahe illi calorem, rigescet,
stabit, durabitur; transit aer in umorem, sed est
nihilominus non sine umore; et aera et aquam facit
terra, sed non magis umquam sine aqua est quam
sine aere. Et ideo facilior est invicem transitus,
quia illis in quae transeundum est iam mixta sunt.
5 Habet ergo terra umorem; hunc exprimit. Habet
aera; hunc umbra hiberni[1] frigoris densat, ut
faciat umorem. Ipsa quoque mutabilis est in umorem; natura sua utitur.

1 11. "Quid ergo," inquit,[2] "si perpetuae sunt
causae quibus flumina oriuntur ac fontes, quare
aliquando siccantur, aliquando quibus non fuerunt
locis exeunt?" Saepe motu terrarum itinera tur-
bantur et ruina interscindit cursum aquis, quae
retentae novos exitus quaerunt et aliquo impetum
faciunt aut ipsius quassatione terrae aliunde alio
transferuntur.

2 Apud nos solet evenire ut amisso canali suo flumina
primum refundantur, deinde quia perdiderunt viam
faciant. Hoc ait accidisse Theophrastus in Coryco
monte, in quo post terrarum tremorem nova vis

---

[1] *inferni* Z.
[2] *inquis* EABV.

of all the elements. What is lost to one passes over into another. And nature balances its parts just as though they were weights on scales, lest the equilibrium of its proportions be disturbed and the universe lose its equipoise. All elements exist in all things. 4 Not only does air pass over into fire but air is never without fire. Take away its heat: it will become rigid, immobile, hard. Air will change into moisture but air is yet not without moisture. Earth creates both air and water, but the earth is never without water any more than it is without air. And so the transition from one thing to another is easier because the elements are already mixed in the things into which the transition must be made. 5 Therefore, the earth contains moisture and forces it out. The earth contains air, and the darkness of winter cold condenses it so that it makes moisture. The earth by itself is capable of changing into moisture; and it makes use of its own capabilities.

11. " But," someone says, " if the causes from 1 which rivers and streams arise are constant, why do they sometimes dry up, sometimes emerge in places where they did not exist before? " Their paths are often disturbed by an earthquake; and landslides cut off channels for water which then searches for a new exit when it is blocked and in some directions does so violently; or rivers are shifted from one place to another by a vibration of the earth itself.

In our experience it usually happens that rivers 2 which have lost their channels at first simply overflow, then because they have lost a route, they make one. Theophrastus says that this happened on Mt. Corycus where the flow of new springs emerged

3 fontium emersit. Sicut alias quoque causas inter-
venire opinatur, quae aliter evocent aquas aut cursu
suo deiciant et avertant. Fuit aliquando aquarum
inops Haemus sed, cum Gallorum gens a Cassandro
obsessa in illum se contulisset et silvas cecidisset,
ingens aquarum copia apparuit, quas videlicet in
alimentum suum nemora ducebant. Quibus eversis[1]
umor qui desiit in arbusta [2] consumi superfusus est.

4 Idem ait et circa Magnesiam accidisse. Sed—pace
Theophrasti dixisse liceat—non est hoc simile veri,
quia fere aquosissima sunt quaecumque umbrosissima.
Quod non eveniret, si aquas arbusta siccarent, quibus
alimentum ex proximo est; fluminum vero vis ex
intimo manat ultraque concipitur quam radicibus
evagari licet. Deinde succisae arbores plus umoris
desiderant; non enim tantum id quo vivant, sed quo
crescant trahunt.

5 Idem ait circa Arcadiam, quae urbs in Creta insula
fuit, fontes et rivos [3] substitisse, quia desierit coli
terra diruta urbe; postea vero quam cultores
receperit,[4] aquas quoque recepisse. Causam siccita-

---

[1] *eversis* Haase, Gercke, Oltramare for *emersis* HPEZ;
excisis ABV.
[2] *angusta* ABV.
[3] *rivos* EO; *viros* HPZ; *lacus* ABV.
[4] *receperit* Erasmus, Gercke, Oltramare for *perceperit* or
exceperit MSS.

---

[1] Pliny 31.54: earthquakes make water break out; thus on
Mt. Corycus a river burst out after an earthquake. The un-
known passage of Theophrastus occurred presumably in his
De Aquis.

after an earthquake.[1] But it is also conjectured **3**
that other causes also intervene which elicit waters
in other ways or stop them in their course or turn
them aside. Mt. Haemus was once lacking in
water, but when a tribe of Gauls, who had been
hemmed in by Cassander,[2] took refuge there and cut
down the woods, a great supply of water appeared,
which evidently the groves were appropriating for
their own nourishment. When the trees were up-
rooted, the moisture overflowed, since it ceased to be
consumed in the vegetation. Theophrastus says **4**
that the same thing happened around Magnesia also.
But—to disagree respectfully with Theophrastus—
this is not likely, because the shadiest areas are
generally the most humid, which would not be the
case if trees dried up the water. Trees get their
nourishment from the immediate vicinity; but the
supply for rivers flows up from deep down and is
derived from far lower than roots can spread. Besides, when trees are lopped more moisture is required, for not only do they draw up the moisture for
living but also for growth.

Theophrastus says that around Arcadia, which **5**
was a city on the island of Crete, fountains and rivers
ceased to exist because the earth ceased to be cultivated after the city was destroyed; but after the

---

[2] Only Seneca and Pliny mentioned this campaign of Cassander (the son of Antipater) who died about 298 B.C. The
Gauls probably came into Illyria from Pannonia about 310 B.C.
Pliny (31.53) reports that springs arise after woods have been
cut down as happened when Cassander was besieging the Gauls
who had cut down the woods on Mt. Haemus to make a ram-
part.

tis hanc ponit quod obduruerit constricta tellus nec
potuerit imbres inagitata transmittere. Quomodo
ergo plurimos videmus in locis desertissimis fontes?

6 Plura denique invenimus quae propter aquas coli
coeperunt quam quae aquas habere coeperint, quia
colebantur. Non esse enim pluvialem hanc quae
vastissima flumina a fonte statim magnis apta[1]
navigiis defert, ex hoc intellegas licet quod per
hiemem aestatemque par est a capite deiectus.
Pluvia potest facere torrentem, non potest amnem
aequali inter ripas suas tenore labentem; quem non
faciunt imbres, sed incitant.

1 12. Paulo repetamus hoc altius, si videtur, et
scies te non habere quod quaeras, cum ad veram
amnium[2] originem accesseris. Flumen nempe facit
copia cursusque aquae perennis. Ergo quaeris a me
quomodo aqua fiat; interrogabo invicem quomodo aer

2 fiat aut terra. Sed si in rerum natura elementa sunt
quattuor, non potes interrogare[3] unde aqua sit;
quarta enim pars naturae est. Quid ergo miraris, si
rerum naturae tam magna portio potest aliquid ex se

3 semper effundere? Quomodo aer, et ipse[4] quarta
pars mundi, ventos et auras movet, sic aqua rivos et
flumina; si ventus est fluens aer, et flumen est fluens
aqua. Satis et multum illi virium dedi, cum dixi,

---

[1] *apta* B; *acta* HEZAV; *actis* P.
[2] Pincianus for *omnium* MSS.
[3] *potest interrogari* ABV; *potest interrogare* λ.
[4] *ipse* ZBV; *ipsa* HPEA.

earth got back its cultivators, it also recovered its waters. He proposed this reason for the dryness: namely, that the constricted earth became hard and while it was not being stirred it was unable to transmit rainwaters. So why do we see very many springs in the most uncultivated areas? Moreover, we find 6 more areas that began to be tilled on account of their water than began to have water because they were tilled. For it is not mere rainwater which carries along great rivers suitable for large ships right from their source, as you may realize from the fact that the flow from the fountainhead is equal in winter and summer. Rainfall can make a torrent but is not able to form a river gliding along with even flow between its banks. Rains do not make a river; they only make it flow faster.

12. Let us go back over this subject a little more 1 deeply, if you are willing, and when you have come to grasp the true origin of rivers you will understand that you do not have any further questions. Of course, an abundant and continuous flow of water makes a river. Therefore, you ask me how the water is made. In reply, I will ask you how air or earth is made. But if there are four elements in 2 nature, you cannot ask where water comes from; for it exists as nature's fourth part. Why, then, are you surprised that so large a portion of nature has the power to pour forth a perpetual supply from itself? Just as air, also a fourth part of the universe, 3 puts into motion winds and breezes, so water moves streams and rivers. If the wind is flowing air, a river is likewise flowing water. I gave it enough power, and more than enough, when I said, " It is

"Elementum est." Intellegis quod ab illo proficiscitur non posse deficere.

1   13. Adiciam,[1] ut Thales ait, "Valentissimum elementum est." Hoc fuisse primum putat, ex hoc surrexisse omnia. Sed nos quoque aut in eadem sententia, aut in vicina[2] eius sumus. Dicimus enim ignem esse qui occupet mundum et in se cuncta convertat; hunc evanidum languentemque considere et nihil relinqui aliud in rerum natura igne restincto quam umorem; in hoc futuri mundi spem

2   latere. Ita ignis exitus mundi est, umor primordium. Miraris ex hoc posse amnes semper exire qui pro omnibus fuit et ex quo sunt omnia? Hic umor in diductione rerum ad quartas redactus est, sic positus ut sufficere fluminibus edendis, ut rivis, ut fontibus posset.

1   14. Quae sequitur Thaletis inepta sententia est. Ait enim terrarum orbem aqua sustineri et vehi more navigii mobilitateque eius fluctuare tunc cum dicitur tremere; non est ergo mirum si abundat umor ad flumina profundenda, cum in umore sit totus.

2   Hanc veterem et rudem sententiam explode. Nec est quod credas in hunc orbem aquam subire per rimas et facere sentinam.

Aegyptii quattuor elementa fecerunt, deinde ex singulis bina.[3] Aera[4] marem iudicant qua[5] ventus

---

[1] *Aqua ait Thales* ABV (instead of *Adiciam, ut Thales ait*).
[2] Oltramare for *ultima* MSS.; *vicinia* Madvig, Gercke. Alexander proposes *aut eandem sententiam aut inulti maius sumimus.*
[3] *bina maria et feminea* E.

an element." You realize that whatever is derived from an element cannot become deficient.

13. I will add, as Thales says, "Water is the 1 most powerful element." He thinks it was the first element, and all things arose from it. We Stoics are also of this opinion, or close to it. For we say that it is fire which takes possession of the universe and changes all things into itself; it becomes feeble, fades, and sinks, and when fire is extinguished nothing is left in nature except moisture, in which lies the hope of the universe to come. Thus, fire is 2 the end of the world, moisture the beginning. Are you amazed that rivers can come continuously from an element which existed before all things and from which all things have existence? In the separation of the elements this moisture was reduced to a fourth part and so placed that it could suffice to produce rivers, just as it can streams, and springs.

14. The following theory of Thales is silly. For 1 he says that this round of lands is sustained by water and is carried along like a boat, and on the occasions when the earth is said to quake it is fluctuating because of the movement of the water. It is no wonder, therefore, that there is abundant water for making the rivers flow since the entire round is in water. Reject this antiquated, unscholarly theory. 2 There is also no reason that you should believe water enters this globe through cracks, and forms bilge.

The Egyptians established four elements, then formed a pair from each one. They consider the

---

[4] *aera* Z; *aerem* most MSS.

[5] *qua ventus . . . qua nebulosus* Z; *quia ventus . . . quia nebulosus* most MSS.

est, feminam qua nebulosus et iners; aquam virilem
vocant mare, muliebrem omnem aliam; ignem vocant
masculum qua [1] ardet flamma, et feminam qua lucet
innoxius tactu; terram fortiorem marem vocant,
saxa cautesque, feminae nomen assignant huic
tractabili et cultae.

3 Mare unum est, ab initio scilicet ita constitutum;
habet suas venas, quibus impletur atque aestuat.
Quomodo maris, sic et huius aquae mitioris vasta in
occulto vis [2] est, quam nullius fluminis cursus ex-
hauriet. Abdita est virium ratio; tantum ex illa
quantum semper fluere [3] possit [4] emittitur.

1 15. Quaedam ex istis sunt quibus assentire
possumus. Sed hoc amplius censeo. Placet natura
regi terram, et quidem ad nostrorum corporum
exemplar, in quibus et venae sunt et arteriae, illae
sanguinis, hae spiritus receptacula. In terra quoque
sunt alia itinera per quae aqua, alia per quae spiritus
currit; adeoque ad similitudinem illa [5] humanorum
corporum natura formavit [6] ut maiores quoque nostri
2 aquarum appellaverint venas. Sed, quemadmodum
in nobis non tantum sanguis est sed multa genera
umoris, alia necessarii, alia corrupti ac paulo pinguio-

---

[1] *qua ardet* HPZλ; *quia ardet* OT; *que ardet* E; *quo ardet*
ABV.
[2] *vis* Gercke, Oltramare for *via* MSS.
[3] *semper fluere* HPZ Oltramare; *superfluum* ABV Gercke.
[4] *possit* Oltramare for *sit* most MSS.; *opus sit* ET; *si*
remittatur G.
[5] *illa* Haase, Gercke, Oltramare, Alexander for *illam* HPEZ;
illam ad similitudinem ABV.

atmosphere male where it is windy, female where it is cloudy and inactive. They call the sea masculine water, all other water feminine. They call fire masculine where a flame burns, and feminine where it glows but is harmless to touch. They call male the firmer earth, such as rocks and crags. They assign the term female to our soil that is tractable for cultivation.

The sea is a unity, undoubtedly established just 3 as it is from the beginning. It has its own sources which keep it filled and cause rough waters. As in the case of the sea, so also in the case of gentler water, there is a vast hidden supply which no river's flow will drain dry. The reason for its strength is obscure. There is emitted from it only as much as is always able to flow.

15. Some of these are theories with which we can 1 agree. But I have this further theory: the idea appeals to me that the earth is governed by nature and is much like the system of our own bodies in which there are both veins (receptacles for blood) and arteries (receptacles for air). In the earth also there are some routes through which water runs, some through which air passes. And nature fashioned these routes so like human bodies that our ancestors even called them " veins " of water.[1] But, 2 just as in us there is not only blood but many kinds of moisture, some essential for life, others tainted and

[1] Pliny 2.166: water penetrates the entire earth by means of a network of veins running within and without above and below.

---

[6] *formavit deus* ABV (instead of *natura formavit*).

ris [1] (in capite cerebrum, in ossibus medullae, muci
salivaeque et lacrimae et quiddam additum articulis
per quod citius flectantur ex lubrico); sic in terra
quoque sunt umoris genera complura,[2] quaedam quae
3 mature durantur.[3] Hinc est omnis metallorum
humus,[4] ex quibus petit aurum argentumque avaritia,
et quae in lapidem ex liquore vertuntur; in quaedam
vero terra umorque putrescunt,[5] sicut bitumen et
cetera huic similia. Haec est causa aquarum secun-
dum legem naturae voluntatemque nascentium.
4 Ceterum, ut in nostris corporibus, ita in illa saepe
umores vitia concipiunt: aut ictus aut quassatio
aliqua aut loci senium aut frigus aut aestus corrupere
naturam, et sulphuratio contraxit umorem, qui modo
5 diuturnus est, modo brevis. Ergo, ut in corporibus
nostris sanguis, cum percussa vena est, tam diu manat
donec omnis effluxit aut donec venae scissura subsedit atque interclusit,[6] vel aliqua alia causa retro
dedit sanguinem, ita in terra [7] solutis ac patefactis
6 venis rivus aut flumen effunditur. Interest quanta
aperta sit vena. Quae modo consumpta aqua deficit;
modo excaecatur aliquo impedimento; modo coit
velut in cicatricem comprimitque quam perfecerat
viam; modo illa vis terrae, quam esse mutabilem

---

[1] *pigrioris* ABV.
[2] *quam plura* HE.
[3] *durantur* Oltramare, Alexander for *durentur* most MSS.
[4] *humus* MSS.; *honos* Oltramare, Alexander; *ortus* Gercke;
genus Fortunatus.
[5] *liquescunt* ABV.
[6] *interclusit* most MSS.; *iter clausit* B; *iter clusit* Oltramare.

rather thick (brain in the head, marrow in the bones, mucus, saliva, tears, and a kind of lubricant added to the joints to make them bend more readily); so, in the earth also there are several kinds of moisture, some which harden soon. Hence comes all metal- 3 producing soil where our avarice seeks gold and silver.[1] And there are the kinds of moisture which change from liquid to stone. In fact, earth and moisture decay into substances such as bitumen and other substances like it. This is the origin of waters, which are produced according to the law and will of nature. But just as in our bodies, the liquids in 4 the earth often develop flaws. A blow or some shock, or the exhaustion of the soil, or cold or heat damage its natural quality. The presence of sulphur, also, draws moisture together, a condition which some- times lasts for a long while, sometimes only briefly. Therefore, just as in our bodies when a vein is cut the 5 blood continues to ooze until it all flows out or until the cut in the vein has closed and shut off the bleed- ing, or some other cause keeps the blood back; so in the earth when veins are loosened or broken open a stream or a river gushes out. It makes a difference 6 how big the open vein is. Sometimes the vein gives out when the water is used up; or it is stopped by some impediment;[2] or it forms a kind of scar and blocks the path it had made; or that characteristic

[1] Aristotle 3.6.378a 27–34: metals are the product of vapor- ous exhalations; they are in one sense water and in another sense not.

[2] Ovid (*Ex Ponto* 4.2.17; *Met.* 15.270–271) refers to the clogged veins of springs.

---

[7] *inter* HPZ; *interim* E.

diximus, desinit posse alimenta in umorem convertere.
7 Aliquando autem exhausta replentur, modo per se
viribus recollectis, modo aliunde translatis. Saepe
enim inania apposita plenis umorem in se avocave-
runt.

Saepe terra, si facilis est in tabem, ipsa solvitur
et umescit; saepe [1] idem evenit sub terra quod in
nubibus, ut spissetur aer [2] graviorque quam ut
manere in natura sua possit gignat [3] umorem;
saepe colligitur roris modo tenuis et dispersus liquor,
qui ex multis in unum locis confluit. Sudorem
aquileges vocant, quia guttae quaedam vel pressura
8 loci eliduntur [4] vel aestu evocantur. Haec tenuis
unda vix fonti [5] sufficit; et ex magnis caveis [6]
magnisque conceptibus excidunt amnes, nonnumquam leviter emissi, si aqua pondere suo se tantum
detulit, nonnumquam vehementer et cum sono, si
illam spiritus intermixtus eiecit.

1   16. Sed quare quidam fontes senis horis pleni
senisque sicci sunt? Supervacuum est nominare
singula flumina quae certis mensibus magna certis
angusta sunt et occasionem singulis [7] quaerere, cum
possim [8] eandem causam omnibus reddere.

2   Quemadmodum quartana ad horam venit, quemadmodum ad tempus podagra respondet, quemadmodum

---

[1] *saepe* supplied by Haase.
[2] *aer* supplied by Haase.
[3] *gignat* T; *gignit* E; *signat* HPZABV.
[4] *eduntur* ABV.
[5] *forti* ABV.
[6] Diels, Oltramare for *causis* MSS.
[7] *fabulis* Z.

of the earth, which I referred to as changeable, ceases to be able to convert ingredients into water. Moreover, the exhausted sources are at times re- 7 plenished by recovering strength on their own account, or by transferring it from elsewhere. For when empty channels are located opposite full channels they frequently attract the moisture to themselves.

The earth itself, if it is easily decomposed, often dissolves and becomes moisture. The same thing frequently happens under the earth that happens in the clouds: the air becomes too thick and heavy to be able to remain in its natural state and brings forth water. Usually, in the manner of dew, a thin-scattered moisture collects and then flows from many sources into one place. Water-finding experts call it sweat because drops, sort of, are either squeezed out by the pressure of the ground or brought out by the heat. This thin trickle is scarcely enough for a 8 spring. Rivers come from large cavities and large reservoirs. Sometimes they flow out gently, if the water carries itself down only by its own weight; at other times, violently and noisily, if air is mixed in and ejects the water.

16. But why are some springs full for six hours and 1 dry for six? It is unnecessary to name individual rivers which are broad in certain months or narrow in certain months and to seek a provenance for each one when I can give the same explanation for them all.

Just as quartain fever comes at the same hour, as 2 gout corresponds to a regular time, as menstruation,

---

8 *possis* λ.

purgatio, si nihil obstitit, statum diem servat,
quemadmodum praesto est ad mensem suum partus,
sic aquae intervalla habent quibus se retrahant et
quibus redeant.[1] Quaedam autem intervalla minora
sunt et ideo notabilia, quaedam maiora nec minus
3 certa. Ecquid hic mirum est, cum videas ordinem
rerum et naturam per constituta procedere? Hiems
numquam aberravit, aestas suo tempore incaluit,
autumni verisque, unde solet, facta mutatio est; tam
solstitium quam aequinoctium suos dies rettulit.

4 Sunt et sub terra minus nota nobis iura naturae,
sed non minus certa. Crede infra quicquid vides
supra. Sunt et illic specus vasti ingentesque recessus
ac spatia suspensis hinc et inde montibus laxa; sunt
abrupti in infinitum hiatus, qui saepe illapsas urbes
receperunt et ingentem ruinam in alto condiderunt.
5 Haec spiritu plena sunt—nihil enim usquam inane
est—et stagna obsessa tenebris et lacus ampli.[2]
Animalia quoque illis innascuntur, sed tarda et in-
formia ut in aere caeco pinguique concepta et aquis
torpentibus situ; pleraque ex his caeca ut talpae et
subterranei mures, quibus deest lumen, quia supervacuum est. Inde, ut Theophrastus affirmat, pisces
quibusdam locis eruuntur.

[1] *redeant* E Gercke; *reddantur* Castiglioni, Oltramare;
reddant HPZABV.
[2] *lacus ampli* Oltramare, Alexander for *locis amplis* MSS.

if nothing interferes, maintains a fixed period, as birth is ready in its proper month; so water has its cycles in which it withdraws and returns. However, some cycles are short and thus noticeable, others are longer but no less fixed. And what is remarkable 3 about this, when you see that in nature the sequence of events proceeds in accordance with established laws? Winter never misses, summer becomes hot at the proper time, the changes of autumn and spring come from habitual causes, the solstice and the equinox alike return on their proper dates.

There are also laws of nature under the earth, less 4 known to us but no less fixed. Believe me that there exists below whatever you see above.[1] There, too, vast caverns exist, and great recesses, and vacant spaces with mountains overhanging here and there. There are gulfs gaping into infinity which have frequently swallowed up cities that fell into them and buried the mighty ruins in the depths. These places 5 are filled with air—for no void exists anywhere— and there are marshes enveloped in darkness, and great lakes. Also, living creatures are born there, but they are slow and deformed since they were conceived in dark, heavy air, and in water made torpid by its inactivity. Many of these creatures are blind, like moles and subterranean rats who have no vision since none is needed. According to Theophrastus, fish are dug up from such depths in certain places.[2]

[1] Lucretius 6.536–542: the earth below as above is everywhere full of windy caverns, bearing many lakes and many pools with rocks and steep cliffs.

[2] Pliny (9.176) reports that Theophrastus says there are kinds of fish that make themselves caves in the ground and are dug up when their movement shows that they are alive.

1   17. Multa hoc loco tibi in mentem veniunt quae
urbane, ut in re incredibili [1] dicas: " Fabulae! [2] non
cum retibus aliquem nec cum hamis, sed cum dolabra
ire piscatum! Expecto ut aliquis in mari venetur." [3]
Quid est autem quare non pisces in terram transeant,
si nos maria transimus, permutabimus sedes?

2   Hoc miraris accidere; quanto incredibiliora sunt
opera luxuriae, quotiens naturam aut mentitur aut
vincit? In cubili natant pisces et sub ipsa mensa
capitur qui statim transferatur in mensam. Parum
videtur recens mullus, nisi qui in convivae manu
moritur. Vitreis ollis inclusi afferuntur et observatur
morientium color, quem in multas mutationes mors
luctante spiritu vertit. Alios necant in garo et con-
3 diunt vivos. Hi sunt qui fabulas putant piscem vivere
posse sub terra, et effodi, [4] non capi. Quam incredibile
illis videretur, si audirent natare in garo piscem nec
cenae causa occidi sed [5] super cenam, cum multum
in deliciis fuit et oculos ante quam gulam pavit!

1   18. Permitte mihi quaestione seposita castigare
luxuriam. " Nihil est," inquis, " mullo expirante

---

[1] *in re credibili* GABV; *in rem credibilem* Z.
[2] "*fabulae!*" Warmington (cf. Terence *Andr.* 1.3.19;
Heauton. 2.3.95); *fabulae* Z; *fabulam* most MSS.; "*fabulam*"
Alexander.
[3] Pincianus for *versetur* MSS.
[4] *effundi* ABV.
[5] *occidi sed* Pincianus for *occidisse* HPEZ; *occisum esse* AV;
occisum B.

17. At this point many ideas are occurring to you 1
which you could express, just as, in commenting on
something incredible, you might say: " Mere story!
Fancy going fishing not with nets or hooks but with
a hoe! I expect next someone may go hunting on
the sea." But what reason is there that fish should
not go onto land if we cross seas and change our place
of residence?

You are surprised at this happening? The 2
achievements of luxury are much more incredible,
as often as they imitate or surpass nature! Fish
swim in a bed and one is caught under the dinner-
table itself for instant transfer to the table. A
surmullet does not seem fresh unless it dies in the
hand of a dinner guest. Surmullets enclosed in
glass jars are brought along and their colour observed
as they die. As they struggle for air death changes
their colour into many hues. Others are killed by
being pickled alive in garum.[1] These are people who 3
think it is fiction that a fish can live under the earth
and be dug up, not caught. How incredible it would
seem to them if they heard that a fish swims in garum
and was killed not for the dinner but during dinner,
when it had furnished great entertainment and
feasted the eyes before the palate!

18. Let me set aside the subject and castigate 1
luxury.[2] " There is nothing," you say, " more

---

[1] On garum see my article " Roman Fish Sauces," *CJ* 58
(February 1963) 204–210, and on the surmullet see A. C.
Andrews, " The Roman Craze for Surmullets," *CW* 42 (1948–
1949), 186–188.

[2] The text of Sec. 1 of Chap. 18 is uncertain in several
places.

formosius;[1] ipsa colluctatione animae deficientis[2]
rubor primum, deinde pallor suffunditur, squamae-
que[3] variantur et in incertas[4] facies inter vitam ac
mortem coloris est vagatio." Longa somniculosae
inertisque luxuriae neglegentia[5] quam sero experrecta[6] circumscribi se et fraudari tanto bono sensit!
Hoc adhuc tam pulchro spectaculo piscatores frue-
2 bantur. "Quo coctum piscem? Quo exanimem?
In ipso ferculo expiret." Mirabamur tantum illis
inesse fastidium ut nollent attingere nisi eodem die
captum, qui, ut aiunt, saperet ipsum mare; ideo cursu
advehebatur, ideo gerulis cum anhelitu et clamore
3 properantibus dabatur via. Quo pervenere deliciae?
Iam pro putrido his est piscis occisus. "Hodie
eductus est?[7] Nescio de re magna tibi credere;
ipsi[8] oportet me credere. Huc afferatur; coram me
animam agat." Ad hunc fastum[9] pervenit venter
delicatorum ut gustare non possint, nisi quem in ipso
convivio natantem palpitantemque viderunt. Tantum[10] ad sollertiam luxuriae superbientis[11] accedit,

---

[1] *expirante illis formosius* HPZG Oltramare; *illic* E Haase;
illo T Gercke; *ullis* Alexander; the word does not appear in
the MSS. of the *Quantum* family.

[2] Gercke, Oltramare for *afficienti* HPZG; *sese afficienti* ET;
efflantis ABV.

[3] Leo, Gercke, Oltramare for *quam aeque* MSS.

[4] *in incertas* Gercke, Oltramare for *in ceteras* HZ; *inter
ceteras* G.

[5] *neglegentia* Z Oltramare, Alexander; most MSS. omit the
word entirely; *expectatio* G.

[6] *experrecta* Warmington for *expressa sero* Oltramare,
Alexander; *expressero* HPZGABV.

beautiful than a dying surmullet. In the very struggle of its failing breath of life, first a red, then a pale tint suffuses it, and its scales change hue, and between life and death there is a gradation of colour into subtle shades." How lately has the long negligence of our somnolent and jaded luxury woken up and realized it has been circumscribed, and cheated of such a great pleasure! Up to this time only fishermen enjoyed such a beautiful spectacle. " Why a fish that is cooked or dead? Let it die on the dinner plate." We used to be amazed at the great fastidiousness in those who were unwilling to touch a fish unless it had been captured that very day and tasted, as they say, of the sea itself. So, the fish was carried at a run; a way had to be made for the carriers as they hurried along breathless and shouting. What has pleasure come to? A fish that has been killed by these people is already considered putrid. " It was caught to-day? I do not know how to trust you in such an important matter. I should trust only the fish. Bring it here. Let it die in front of me." The belly of gourmets has reached such daintiness that they cannot taste a fish unless they see it swimming and palpitating in the very dining-room. What a lot is being added to the ingenuity of excessive extravagance!

---

⁷ is pro putido iam piscis offertur qui non hodie eductus, hodie occisus est AV (for Iam pro putrido . . . eductus est).

⁸ ipsi Oltramare for ipse MSS.; tibi ipse credere, me credas Z; ipse oportet ne credas Alexander.

⁹ fastum ET; festum most MSS.

¹⁰ tantum Haase, Oltramare for quantum HPEZ; quanti ABV.

¹¹ Oltramare for pereunt his most MSS.; pereuntis Gronovius, Alexander.

tantoque subtilius cotidie et elegantius aliquid
4 excogitat furor usitata contemnens! Illa audiebamus: "Nihil est melius saxatili mullo." At nunc
audimus: "Nihil est moriente formosius. Da mihi
in manus vitreum, in quo exultet trepidet." Ubi
multum diuque [1] laudatus [2] est, ex illo perlucido
5 vivario extrahitur. Tunc, ut quisque peritior est,
monstrat: "Vide quomodo exarserit rubor omni
acrior minio! Vide quas per latera venas agat!
Ecce sanguineum [3] putes ventrem! Quam lucidum
quiddam caeruleumque sub ipso tempore effulsit! Iam
porrigitur et pallet et in unum colorem componitur."
6 Ex his nemo morienti amico assidet; nemo videre
mortem patris sui sustinet, quam optavit. Quotusquisque funus domesticum ad rogum prosequitur?
Fratrum propinquorumque extrema hora deseritur;
ad mortem mulli [4] concurritur. "Nihil est enim illa
formosius."
7 Non tempero mihi quin utar interdum temerarie
verbis et proprietatis modum excedam. Non sunt ad
popinam dentibus et ventre et ore contenti; oculis
quoque gulosi sunt.
1 19. Sed ut ad propositum revertar, accipe argumentum, magnam vim aquarum in subterraneis occuli [5]
fertilem foedorum situ piscium; si quando erupit,

---

[1] *ubique* HPEGZ.
[2] *luctatus* g Haase, Gercke.
[3] *sanguinem* Warmington.
[4] *nulli* ZAB λ.
[5] *occultis* HPEZ.

---

[1] *ipso tempore* could also mean "just before death."

And how much more delicately and elegantly does our madness invent something while despising anything ordinary! We used to hear this: "Nothing is better than a surmullet caught under a rock." But now we hear: "Nothing is more beautiful than a dying surmullet. Let me hold in my hands the glass jar where the fish may leap and quiver." When the fish has been much admired for a long time it is taken from its transparent fishpond. Then any experienced guest points: "See how the red becomes inflamed, more brilliant than any vermilion! Look at the veins which pulse along its sides! Look! You would think its belly were actual blood! What a bright kind of blue gleamed right under its brow![1] Now it is stretching out and going pale and is settling into a uniform hue."

No one of them would sit by a dying friend; no one of them would endure to watch the death of his own father, even though he hoped for it. How few would follow the funeral of a member of the family to the graveyard? They desert the last hours of a brother or close relative; yet they all run to the death of a surmullet. "For nothing is more beautiful than this."

At times I do not restrain myself from using words rashly and I exceed the bounds of propriety. They are not content with their teeth and belly and mouth at the eating place; they are also gluttonous with their eyes.

19. But to return to the subject. Here is proof that in underground regions a great quantity of water is concealed which is teeming with fish that are foul because of their inactivity. If any time the

effert secum immensam animalium turbam, horridam
2 aspici et turpem ac noxiam gustu. Certe cum in
Caria circa Idymum urbem talis exiluisset unda,
perierunt quicumque illos ederant pisces quos ignoto
ante eam diem caelo novus amnis ostendit. Nec id
mirum. Erant enim pinguia et differta, ut ex longo
otio, corpora, ceterum inexercitata et tenebris sagin-
ata et lucis expertia, ex qua salubritas ducitur.
3 Nasci autem posse pisces in illo terrarum profundo sit
indicium quod anguillae latebrosis locis nascuntur,
gravis et ipsae cibus ob ignaviam, utique si altitudo
illas luti penitus abscondit.

4 Habet ergo non tantum venas aquarum terra, ex
quibus conrivatis flumina effici possint, sed amnes
magnitudinis vastae, quorum aliis semper in occulto
cursus est, donec aliquo sinu terrae devorentur; alii
sub aliquo lacu emergunt. Nam quis ignorat esse
quaedam stagna sine fundo? Quorsus hoc pertinet?
Ut appareat hanc aquam magnis amnibus aeternam
esse materiam, cuius non tanguntur extrema, sicut
fluminum fontes.

1 20. At quare aquis sapor varius? Propter quattuor causas. Ex solo prima est per quod fertur;
secunda ex eodem, si mutatione[1] eius nascitur;

---

[1] *si mutatione* Gronovius, Oltramare for *simulatione* PEZ;
similitudine ABV.

water bursts forth it carries with it an immense mass of creatures that are ugly to look at, disgusting, and poisonous to taste. Certainly, in Caria, near the 2 city of Idymus, when such waters leaped forth, all died who had eaten the fish which were discharged by a river which was new and unaccustomed to the daylight before that time. And no wonder. Their bodies were full of oil and swollen as from long inactivity; moreover, they had been fattened in the dark without exercise and deprived of the light from which health is acquired.[1] Yet let a proof that fish can be born in those depths of the earth be the fact that eels are bred in secret hiding-places; and they themselves are a heavy food because of lack of exercise, especially if a deep layer of mud has hidden them entirely.

Therefore, the earth has not only veins of water 4 from the confluence of which rivers can be formed, but also streams of vast size. Some of them have channels always hidden, until they are swallowed up in some recess of the earth. Others emerge under some lake. Everyone knows that there are certain swamps without a bottom. What does all this prove? It proves that such water is an unending supply for great rivers. The limits of this supply are untouched, just as the sources of rivers are.

20. But why the variety of taste in water? There 1 are four causes. The first is from the soil through which the water is carried; the second also depends on the soil if the water is produced by a transmutation

---

[1] Perhaps Seneca is drawing his information about fish of underground regions from Theophrastus, whom Pliny cites (9.175–178) as a source.

tertia ex spiritu qui in aquam transfiguratus est;
quarta ex vitio quod saepe concipiunt corruptae per
2 iniuriam. Hae causae saporem dant aquis varium,
hae medicatam potentiam, hae gravem spiritum
odoremque[1] pestiferum gravitatemque, hae[2] aut
calorem aut nimium rigorem. Interest utrum loca
sulphure an nitro an bitumine plena transierint; hac
ratione corruptae cum vitae periculo bibuntur.
3 Illinc illud de quo Ovidius ait:

Flumen habent Cicones quod potum saxea reddit
Viscera, quod tactis inducit marmora rebus.

Medicatum est et eius naturae habet limum ut
corpora adglutinet et obduret. Quemadmodum
Puteolanus pulvis, si aquam attigit, saxum est, sic e
contrario haec aqua, si solidum tetigit, haeret et
4 affigitur. Inde est quod res abiectae in eiusmodi[3]
lacum lapideae subinde extrahuntur. Quod in
Italia quibusdam in locis evenit: sive virgam, sive
frondem demerseris, lapidem post paucos dies
extrahis; circumfunditur enim corpori limus adlini-
turque paulatim. Hoc minus tibi videbitur mirum,

---

[1] *odorem* EZT; *colorem* most MSS.
[2] *hae* supplied by Haase.
[3] *eiusmodi* Gertz; *eiusdem* Alexander; *eundem* MSS.;
Euryminaeum Garrod (cf. Pliny 31.29: *In Eurymenis deiectae
coronae in fontem lapideae fiunt*).

of earth into water; the third comes from the air which
was transformed into water; the fourth from a pollu-
tion which water often receives when it has been
corrupted by harmful substances. These causes 2
give water its different taste, its medicinal power, its
disagreeable exhalation and pestilential odour, as
well as its unwholesomeness, heat or excessive cold.
It makes a difference whether it passes through
places full of sulphur, nitre,[1] or bitumen. When water
is polluted this way it is a risk of life to drink it.
Accordingly, this is what Ovid means when he says: 3

> The Cicones have a river
> Which when drunk
> Turns the viscera to stone
> And puts a layer of marble
> On everything it touches.[2]

The water is adulterated and has mud of such a
nature that it cements and hardens objects. Just as
the dust of Puteoli becomes rock if it touches water
so, on the contrary, if this water touches a solid
object it clings and attaches itself to it. This is why 4
objects thrown into a lake of that type[3] are sub-
sequently extracted as rock-like substances. This
happens in certain localities in Italy. If you
immerse a twig or a branch, after a few days you
take out a stone. For the mud flows around the

---

[1] Soda.
[2] Ovid *Met.* 15.313–314. The river is the Hebrus (Maritza).
[3] Or accept Alexander's reading *eiusdem* (sc. *aquae*) and
translate, as he does, "into a tank of the same water."

si notaveris Albulas [1] et fere sulphuratam aquam circa canales suos ripasque [2] durari.

5   Aliquam harum habent causam illi lacus " quos quisquis faucibus hausit," ut idem poeta ait:

Aut furit aut patitur mirum gravitate soporem.

Similem habent vim mero, sed vehementiorem. Nam, quemadmodum ebrietas, donec exiccetur, dementia est et nimia gravitate defertur in somnum, sic huius aquae sulphurea vis habens quoddam acrius ex aere noxio virus mentem aut furore movet aut 6 sopore opprimit.   Hoc habet mali:

Lyncestius [3] amnis
Quem quicumque parum moderato gutture traxit,
Haud aliter titubat quam si mera vina bibisset.

---

[1] *Albulam* ABV.
[2] *ripasque* ET; *rivosque* ABV; *cibosque* HPZ.
[3] The MSS. of Ovid have *lincestius,* that is, Lyncestius. Whether Seneca also wrote Lyncestius is doubtful.   Of the MSS of Seneca H²PZA have *linceius,* H¹ B *liceius,* EV *linceus.*

---

[1] The effects described by Seneca are those produced by water which transfers minerals on to objects, or infuses minerals into objects (which are thus hardened), often substituting the intruded minerals for the object's material which is dissolved away; or deposits minerals free-standing such as stalactites and stalagmites.

object and gradually coats it all over.[1] This will seem less surprising to you if you have noticed that the waters of Albula [2] and almost all water containing sulphur are encrusted around their channels and banks.

One or another of these causes is present in those 5 lakes so that, as the same poet says:

> Whoever lets them go down his throat
> Either goes mad
> Or suffers
> A strange deep coma.[3]

They have a power similar to neat wine, but stronger. For, just as drunkenness is madness, until it dries out and results in a sleep that is excessively heavy, so the sulphuric force of this water containing a kind of poison, made more severe by the noxious air, either unhinges the mind with frenzy or oppresses it with sleep. The following has this harmful effect: 6

> ... the river in Lyncestis.
> Anyone who consumes it
> With immoderate thirst
> Staggers,
> As if he had drunk
> Strong wine.[4]

[1] The *Albula*, or *Albulae* (sc. *aquae*) was water from several sulphur springs near Tibur, now Tivoli, a few miles east of Rome. The water was considered a cure for almost every ailment (Pliny 31.10; Suet. *Aug.* 82; *Nero* 31), as it is still to-day in Italy at the Bagni di Tivoli with the Stabilimento delle Acque where two lakes, fed by hot springs, are redolent with sulphuretted hydrogen.

[3] Ovid, *Met.* 15.320–321.

[4] Ovid, *Met.* 15.329–331. The name Lyncestius is connected with the Lyncestae of Macedonia.

1 21. In quosdam specus qui despexere moriuntur; tam velox malum est ut transvolantes aves deiciat. Talis est aer, talis locus ex quo letalis aqua destillat. Quod si remissior fuit aeris et loci pestis, ipsa quoque temperatior noxa nihil amplius quam temptat nervos
2 velut ebrietate torpentes. Nec miror si locus atque aer aquas inficit similesque regionibus reddit per quas et ex quibus veniunt: pabuli sapor apparet in lacte et vini vis existit in aceto. Nulla res est quae non eius quo nascitur notas reddat.

1 22. Aliud est aquarum genus quod nobis placet coepisse cum mundo. Sive ille aeternus est, haec quoque aqua [1] fuit semper; sive initium [2] aliquod est illi, haec quoque cum toto disposita est. Quae sit haec quaeris? Oceanus et quodcumque ex illo mare terras interluit.[3] Iudicant quidam flumina quoque quorum inenarrabilis natura est cum ipso mundo traxisse principia, ut Histrum, ut Nilum, vastos amnes

---

[1] *aqua* supplied by Oltramare.
[2] *fuit sine initio. Initium* ABV (instead of *fuit semper; sive initium*).
[3] *interfluit* A[1]B.

---

[1] Lucretius (6.738–748) says that such places had the generic name of Avernus because they were dangerous to all birds as at Cumae. Pliny 31.21, "Caelius says in our Avernus leaves sink, and Varro that the birds fly to it to die."

21. People die who have looked down into certain 1
caves.[1] The deadliness is so swift that it brings down
birds flying by. Such is the atmosphere, such is the
place from which lethal water discharges. But if the
deadliness of the atmosphere or of the place is less
severe, the poison itself is less harmful and affects
little more than the sinews as though they were
asleep because of drunkenness. I am not surprised 2
that locality and atmosphere infect water and make
it similar to the regions through which and from
which it comes. The taste of fodder appears in milk,
and the essence of wine stands out in vinegar.
There is nothing which does not render traces of that
from which it is derived.

22. There is another type of water which we Stoics 1
like to think began with the universe. If the universe
is eternal, this water, too, always existed. Or, if
there was some beginning for the universe, this
water also was set down along with everything else.
You ask what water this is? The ocean and any sea
from it that flows between the lands.[2] Some
judge that also the rivers whose nature is inexplicable
take their beginning along with the universe itself;
such as the Danube and the Nile, rivers so vast and

[2] Crates (*fl. c.* 150 B.C.) and Hipparchus (also *fl. c.* 150 B.C.)
and others imagined that the Atlantic Ocean is a kind of gulf
between continents and that two such continents, divided by
an equatorial sea, exist on either side of the earth's sphere
(Strabo I.1.3–9, C 26 disagrees). However, Seneca may more
likely have in mind the Mediterranean Sea, the Red Sea, and
the Persian Gulf which are inlets into the continents Europe,
Asia and Africa of the one inhabited world.

magisque insignes quam ut dici possit eandem illis originem quam ceteris esse.

1   23. Haec est ergo aquarum, ut videtur, divisio: quaedam ex his posterioribus caelestes, quas nubila excutiunt; ex terrenis aliae sunt, ut ita dicam, supernatantes, quae in summa humo repunt; alia abditae, quarum reddita est ratio.

1   24. Quare quaedam aquae caleant, quaedam etiam ferveant in tantum ut non possint esse usui, nisi aut in aperto evanuerunt aut mixtura frigidae intepuerunt, plures causae redduntur. Empedocles existimat ignibus quos multis locis terra opertos tegit aquam calescere, si subiecti sunt ei[1] solo per quod aquis transcursus est.

2   Facere solemus dracones et miliaria et complures formas in quibus aere tenui fistulas struimus per declive circumdatas, ut saepe eundem ignem ambiens aqua per tantum fluat spatii quantum efficiendo calori sat est; frigida itaque intrat, effluit calida.

3   Idem sub terra Empedocles existimat fieri, quem non

[1] Gercke, Oltramare for *et* HPEZ.

---

[1] Lucan 10.263–267: some waters burst forth as a consequence of earthquakes long after the world was created while others had their origin along with the universe.

so remarkable that they cannot be said to have the same origin as the other rivers.

23. This, then, is the classification of waters, as it 1 seems to some: of the waters that are later[1] than the ocean some are celestial, others are terrestial. Celestial waters are discharged by the clouds. Some terrestial waters swim on the surface, so to speak, and creep along the top of the ground; others are hidden; and of these I have already given an account.

24. Several explanations are given why some 1 waters are hot and some even boil so much that they cannot be used unless they either dissipate their steam in the open or become tepid by mixing with cold water. Empedocles[2] thinks that the water is heated by fires which the earth covers and conceals in many places, especially if the water lies under earth such as waters can pass through.

We commonly construct serpent-shaped con-2 tainers,[3] cylinders, and vessels of several other designs, in which we arrange thin copper pipes in descending spirals so that the water passes round the same fire over and over again, flowing through sufficient space to become hot. So the water enters cold, comes out hot. Empedocles conjectures that 3 the same thing happens under the earth. The

[2] This is the famous Empedocles of Acragas, Agrigentum, who developed the concept of the four elements, earth, air, fire, and water, whose combination and dissociation produce the objects of the world we know. He lived from about 494 to 434 B.C.

[3] *dracones* were snake-shaped water-holders, *miliaria* tall cylindrical hot-water-holders used in bathrooms.

falli crede Baianis,[1] quibus balnearia sine igne cale-
fiunt. Spiritus in illa fervens loco aestuanti infunditur; hic per tubos [2] lapsus non aliter quam igne
subdito parietes et vasa balnei calefacit; omnis
denique frigida transitu mutatur in calidam nec
trahit saporem e vaporario,[3] quia clausa praelabitur.

4 Quidam existimant per loca sulphure plena vel
nitro euntes [4] aquas calorem beneficio materiae per
quam fluunt trahere. Quod ipso odore gustuque
testantur; reddunt enim qualitatem eius qua caluere
materiae. Quod ne accidere mireris, vivae calci
aquam infunde, fervebit.

1 25. Quaedam aquae mortiferae sunt nec odore
notabiles nec sapore. Circa Nonacrin [5] in Arcadia
Styx appellata ab incolis advenas fallit, quia non facie,
non odore suspecta est, qualia sunt magnorum
artificum venena quae deprehendi nisi morte non

[1] *crede Baianis* Gercke, Oltramare for *credebant. In* MSS.;
credent ii Haase.
[2] Muret, Oltramare for *per rivos* ABV; *pertusos* HPZG.
[3] Koeler, Oltramare for *evaporatio* MSS.
[4] *nitro euntes* H; *introeuntes* most MSS.
[5] *Nonacrin* Fortunatus, Gercke, Oltramare for *Nonacrinum*
ZAV; *Nonacriam* E; *non acrinum* HP.

---

[1] Pliny says (31.4) that nowhere is water more bountiful or
beneficial than in the Bay of Naples.
[2] Pliny (2.231; 31.27) reports that one drink of this River
Styx causes death on the spot and that according to Theophrastus it has equally deadly fish.
[3] [The vagueness of the words *magnorum artificum* suggests
that we might read here *Magorum* and even delete *artificum* as
an intruded explanatory word, and that we might translate
" poisons " (*venena*) " of the Magi," however unjust may be the
implication against those much abused " Wise Men;" who, as

inhabitants of Baiae,[1] whose baths are heated without fire, can attest that Empedocles is right. Warm air flows from a hot place into the baths; here it circulates through conduits and heats the walls and basins of the bath just as if fire had been applied. In short, all the cold water is changed to hot water in transit, and because it flows through enclosed conduits it does not take on any flavour from a steam pipe.

Some suppose that water passing through places 4 full of sulphur or nitre takes on heat from the properties of the material through which it flows. The water indicates this by its special odour and taste, for it reproduces the quality of the material which made it become warm. If you are surprised that this happens, pour water on quicklime; it will boil.

25. Some waters are deadly and yet are not distinctive in odour or taste. Near Nonacris in Arcadia the Styx,[2] as it is called by the inhabitants, fools strangers because it is not suspected by its appearance or odour. Such waters are like the poisons of high-and-mighty tricksters,[3] which cannot be detected

obscurely suggested by Pliny's words in *NH*. 30.17, might be capable of practising the art of poisoning; we have also the statement *magicae artes earumque artifices extiterunt* in Augustine, *de Civitate Dei* 21.6. But in Seneca here *magnorum artificum* is probably right because in Bk. 4A, Praef. section 5 (cf. 3 and indeed all of 3–6), of the *Natural Questions*, one Plancus, though he was neither a Magus nor a poisoner but a flatterer, is called by Seneca *artifex maximus*. Moreover we have in 1. Praef. 16 *magno artifice* used for an honourable expert such as a real artist or an artistic creator. So for Seneca *magnus artifex* can be a clever man in a good or in a bad sense, " a clever trickster," applicable according to such and such a context—real poisoning in 3.25.1, mere flattering in 4A, Praef. 5 (cf. 3). —E.H.W.]

possunt. Haec autem de qua paulo ante rettuli aqua
summa celeritate corrumpit, nec remedio locus est,
quia protinus hausta duratur nec aliter quam gypsum
2 sub umore constringitur et alligat viscera. Est
aeque noxia aqua in Thessalia circa Tempe, quam et
fera et pecus omne devitat. Per ferrum et aes exit,
tanta vis illi est etiam dura mordendi; ne arbusta
quidem ulla alit, herbas necat.

3 Quibusdam fluminibus vis inest mira; alia enim
sunt quae pota inficiunt greges ovium intraque
certum[1] tempus quae fuere nigra, albam ferunt
lanam, quae albae venerant nigrae abeunt. Hoc in
Boeotia amnes duo efficiunt, quorum alteri ab effectu
Melas nomen est; utrique ex eodem lacu exeunt
4 diversa facturi. In Macedonia quoque, ut ait
Theophrastus, qui[2] facere albas oves volunt, ad
Haliacmonem[3] adducunt; quem ut diutius potavere,
non aliter quam infectae mutantur. At si illis lana
opus fuit pulla, paratus gratuitus infector est: ad
Peneion eundem gregem appellunt. Auctores
bonos[4] habeo esse in Galatia flumen quod idem in
omnibus[5] efficiat, esse in Cappadocia quo poto equis,
nec ulli praeterea animali, color mutetur et spargatur
albo cutis.

5 Quosdam lacus esse qui nandi imperitos ferant

---

[1] *breve* ABV.

[2] *Theophrastus, amnis est ad quem, qui* ET; *Theophrastus,
est flumen ad quod, qui* ABV.

[3] *ad Haliacmonem* supplied by Gercke, Oltramare (cf. Pliny
21.14).

except by death. Moreover, this water, which I just referred to, corrupts with amazing speed. There is no time for an antidote because as soon as it is drunk it hardens and is congealed by moisture like gypsum and binds the bowels. There is equally 2 poisonous water in Thessaly, around Tempe, which wild animals and all cattle avoid. It has so much power it even softens hard objects and passes through iron and copper; it does not nourish any trees and it kills plants.

There is a strange power in some rivers. For there 3 are some which, when drunk, dye flocks of sheep, and within a specific time the sheep which were black wear white wool and those which had come white go away black. Two rivers in Boeotia do this. One of them is named Black River from the effect it produces. Both come from the same lake to do different things. Also in Macedonia, as Theophrastus says, people 4 who want to make their sheep white lead them to the Haliacmon River. Sheep that drink it for any length of time are changed just as if they had been dyed. But if there is need of dark wool there is a free dyer near by: they drive the same flock to the Peneus River. I have it from reliable authorities that there is a river in Galatia which does the same for all animals, and a river in Cappadocia changes the colour of horses that drink it but not of any other animal. The skins of the horses become dappled with white.

It is well known that there are certain lakes which 5 support people who do not know how to swim. There

---

[4] Gronovius, Gercke, Oltramare for *novos* most MSS.
[5] *ovibus* EZABVT.

notum est; erat in Sicilia, est adhuc in Syria stagnum in quo natant lateres et mergi proiecta non possunt, licet gravia sint. Huius rei palam causa est. Quamcumque vis rem expende et contra aquam statue, dummodo utriusque par sit modus; si aqua gravior est, leviorem rem quam ipsa est fert et tanto supra se extollet quanto erit levior; graviora descendent. At si aquae et eius rei quam contra pensabis par pondus erit, nec pessum ibit nec extabit, sed exaequabitur aquae et natabit quidem sed paene mersa ac

6 nulla eminens parte. Hoc est cur quaedam tigna supra aquam paene tota efferantur,[1] quaedam ad medium submissa sint, quaedam ad aequilibrium aquae descendant. Namque, cum utriusque pondus par est, neutra res alteri cedit; graviora descendunt; leviora gestantur. Grave autem et leve est, non aestimatione nostra, sed comparatione eius quo vehi

7 debet. Itaque, ubi aqua gravior est hominis corpore aut saxo, non sinit id quo non vincitur mergi; sic evenit ut in quibusdam stagnis ne lapides quidem pessum eant. De solidis et duris loquor. Sunt enim multi pumicosi et levis, ex quibus quae constant insulae in Lydia natant; Theophrastus est auctor.

[1] Those MSS. which begin with the word *Quantum* skip from *efferantur* to the first word (*Grandinem*) of Book Four B.

---

[1] This "*stagnum*" is not necessarily the Dead Sea.

used to be a pond in Sicily, and there still is one in Syria,[1] where bricks float and no objects thrown in sink no matter how heavy they are. The reason for this is obvious. Weigh anything you like and compare it with water, provided the volume of both is equal. If the water is heavier it will support the object which is lighter and lift it as high above the surface as it is lighter. Objects heavier than the water will sink. But if the weight of the water is equal to the weight of the object you measure it against, the object will neither go to the bottom nor stick up. It will be in balance with the water and in fact will float but almost submerged and without any part sticking up. This is why some logs are elevated almost entirely above water, others are halfway submerged, others go down to the point of equal balance in the water. For, when the weight of both is equal neither yields to the other, but objects heavier than water sink, the lighter objects are supported. However, heavy or light derives not from our own estimate but from a comparison with the water in which the object is to be carried. So, when water is heavier than a man's body or a stone it does not permit anything to sink which does not overcome the water's own heaviness. Thus it happens that in some ponds not even stones go to the bottom. I am talking about solid, hard stones. For there are many light, pumice-like stones of which islands are composed, namely those which float in Lydia.[2] Theophrastus is my authority for this.

6

7

---

[2] Pliny (2.209) refers to the islands in Lydia named Reed Islands which are not only driven by winds but can be punted in any direction with poles.

8 Ipse ad Cutilias natantem insulam vidi,[1] et alia
in Vadimonis [2] lacu vehitur (lacus in Statoniensi est).
Cutiliarum insula et arbores habet et herbas nutrit;
tamen aqua sustinetur et in hanc atque illam partem
non vento tantum sed aura compellitur, nec umquam
illi per diem ac noctem uno loco statio est; adeo
9 movetur levi flatu. Huic duplex causa est: aquae
gravitas medicatae et ob hoc ponderosae, et ipsius
insulae materia vectabilis, quae non est corporis
solidi, quamvis arbores alat. Fortasse enim leves
truncos frondesque in lacu sparsas pinguis umor
10 apprehendit ac vinxit. Itaque, etiam si qua in illa
saxa sunt, invenies exesa [3] et fistulosa, qualia sunt
quae duratus umor efficit, utique circa medicatorum
fontium rivos, ubi purgamenta aquarum coaluerunt
et spuma solidatur. Necessario leve est quod ex
ventoso inanique concretum est.

11 Quorundam causa non potest reddi: quare aqua
Nilotica fecundiores feminas faciat, adeo ut quarun-
dam viscera longa sterilitate praeclusa ad conceptum

---

[1] Fortunatus for *vado* MSS.
[2] Fortunatus for *vadosis* MSS.
[3] *exesa* H²FλZ; *aquosa* H¹PEJ².

I myself saw a floating island near Cutiliae,[1] and 8
another floats around in the Lake of Vadimo [2] (the
lake is in the Statonia region).[3] The island at
Cutiliae has trees and grows plants; none the less
it is supported on water and is driven in this or that
direction not only by the wind but even by the
breeze, and never has a position in one place day
or night; it is moved by any light puff. There are 9
two explanations for it: the density of the water,
which is full of minerals and for this reason heavy;
and the movable material of the island itself, which
is not composed of solid substance, although it does
support trees. Perhaps the thick water caught and
held light tree-trunks and their leaves scattered on
the lake. So, even if there are any rocks on the 10
island you will find them hollow and porous like
those which hardened moisture has formed, certainly
along the banks of mineral springs where the deposits
from the water coalesce and the foam solidifies.
Such deposits are necessarily light because they are
an accretion of airy, empty substances.

An explanation cannot be given for some pheno- 11
mena: for example, why Nile water should make
women more fertile, and so effectively that the
innards of some women which have become closed
by a long period of sterility have relaxed for

---

[1] Pliny (2.209) mentions a dense wood near the springs of
Cutiliae which is never seen in the same place day or night.
[2] Pliny the Younger (8.20) describes several grassy islands
floating around the Lake of Vadimo.
[3] [Probably an intruded remark (the Latin is corrupted in
the MSS.) of a later date and not written by Seneca—E.H.W.]

relaxaverit; quare quaedam in Lycia aquae conceptum feminarum custodiant, quas solent petere quibus parum tenax vulva est. Quod ad me attinet, pono ista inter temere vulgata. Creditum est quasdam aquas scabiem afferre corporibus, quasdam vitiliginem et foedam ex albo varietatem, sive infusa, sive pota sit; quod vitium dicunt habere aquam ex rore collectam.

12 Quis non gravissimas esse aquas credat quae in crystallum coeunt? Contra autem est. Tenuissimis enim hoc evenit, quas frigus ob ipsam tenuitatem facillime gelat. Unde autem fiat eiusmodi lapis, apud Graecos ex ipso nomine apparet; κρύσταλλον enim appellant aeque hunc perlucidum lapidem quam illam glaciem ex qua fieri lapis creditur. Aqua enim caelestis minimum in se terreni habens, cum induruit, longioris frigoris pertinacia spissatur magis ac magis, donec omni aere excluso in se tota compressa est, et umor qui fuerat lapis effectus est.

1 26. Aestate quaedam flumina augentur, ut Nilus, cuius alias ratio reddetur. Theophrastus est auctor in Ponto quoque quosdam amnes crescere tempore aestivo. Quattuor esse iudicant causas: aut quia tunc maxime in umorem mutabilis terra sit; aut quia maiores in remoto imbres sint, quorum aqua per

---

[1] A number of Greek authors, including Athenaeus (2.15), who cites Theophrastus as an authority, say the waters of the Nile stimulate fertility. Pliny simply repeats the saying, without comment (7.33).

[2] That is, a quartz resembling ice.

conception.[1] Why should some waters in Lycia protect the pregnancy of women? Women whose wombs do not hold a pregnancy customarily seek these waters. As far as I am concerned, I put such beliefs among unfounded rumours. It has been believed that some waters, whether taken internally or externally, cause scabs on the body, others cause sores and unpleasant blotches in place of white skin. Water collected from dew, they say, has this unpleasant effect.

Anyone would suppose that water which turns into 12 *crystallus* or ice is the heaviest. But the opposite is true. For this happens to the thinnest water, which the cold easily freezes because of its very thinness. Incidentally, where a stone of this type [2] comes from is obvious from the very term among Greeks: for they call " crystal " both this transparent stone and the ice from which it is believed to be formed. Rainwater has very little in it of earthly element, but when it has frozen it becomes more and more condensed by the persistence of prolonged cold until all the air is excluded and it is entirely compressed upon itself, and what had been moisture has become stone.

26. Some rivers rise in the summer, as the Nile 1 does, of which an account will be given elsewhere.[3] Theophrastus is my authority that in the Pontus also some rivers rise in the summertime. Authorities conclude that there are four causes: first, because the earth is at the time especially changeable into water; second, because there are heavier rains in remote districts and their water passes through hidden underground channels and pours unnoticed into the

[3] In Book Four-A.

2 secretos cuniculos reddita tacite suffunditur.   Tertia
   si crebrioribus ventis ostium caeditur et reverberatur[1]
   fluctu amnis resistit, qui crescere videtur, quia non
   effunditur.   Quarta siderum ratio est.   Haec enim
   quibusdam mensibus magis urgent et exhauriunt
   flumina.   Cum longius recesserunt, minus consumunt
   atque trahunt; ita, quod impendio solebat, id
   incremento accidit.

3   Quaedam flumina palam in aliquem specum decidunt et sic ex oculis auferuntur.   Quaedam consu-
   muntur paulatim et intercidunt; eadem ex intervallo
   revertuntur recipiuntque et nomen et cursum.
   Causa manifesta est: sub terra vacat[2] locus; omnis
   autem natura umor ad inferius et ad inane defertur.
   Illo itaque recepta flumina cursus egere secreto, sed,
   cum primum aliquid solidi quod obstaret occurrit,
   perrupta parte quae minus ad exitum repugnavit,
   repetiere cursum suum.

4   Sic, ubi terreno Lycus est potatus[3] hiatu,
       Existit procul hinc alioque renascitur ore.
       Sic modo combibitur, tacito[4] modo gurgite lapsus
       Redditur Argolicis ingens Erasinus in undis.[5]

       [1] *reverberatus* EZ Oltramare.
       [2] Fortunatus for *vagatur* MSS.
       [3] *epotus* Ovid MSS.
       [4] *tecto* or *toto* Ovid MSS.
       [5] *arvis* Ovid MSS.

[1] Ovid *Met.* 15.273–276.   Herodotus (7.30) says the river
Lycus disappears underground to reappear about a half mile
farther on where it joins the Meander.   Pliny (2.225) includes
the Lycus in Asia and the Erasinus in Argos among the rivers

rivers.   Third, if the mouth of the river is beaten by   2
more frequent winds and lashed by the sea-waves the
river stops and seems to rise because it cannot flow
out.   The fourth cause is that of the stars, for in
certain months these bodies exert more force and
drain rivers.   When they recede farther away they
absorb and draw off less water.   So, what used to be
expended turns up as an increase.

Certain rivers fall visibly into some cave and so are   3
carried out of sight.   Others diminish gradually and
are lost but return after some distance and recover
their name and course.   The reason is obvious: there
is a vacant space underground; moreover, all liquid
by its nature is carried to a lower and empty region.
And so the rivers received into that empty region
continue their course out of sight, but as soon as
anything solid meets them so as to obstruct them
they burst through the section that offers the least
resistance to their exit and recover their course on
the surface.

> Thus, when Lycus is drunk up   4
> By the yawning earth
> It comes out far from here
> And is reborn
> From another source.
> Thus, the mighty Erasinus
> Is sometimes drunk up,
> Sometimes glides along in silent flow
> And is restored
> In the waters of Argos.[1]

that flow underground and come to the surface again, as the
Tigris does in Mesopotamia.   Seneca misquotes Ovid somewhat.

Idem et in Oriente Tigris facit; absorbetur et desideratus diu tandem longe remoto loco, non tamen dubius an idem sit, emergit.

5 Quidam fontes certo tempore purgamenta eiectant, ut Arethusa in Sicilia quinta quaque aestate per Olympia. Inde opinio est Alpheon ex Achaia eo usque penetrare et agere sub mari [1] cursum nec ante quam in Syracusano litore emergere, ideoque his diebus quibus Olympia sunt victimarum stercus 6 secundo traditum flumini illic redundare. Hoc et a te creditum est, ut in prima parte dixi,[2] Lucili carissime, et a Vergilio, qui alloquitur Arethusam:

Sic tibi, cum fluctus subter labere Sicanos,
Doris amara suas non intermisceat undas.[3]

Est in Chersoneso Rhodiorum fons qui post magnum intervallum temporis foeda quaedam turbidus ex intimo fundat, donec liberatus eliquatusque est. 7 Hoc quibusdam locis fontes faciunt, ut non tantum lutum sed folia testasque et quicquid putre iacuit expellant. Ubique autem facit mare, cui haec natura est ut omne immundum stercorosumque litoribus impingat. Quaedam vero partes maris

[1] *mari* Z Oltramare, Alexander; *mare* most MSS. Gercke.
[2] *dixi* supplied by Gercke, Oltramare; *in poemate* Haase (for *in prima parte*).
[3] *suam . . . undam* Virgil MSS. Z.

[1] Pliny 31.55: the Arethusa at Syracuse smells of dung during the Olympic games, for the Alpheus crosses to Sicily under the sea. Cf. Pliny 2.226; Strabo 6.2.4.

Also, in the East the Tigris does the same thing. It is absorbed and after a long disappearance it finally emerges far away in a remote place yet undoubtedly the same river.

Some springs cast out impurities at a specific time, 5 as the Arethusa does in Sicily every fifth summer during the Olympic festival.[1] Hence there is the belief that the Alpheus penetrates all the way to Sicily from Achaia and maintains its course under the sea and re-emerges only at the coast of Syracuse. So, on those days when the Olympic festival is held the excrement of sacrificial animals consigned to the current of the River Alpheus overflows in Sicily. Even you believe this legend, my dear Lucilius, as 6 I said in the first part of this work; and so does Virgil, who addresses Arethusa:

> So, when you glide beneath Sicilian waters
> May the sea nymph Doris
> Never mingle her bitter waves
> With yours.[2]

In the Chersonese which belongs to the Rhodians there is a spring which after a long interval of time[3] becomes stirred up from its depths and pours out some foul stuff, until it is freed of it and cleansed. In some other places springs do this, so that they not 7 only expel mud but also leaves and bottles and any trash lying in them. However, the sea does this everywhere. It is its nature to wash ashore all impurities and filth. In fact some regions of the

[2] Virgil *Ec.* 10.4–5. See also Seneca, *N.Q.*, 3.1.1.
[3] A spring in the Rhodian Chersonesus, Pliny says (31.55), pours out refuse every ninth year.

certis temporibus hoc faciunt, ut circa Messenen et
Mylas fimo[1] quiddam simile turbulenta aequinoctii
vice[2] mare profert fervetque et aestuat non sine
colore foedo, unde illic stabulare Solis boves fabula
8 est. Sed difficilis ratio est quorundam, utique ubi
tempus eius rei de qua quaeritur non[3] inobservatum
sed incertum est; itaque proxima quidem inveniri
et vicina non potest causa. Ceterum publica est
illa: omnis aquarum stantium clausarumque natura
se purgat. Nam in his quibus cursus est non possunt
vitia consistere, quae secunda vis defert et exportat;
illae quae non emittunt quicquid insedit magis
minusve aestuant. Mare vero cadavera stramenta-
que et naufragorum reliqua similia ex intimo trahit,
nec tantum tempestate fluctuque sed tranquillum
quoque placidumque purgatur.

1 27. Sed monet me locus ut quaeram, cum fatalis
dies diluvii venerit, quemadmodum magna pars
terrarum undis obruatur; utrum oceani viribus fiat et
externum in nos pelagus exurgat, an crebri sine
intermissione imbres et elisa aestate hiems pertinax
immensam vim aquarum ruptis nubibus deiciat, an

[1] Fortunatus for *fimum* MSS.
[2] *turbulenta aequinoctii vice* Oltramare for *turbulentae avis*
HPE; *turbulenti avis* Z; *turbulente alternis annis* Alexander;
turbulentis aquis Haase.
[3] *non* supplied by Oltramare.

sea do this periodically, as in the turbulent season of
the equinox [1] the sea around Messana and Mylae
throws up something like excrement and boils and
seethes with a vile colour. Hence the legend that
the cattle of the Sun are stabled there. But the 8
explanation for some of these is difficult, especially
when the time of the occurrence—a subject of inquiry—has not been unwitnessed but is still uncertain,
and so the immediate and related cause cannot be
discovered. However, there is a common cause:
all standing and enclosed water naturally purges
itself. For, in water that has a current, impurities
are not able to settle; the force of the current
sweeps them along and carries them away. Water
which does not emit whatever settles in it more or
less boils. As for the sea, it drags from the depths
dead bodies, litter, and similar debris of shipwrecks,
and purges itself of them, not only in storms and
waves but also when the sea is tranquil and calm.

27. But this subject reminds me to wonder how a 1
great part of the earth will be covered over by water
when the fated day of the deluge comes.[2] Will it be
by the force of the ocean and the rising of the outer
sea against us or will heavy rains fall without ceasing
and persistent winter eliminate summer and hurl
the full force of water down from burst clouds?

---

[1] The text is very doubtful here. Pliny 2.220: in the
neighbourhood of Messana and Mylae scum resembling dung is
cast out on to the shore, which is the origin of the story that
this is the place where the cattle of the Sun were stabled.

[2] Seneca's treatment of the universal catastrophe as if
occurring in his time may be caused by the idea that it recurs;
and thus can be thought of as a permanent feature of the universe. Hence his present tenses.

flumina tellus largius fundat aperiatque fontes novos,
an non sit una tanto malo causa sed omnis ratio
consentiat et simul imbres cadant, flumina increscant,
maria sedibus suis excita procurrant et omnia uno
2 agmine ad exitium humani generis incumbant. Ita
est. Nihil difficile naturae est, utique ubi in finem
sui properat. Ad originem rerum parce utitur
viribus dispensatque se incrementis fallentibus;
subito ad ruinam toto impetu venit. Quam longo
tempore opus est ut conceptus ad puerperium per-
duret infans; quantis laboribus tener educatur;
quam diligenti nutrimento obnoxium novissime corpus
adolescit! At quam nullo negotio solvitur! Urbes
constituit aetas, hora dissolvit; momento fit cinis,
diu silva; magna tutela stant ac vigent omnia, cito ac
repente dissiliunt.

3 Quicquid ex hoc statu rerum natura flexerit, in
exitium mortalium satis est. Ergo, cum affuerit illa
necessitas temporis, multas simul fata causas movent.
Neque enim sine concussione mundi tanta mutatio
est, ut quidam putant, inter quos Fabianus est.

4 Primo immodici cadunt imbres et sine ullis solibus
triste nubilo caelum est nebulaque continua et ex
umido spissa caligo numquam exiccantibus ventis.
Inde vitium satis est, segetum sine fruge surgentium

---

[1] Servius Flavius Papirius Fabianus lived in the first century
of the Christian era and wrote *Naturalium Causarum Libri*.

Or will the earth pour out rivers far and wide and open new springs? Or will there be no single cause for such a catastrophe but rather all principles working together; at the same time the rains will descend, the rivers rise, the seas rush violently from their places, and all things in a united effort will apply themselves to the destruction of the human race? And so it will be. Nothing is difficult for 2 nature, especially when she rushes to destroy herself. At the beginning of things she uses her strength sparingly and apportions herself out in imperceptible increases. For destruction she comes suddenly with all her violence. A long time is needed so that a child, once conceived, may come to be born. The tender infant is reared only with great toil. The frail body finally develops only with diligent nurture. But how with no effort it is all undone! It takes an age to establish cities, an hour to destroy them. A forest grows for a long time, becomes ashes in a moment. Great safeguards may exist and all things may be flourishing, but quickly and suddenly they all fall apart.

Any deviation by nature from the existing state of 3 the universe is enough for the destruction of mankind. So, when that destined time comes the fates put into motion many causes at the same time. For according to some thinkers, among them Fabianus,[1] such a great change does not occur without a shattering of the universe.

At first, excessive rain falls. There is no sunshine, 4 the sky is gloomy with clouds, and there is continuous mist, and from the moisture a thick fog which no winds will ever dry out. Next, there is a blight on

marcor. Tunc corruptis quae seruntur manu palus-
5 tris omnibus campis herba succrescit. Mox iniuriam
et validiora sensere. Solutis quippe radicibus arbusta
procumbunt et vitis atque omne virgultum non
tenetur solo, quod molle fluidumque est. Iam
nec gramina aut pabula laeta aquis sustinet. Fame
laboratur et manus ad antiqua alimenta porrigitur;
qua ilex est et quercus excutitur et quaecumque in
arduis arbor commissura astricta lapidum stetit.
6 Labant ac madent tecta et, in imum usque receptis
aquis, fundamenta desidunt ac tota humus stagnat.
Frustra titubantium fultura temptatur; omne enim
firmamentum in lubrico figitur et lutosa humo;
nihil stabile est.
7   Postquam magis magisque ingruunt nimbi et
congestae saeculis tabuerunt nives, devolutus torrens
altissimis montibus rapit silvas male haerentes et
saxa resolutis remissa compagibus rotat, abluit villas
et intermixtos dominis greges devehit; vulsisque
minoribus tectis quae in transitu abduxit, tandem in
maiora violentus aberrat, urbes et impactos [1] trahit
moenibus suis populos, ruinam an naufragium queren-
tur incertos. Adeo simul et quod opprimeret et
quod mergeret venit. Auctus deinde processu
aliquot in se torrentibus raptis plana passim popula-

---

[1] Oltramare for *implicitos* most MSS.; *implictos* Z.

the crops, a withering of fields of standing grain as it grows without fruit. Then all things sown by hand rot and swamp plants spring up in all the fields. Next the stronger plants also feel the blight. For, 5 indeed, trees fall when their roots are loosened, and vines and all shrubs are not held by the soil, which becomes soft and fluid. No longer does the ground sustain grazing land and water-loving pasturage. There is suffering from famine, and recourse is had to the diet of ancient times: food is shaken down wherever there is an ilex or an oak or where any tree on a hillside stands, still held firm by tightly joined rocks. Houses sag and drip, and when the moisture 6 penetrates deeply the foundations settle and all the ground becomes marshy. Props are tried for collapsing houses, uselessly; for every foundation is set in slipping and muddy soil. Nothing is stable.

After the clouds have massed more and more, and 7 the accumulated snows of centuries have melted, a torrent which has rolled down from the highest mountains carries off forests that are unable to cling fast and tears boulders free from their loosened structures and rolls them along, washes away villas and carries down sheep and owners intermixed. The smaller houses are plucked up by the torrent which carries them off as it passes. Finally the torrent is diverted violently against larger dwellings and drags along cities and peoples who are forced back to their city walls and uncertain whether they should complain of a cave-in or a shipwreck. In such a way the disaster comes, which both crushes and submerges them at the same time. Eventually, as the torrent passes along it is increased by the absorbtion

tur; novissime [in] materia[1] magna gentium onustus [2] diffunditur.

8   Flumina vero suapte natura vasta et tempestatibus rapida alveos reliquerunt.   Quid tu esse Rhodanum, quid putas Rhenum atque Danuvium, quibus torrens etiam in canali suo cursus est, cum superfusi novas sibi fecere ripas ac scissa humo simul excessere alveo?

9   Quanta cum praecipitatione volvuntur, ubi per campestria fluens Rhenus ne spatio quidem languit, sed[3] latissimas velut per angustum aquas impulit;[4] cum Danuvius non iam radices nec media montium stringit, sed iuga ipsa sollicitat ferens secum madefacta montium latera rupesque disiectas et magnarum promontoria regionum, quae fundamentis laborantibus a continenti recesserunt, deinde non inveniens exitum—omnia enim ipse sibi praecluserat—in orbem redit, ingentemque terrarum ambitum atque urbium uno vertice involvit.

10   Interim permanent imbres, fit caelum gravius ac sic diu malum ex malo colligit.   Quod olim fuerat nubilum, nox est et quidem horrida ac terribilis intercursu luminis diri.   Crebra enim micant fulmina, procellaeque quatiunt mare tunc primum auctum[5]

---

[1] *materiam magnam* E; *miseriam* Haase; *maestitia* Castiglioni.

[2] *magna gentium clarus honustusque* most MSS.; *magna gentium cadaveribus onustus* Oltramare; *magna ruina gentium clarus onustusque* Alexander.

[3] *languit, sed* Oltramare, Alexander for *languisset* Z; *languidus* most MSS.

[4] *impulit* Oltramare, Alexander for *impluit* Z; *implet* HPFEG.

into itself of several other torrents and spreads out in scattered devastation on the plain. Finally, it pours out in all directions, loaded with the vast stuff of nations.

The rivers, also, which are vast by their own nature, 8 and are hurried along by the storm, leave their beds. The Rhone, the Rhine, and the Danube have a torrential current even when in their channels. What do you suppose they are when they have overflowed and made new banks for themselves and, cutting through the ground, have all left their usual bed ? The 9 rivers roll forth with unchecked force. The Rhine flowing over the plains has not been slowed down even by the wide open spaces but has driven its spreading waters as if through a narrow gorge. The Danube no longer touches the base nor even the middle of the mountains but attacks the summits themselves, carrying with it the mountain-sides it has flooded, the crags it has hurled apart, and the promontories of whole regions which have their foundations weakened and are detached from the continent. The Danube, finding no exit—for it has itself closed off all passages for itself—returns in a circle and envelops in one whirlpool the great circuit of lands and cities.

Meanwhile, the rains continue, the sky becomes 10 heavier and in this way for a long time reaps disaster from disaster. What was formerly a cloud is now black night, and a night that is dreadful and terrible with flashes of awful illumination. Lightning flashes frequently, and squalls shake the sea which,

---

⁵ *auctum* ET; *actum* HPZG.

fluminum accessu et sibi angustum. Iam enim
promovet litus nec continetur suis finibus; sed
prohibent exire torrentes aguntque fluctum retro.
Pars tamen maior ut maligno ostio retenta restagnat
11 et agros in formam unius laci redigit. Iam omnia,
qua prospici potest, aquis obsidentur; omnis tumulus
in profundo latet et immensa ubique altitudo est.
Tantum in summis montium iugis vada sunt; in ea
excelsissima cum liberis coniugibusque fugerunt actis
ante se gregibus. Diremptum inter miseros com-
mercium ac transitus, quoniam, quicquid submissius
12 erat, id unda complevit. Editissimis quibusque
adhaerebant reliquiae generis humani, quibus in
extrema perductis hoc unum solacio fuit quod tran-
sierat in stuporem metus. Non vacabat timere
mirantibus, nec dolor quidem habebat locum; quippe
vim suam perdit in eo qui ultra sensum mali miser est.
13 Ergo insularum modo eminent

montes, et sparsas Cycladas augent,

ut ait ille poetarum ingeniosissimus egregie. Sicut
illud pro magnitudine rei dixit:

Omnia pontus erat, deerant quoque litora ponto,

---

[1] Ovid *Met.* 2.264.
[2] Ovid *Met.* 1.292.

for the first time, is increased by the influx of the rivers and is too narrow for itself. Now it advances its own shores and is no longer contained within its own boundaries; yet the torrents prevent the sea from leaving its place and drive its waves back. Yet the greater part of the torrents is as if stopped by the narrow mouth and swirls backwards, reducing the fields to the form of a single lake. Now every- 11 thing in sight is filled with water; every little hill lies hidden in the depths, and the height of the water is everywhere immense. Only on the highest ranges of mountains are there shallows. To these heights men have fled with children and wives, driving their cattle before them. Communication and exchange has been cut off among the miserable survivors, since the water has filled all the ground that lies lower. The remnants of the human race clung to 12 whatever peaks are highest. Reduced to extremities they had this one thing for solace: namely, that fear had passed into stupor. In their astonishment there was no room for fear nor, in fact, did sorrow have any place; since it loses its meaning in the case of a man who is miserable beyond the realization of misfortune. So, mountains rise up like islands 13

> And they add to the number of
> The scattered Cyclades [1]

as the most ingenious of poets says beautifully. Just as he also said this, appropriate to the magnitude of his theme:

> All was sea,
> And the sea
> Had no shores. [2]

ni tantum impetum ingenii et materiae ad pueriles ineptias reduxisset:

Nat lupus inter oves, fulvos vehit unda leones.

14 Non est res satis sobria lascivire devorato orbe terrarum. Dixit ingentia et tantae confusionis imaginem cepit, cum dixit:

Expatiata ruunt per apertos flumina campos,
    pressaeque labant [1] sub gurgite turres.

Magnifice haec, si non curaverit quid oves et lupi faciant. Natari autem in diluvio et in illa rapina potest? Aut non eodem impetu pecus omne quo raptum erat mersum est?

15 Concepisti imaginem quantam debebas, obrutis omnibus terris caelo ipso in terram ruente. Perfer. Scies quid deceat, si cogitaveris orbem terrarum natare.

1 28. Nunc ad propositum revertamur. Sunt qui existiment immodicis imbribus vexari terras posse, non obrui; magno impetu magna ferienda sunt. Faciet pluvia segetes malas, fructum grando decutiet, intumescent rivis flumina, sed resident.

---

[1] Ovid has *latent* Fλ.

Yet he reduced his great inspiration and subject to childish silliness:

> The wolf swims among the sheep,
> The water carries tawny lions.[1]

It is not a sufficiently serious attitude to make fun 14 of the whole world now swallowed up.   He spoke grandly and caught the image of such vast confusion when he said:

> The widespread rivers
> Rush through open plains.
> . . . Towers totter
> And sink
> Under the flood.[2]

This is magnificently said.   If only he had not been concerned with what the sheep and the wolves were doing.   But could anything be swimming in this deluge and destruction? Were not all beasts drowned by the same force which carried them off?

You conceived the great image you should have, 15 with all the lands overwhelmed and the sky itself rushing into the earth.   Keep it up.   You will know what is fitting if you bear in mind that the entire earth is swimming.

28. Now let us return to the discussion.   There 1 are those who think that the earth can be damaged but not destroyed by excessive rains.   Mighty things must be stricken by a mighty blow.   Rain will make the crops bad, hail will knock down the fruit, rivers will swell in their channels but will subside again.

---

[1] Ovid *Met.* 1.304.
[2] Ovid *Met.* 1.285 and 290.

2   Quibusdam placet moveri mare et illinc causam tantae cladis accersere. Non potest torrentium aut imbrium aut fluminum iniuria fieri tam grande naufragium. Ubi instat illa pernicies mutarique humanum genus placuit, fluere assiduos imbres et non esse modum pluviis concesserim, suppressis aquilonibus et flatu sicciore austris nubes et amnes abundare. Sed adhuc in damna profectum est:

> Sternuntur segetes et deplorata colonis
> Vota iacent longique perit labor irritus anni.

3   Non laedi terrae debent sed abscondi. Itaque, cum per ista prolusum est, crescunt maria, sed super solitum, et fluctum ultra extremum tempestatis maximae vestigium mittunt. Deinde, a tergo ventis surgentibus, ingens aequor evolvunt, quod longe a conspectu veteris [1] litoris frangitur. Deinde, ubi litus bis terque prolatum est et pelagus in alieno constitit, velut amota mole,[2] comminus procurrit
4 aestus ex imo recessu maris. Nam, ut aeris, ut aetheris, sic huius elementi larga materia est multoque in abdito plenior. Haec fatis mota (non aestu—nam aestus fati ministerium est) attollit vasto sinu fretum agitque ante se. Deinde in miram alti-

---

[1] *interioris* P; *antiqui* Z.
[2] *amota mole* Warmington for *admoto malo* most MSS.; *amoto* FZ Oltramare; *admoto cumulo* Garrod.

---

[1] Ovid *Met.* 1.272–273.

Some are satisfied that the sea will be displaced 2
and hence they derive the cause of the great calamity.
Such a great shipwreck of the world cannot come
about from the damages of torrents, rains, or rivers.
I would concede that when that catastrophe threatens
and it is decided that the human race is to be changed,
continuous rains will fall and there will be no limit to
the floods; the north winds, and the south winds too
with their drier air, will be checked and clouds and
streams abound. But up to this time the effect is
mere damage:

> Crops are flattened to the ground
> And hopes lie mourned by farmers
> And the labour of a long year perishes,
> Worthless.[1]

The land ought not to be merely damaged but 3
submerged. And so, when the prelude has occurred
through these disasters, the seas will swell far beyond
usual and send waves past the last watermark of the
most violent storm. Then, when the winds surge up
from the rear, the seas roll out a great expanse of
water which is broken far from the sight of the old
shore. Then, when the shore has been shifted for-
ward two or three times and the sea stands in a
place that is not its own, just as though an obstruction
were removed the tide will rush forth at close
quarters from the deepest recess of the sea. For, 4
like the air and the upper atmosphere, the element
water also has a great reserve, and more plentiful in
hidden regions. Once this reserve is moved by the
fates (not by the tide—for the tide is only an agency
of fate) it lifts the sea in a vast fold and drives it ahead.

SENECA

tudinem erigitur et illis tutis hominum receptaculis
superest. Nec id aquis arduum est, quoniam aequo
5 terris fastigio ascendunt.[1] Si quis excelsa perlibret,
maria paria sunt. Nam par undique sibi ipsa tellus
est (cava eius et plana exiguo inferiora sunt, sed
istis adeo in rotundum orbis aequatus est) in parte
autem eius et maria sunt, quae in unius aequalitatem
pilae coeunt. Sed, quemadmodum campos intuen-
tem quae paulatim devexa sunt fallunt, sic non[2]
intellegimus curvaturas maris et videtur planum
quicquid apparet; at illud aequale terris est ideoque,
ut effluat, non magna mole tollendum:[3] satis est
illi, ut supra paria[4] veniat, leviter exurgere. Nec a
litore, ubi inferius est, sed a medio, ubi ille cumulus
est, defluit.

6 Ergo, ut solet aestus aequinoctialis sub ipsum
lunae solisque coitum omnibus aliis maior undare, sic
hic qui ad occupandas terras emittitur, solitis maxi-
misque violentior, plus aquarum trahit nec, antequam
supra cacumina eorum quos perfusurus est montium
crevit, devolvitur. Per centena milia quibusdam
locis aestus excurrit innoxius et ordinem servat; ad
7 mensuram enim crescit iterumque decrescit. At illo
tempore solutus legibus sine modo fertur. " Qua
ratione?" inquis. Eadem qua conflagratio futura
est. Utrumque fit, cum deo[5] visum ordiri meliora,

[1] Gronovius for *ascendet* HPEZG.
[2] *sic non* T Oltramare, Alexander; *sic cum non* most MSS.
[3] *mole tollendum* Oltramare for *mole tollet dum* P; *mole se tollet dum* HG; *mole se tollit dum* EF.
[4] *maria* EJ[1]K.   [5] *adeo* λ.

Then it rears up to an astounding height and over-
tops those safe little refuge-places of men. Nor is
this difficult for the waters, since they ascend at a
height equal to the lands. If the high points are 5
flattened down the seas are level. For the earth
itself has the same elevation everywhere (its hollows
and plains are a very little below the level, but
through these it is about equalized into the round-
ness of a sphere), but in part of it are also the seas,
which combine into the uniformity of a single ball.
But when we look out over a plain the ground de-
ceives us as it curves down gradually. In the same
way we do not realize the curvature of the sea; whatever is visible appears flat. The sea is so level with
the land that, to overflow, it does not need to rise
with any great effort. To come over what is equal
in level it is enough for the sea to rise only slightly.
It does not flow from the shore, where the sea is lower,
but from the middle, where the accumulation is.

Therefore, just as the equinoctial tide following 6
the conjunction of the moon and the sun usually
rises higher than at any other time, so the tide which
is sent to overwhelm the lands is more violent than
the greatest of ordinary tides and carries more water
and does not ebb before it has risen above the peaks
of the mountains which it intends to flood. In some
regions the tide runs up harmlessly for a hundred
miles and maintains regularity; for it rises to its
intended limit and subsides again. But at the time 7
of the deluge the tide, freed from its laws, advances
without limit. "On what principle?" you ask. In the
same principle in which the conflagration will occur.
Both will occur when it seems best to god for the

vetera finiri. Aqua et ignis terrenis dominantur; ex his ortus, ex his interitus est. Ergo, quandoque placuere res novae [1] mundo, sic in nos mare emittitur desuper, ut fervor ignisque cum aliud genus exitii placuit.

1 29. Berosos, qui Belum [2] interpretatus est, ait ista cursu siderum fieri. Adeo quidem affirmat ut conflagrationi atque diluvio tempus assignet. Arsura enim terrena contendit, quandoque omnia sidera quae nunc diversos agunt cursus in Cancrum convenerint, sic sub eodem posita vestigio ut recta linea exire per orbes omnium possit; inundationem futuram, cum eadem siderum turba in Capricornum convenerit. Illic solstitium, hic bruma conficitur; magnae potentiae signa, quando in ipsa mutatione anni momenta sunt.

Quidam existimant terram quoque concuti et dirupto solo nova fluminum capita detegere, quae
2 amplius ut e pleno profundant. Et istas ego receperim causas—neque enim ex uno est tanta pernicies— et illam quae in conflagratione nostris placet hoc

---

[1] Fortunatus for *novo* MSS.
[2] Fortunatus for *bellum* HPEZ.

old things to be ended and better things to begin. Water and fire dominate earthly things. From them is the origin, from them the death. Therefore whenever a renewal for the universe is decided, the sea is sent against us from above, like raging fire, when another form of destruction is decided upon.

29. Berosos,[1] who translated Belus, says that these catastrophes occur with the movements of the planets.[2] Indeed, he is so certain that he assigns a date for the conflagration and the deluge. For earthly things will burn, he contends, when all the planets which now maintain different orbits come together in the sign of Cancer, and are so arranged in the same path that a straight line can pass through the spheres of all of them. The deluge will occur when the same group of planets meets in the sign of Capricorn. The solstice is caused by Cancer, winter by Capricorn; they are signs of great power since they are the turning-points in the very change of the year.

Some think that the earth also is shaken and when the ground is disrupted uncovers new sources of rivers which pour forth a greater volume of water as if from a full reservoir. And I would accept these explanations also—for such enormous destruction will not come from a single cause—but I think the view that appeals to us Stoics in regard to a conflagration

[1] Berosos was a contemporary of Alexander the Great. Pliny tells us (6.121) that the temple of Jupiter Belus in Babylon is still standing and that Belus was the discoverer of the science of astronomy.

[2] In astrology the sun and the moon are counted among the planets.

quoque transferendam puto: sive animal[1] est
mundus, sive corpus natura gubernabile, ut arbores,
ut sata, ab initio eius usque ad exitum quicquid
3 facere quicquid pati debeat, inclusum est. Ut in
semine omnis futuri hominis ratio comprehensa est et
legem barbae canorumque nondum natus infans
habet. Totius enim corporis et sequentis actus in
parvo occultoque liniamenta sunt. Sic origo mundi
non minus solem et lunam et vices siderum et animalium ortus quam quibus mutarentur terrena continuit.
In his fuit inundatio, quae non secus quam hiems,
quam aestas, lege mundi venit.

4 Itaque non pluvia istud fiet, sed pluvia quoque;
non incursu maris, sed maris quoque incursu; non
terra motu, sed terrae quoque motu. Omnia adiuva-
bunt naturam, ut naturae constituta peragantur.
Maximam tamen causam ad se inundandam terra
ipsa praestabit, quam diximus esse mutabilem et
5 solvi in umorem. Ergo, quandoque erit terminus
rebus humanis, cum partes eius interire debuerint
abolerive funditus totae ut de integro totae rudes
innoxiaeque generentur nec supersit in deteriora
praeceptor, plus umoris quam semper fuit fiet.
Nunc enim elementa ad id quod debetur pensa sunt;

[1] Koeler, Oltramare for *anima* MSS.

must also be applied here. Whether the world is an animated being, or a body governed by nature, like trees and plants, there is incorporated in it from its beginning to its end everything it must do or undergo. In the semen there is contained the en- 3 tire record of the man to be, and the not-yet-born infant has the laws governing a beard and grey hair. The features of the entire body and its successive phases are there, in a tiny and hidden form. In the same way, the origin of the universe included the sun and the moon and the revolutions of the heavenly bodies and the rise of animal life no less than the changes which the earth's materials undergo. Among these changes was flood, which occurs by a universal law just as winter and summer do.

So, the rain will not make that catastrophe, but 4 rain will also contribute; the advance of the sea will not cause it, but the sea's advance will also contribute to it; and earthquake will not be the catastrophe, but an earthquake will also be a contributor. All elements will help nature so that nature's decrees may be carried out. Earth will furnish to itself the greatest cause of the flood since, as I said, earth is susceptible to changing and being dissolved into liquid. There- 5 fore, whenever the end comes for human affairs, when parts of the world must pass away and be abolished utterly so that all may be generated from the beginning again,[1] new and innocent, and no tutor of vice survives, there will be more water than there ever was. At present the elements are balanced out for

[1] In *Ad Marciam* (126.6) Seneca describes the end of the universe as caused by the sea combined with the clashing of stars and a general conflagration.

aliquid oportet alteri accedat, ut quae libramento
stant inaequalitas turbet. Accedet umori. Nunc
enim habet quo ambiat terras, non quo obruat;
quicquid illi adieceris, necesse est in alienum locum
exundet.

6 Vide ergo ne terra debeat minui,[1] ut validiori infirma
succumbat. Incipiet ergo putrescere, dehinc laxata
ire in umorem et assidua tabe defluere. Tunc
exilient sub montibus flumina ipsosque impetu[2]
7 quatient; inde ora nacta[3] manabunt. Solum omne
aquas reddet; summi scaturient montes. Quemadmodum in morbum transeunt sana et ulceri vicina
consentiunt, ut quaeque proxima terris fluentibus
fuerint, ipsa eluentur stillabuntque, deinde decurrent
et, hiante pluribus locis saxo, fretum saliet et maria
inter se componet. Nihil erunt Adria, nihil Siculi
aequoris fauces, nihil Charybdis, nihil Scylla; omnes
novum mare fabulas obruet et hic qui terras cingit
oceanus extrema sortitus veniet in medium.

8 Quid ergo est? Nihilominus tenebit alienos
menses hiems, aestas prohibebitur, et quodcumque
terras sidus exiccat compresso ardore cessabit.

---

[1] Madvig, Gercke, Oltramare for *minus* HPEZ.
[2] Fortunatus for *impetus* HPEFZ.

whatever is required; for inequality to disturb the things which stand in balance a surplus must be added to one element or the other. A surplus will be added to water. At present it has the power to surround the lands, not the power to submerge them. Whatever you add to water necessarily overflows into another place strange to the waters.

Surely then the earth must be diminished, and **6** when weak it will succumb to a stronger element. It will therefore begin to decompose, then loosen and liquify and wash away in a continuous melting. Rivers will leap out from the base of mountains and by their impetus cause the mountains to shake; and the waters will then pour out of the openings they gained. The soil everywhere will ooze water; the **7** tops of mountains will gush it out. Just as a disease corrupts healthy bodies and as sores infect the adjacent areas, so all that is closest to the liquifying soil will wash away and dissolve and finally run off; and in many places the rock will split open, the strait will leap and join the seas to each other. There will be no Adriatic, no strait of the Sicilian Sea, no Charybdis, no Scylla; a new sea will wash away all the fables and the existing ocean which encircles the land, though allotted the outside parts, will come into the centre.

Well, then, what is next? As if this were not **8** enough, winter will hold strange months, summer will be prohibited, and all the stars that dry up the earth will have their heat repressed and will cease.

---

[3] *ora nacta* Oltramare for *aura tacta* MSS.

Peribunt tot nomina, Caspium et Rubrum mare,
Ambracii et Cretici sinus, Propontis et Pontus;
peribit omne discrimen; confundetur quicquid in
suas partes natura digessit. Non muri quemquam,
non turres tuebuntur. Non proderunt templa
supplicibus nec urbium summa, quippe fugientes
9 unda praeveniet et ex ipsis arcibus deferet. Alia
ab occasu, alia ab oriente concurrent. Unus humanum genus condet dies; quicquid tam longa fortunae
indulgentia excoluit, quicquid supra ceteros extulit,
nobilia pariter atque adornata magnarumque gentium regna pessum dabit.

1 30. Sunt omnia, ut dixi, facilia naturae, utique quae
a primo facere constituit, ad quae non subito sed ex
denuntiato venit. Iam autem a primo die mundi,
cum in hunc habitum ex informi unitate discederet,
quando mergerentur terrena decretum est; et, ne
sit quandoque velut in novo opere dura molitio,
2 olim ad hoc maria se exercent. Non vides ut fluctus
in litora tamquam exiturus incurrat? Non vides ut
aestus fines suos transeat et in possessionem terrarum
mare inducat? Non vides ut illi perpetua cum

---

[1] Seneca starts with the final catastrophe tracing the
sequence of events backwards from the merging of the waters
of the Caspian Sea and the Red Sea (in the northern and
southern parts of the known world—Seneca probably shared in
an erroneous belief that the Caspian was a gulf or inlet of a
" northern ocean "), preceded by the lesser catastrophe of the
joining of the Ambracian Gulf and the Cretan Gulf (cutting
north-west to south-east diagonally across Greece), preceded
by the flowing together of the adjacent Propontis and Pontus.

All these names will pass away: the Caspian and the Red Sea, the Ambracian and Cretan Gulf, the Propontis and the Pontus;[1] all distinctions will disappear; all that nature has separated into individual parts will be jumbled together. Neither walls nor towers will protect anyone. Temples will not help worshippers, nor will the heights of cities help refugees, since the wave will anticipate the fugitives and sweep them down from the very citadels. The destructive forces will rush together, some from 9 the west, some from the east. A single day will bury the human race; all that the long indulgence of fortune has cultivated, all that it has lifted to eminence above the rest, all that is noble and beautiful, even the kingdoms of great nations—fortune will send all down to ruin at the same time.

30. All things are easy for nature, as I said,[2] 1 especially the things she has decided to do from the beginning, which she approaches not suddenly but after giving warning. But from the very first day of the universe, when out of shapeless unity it separated into the appearance it now has, nature at that time decreed when earthly things would be submerged. And the seas have long trained themselves for this, so that the effort would not be difficult when the time comes, as it would be if the task were unfamiliar. Do you not see that the wave rushes as though it were 2 intending to run up on shore? Do you not see that the tide crosses its boundaries and leads the sea into possession of the land? Do you not see that its fight against its barriers is unceasing? What then?

[2] Above, Chapter 27.2.

claustris suis pugna sit? Quid porro? Istinc unde
tantum tumultum vides metus est, e mari et magno
spiritu erumpentibus fluviis?

3 Ubi non umorem natura disposuit, ut undique
nos, cum voluisset, aggredi posset? Mentior,
nisi eruentibus terram umor occurrit et, quotiens
nos aut avaritia defodit aut aliqua causa penetrare
altius cogit, eruendi finis aliquando [1] est. Adice
quod immanes sunt in abdito lacus et multum maris
conditi, multum fluminum per operta labentium.

4 Undique ergo erit causa diluvio, cum aliae aquae
subterfluant terras, aliae circumfluant, quae diu
coercitae vincent et amnes amnibus iungent, paludi-
bus stagna. Omnium tunc mare ora fontium imple-
bit et maiore hiatu solvet. Quemadmodum corpora
nostra ad egestum venter exhaurit, quemadmodum
in sudorem eunt vires, ita tellus liquefiet et, aliis
causis quiescentibus, intra se quo mergatur inveniet.
Sed magis omnia coitura crediderim.

5 Nec longa erit mora exitii. Temptatur divellitur-
que concordia. Cum semel aliquid ex hac idonea
diligentia remiserit mundus, statim undique ex
aperto et abdito, superne, ab infimo, aquarum fiet
6 irruptio. Nihil est tam violentum, tam incontinens
sui, tam contumax infestumque retinentibus quam

---

[1] *a liquido* Z Alexander; *aliquando* ⟨*aqua*⟩ Warmington.

Have you fear from that quarter where you see such great turmoil, while floods of water burst forth with great blast from the sea?

Nature has put water everywhere so that she can 3 attack us from all sides when she chooses. I am telling the truth that water meets us as we dig up the ground, and whenever our avarice sends us down into the earth or some motive compels us to dig deep, it is sooner or later water that makes an end of the digging. Add the fact that there are immense lakes hidden underground, a vast quantity of hidden sea there, and many rivers flowing through concealed channels. On all sides, then, there will exist causes 4 for the deluge, since some waters flow beneath the lands, others flow around them. For a long time they have been restrained: but they will conquer, joining streams to streams, swamps to marshes. Then the sea will fill up the mouths of all the springs and expand them in wider openings. Just as the belly drains our bodies in voiding wastes, just as our strength goes off in sweat, so the earth will liquify and, even though other causes are inoperative, the earth will find within itself the cause by which it is to be submerged. Still, I am more inclined to believe, all things will combine in the catastrophe.

There will be no long delay in the destruction. 5 The equilibrium is now being attacked and disrupted. As soon as the universe relaxes a little from the present proper diligent surveillance, immediately from all sides, from the open and the hidden, from above, from below, there will be an irruption of the waters. There is nothing so violent as the full force 6 of water, nothing so uncontrollable, so unyielding,

magna vis undae; utetur libertate permissa et, iubente natura, quae scindit circuitque complebit. Ut ignis diversis locis ortus cito miscet incendium flammis coire properantibus, sic momento se redundantia pluribus locis maria committent.

7 Nec ea semper licentia undis erit sed, peracto exitio generis humani extinctisque pariter feris, in quarum homines ingenia transierant, iterum aquas terra sorbebit, terra pelagus stare aut intra terminos suos furere coget, et reiectus e nostris sedibus in sua secreta pelletur oceanus, et antiquus ordo revocabi-

8 tur. Omne ex integro animal generabitur [1] dabiturque terris homo inscius scelerum et melioribus auspiciis natus. Sed illis quoque innocentia non durabit, nisi dum novi sunt. Cito nequitia subrepit. Virtus difficilis inventu est, rectorem ducemque desiderat; etiam sine magistro vitia discuntur.

[1] Fortunatus, Oltramare for *gloriabitur* HP Alexander; *orietur* Z.

so destructive against any restraints. It will utilize any freedom permitted to it and, as its nature dictates, it will fill up whatever it has divided and surrounded. Just as fire starting in different separate areas will quickly unite its blaze with flames that hurry to meet each other, so in a moment the seas, overflowing at numerous places, will come together.

But the water will not have this freedom for ever. **7** When the destruction of the human race is completed and the wild animals, into whose savagery men will have passed, are equally extinct, again the earth will absorb the waters. The earth will force the sea to stay in its place or to rage within its own boundaries, and the ocean will be ejected from our abode and driven back to its own secret dwelling-place, and the ancient order of things will be re-established. Every **8** living creature will be created anew and the earth will be given men ignorant of sin, and born under better auspices. But their innocence, too, will not last, except as long as they are new. Vice quickly creeps in. Virtue is difficult to find; it needs a director and guide. Vices can be learned even without a teacher.

PRINTED IN GREAT BRITAIN BY
RICHARD CLAY (THE CHAUCER PRESS), LTD.,
BUNGAY, SUFFOLK.

THE LOEB CLASSICAL LIBRARY

VOLUMES ALREADY PUBLISHED

Latin Authors

AMMIANUS MARCELLINUS. Translated by J. C. Rolfe. 3 Vols.

APULEIUS: THE GOLDEN ASS (METAMORPHOSES). W. Adlington (1566). Revised by S. Gaselee.

ST. AUGUSTINE: CITY OF GOD. 7 Vols. Vol. I. G. E. McCracken. Vol. II. W. M. Green. Vol. III. D. Wiesen. Vol. IV. P. Levine. Vol. V. E. M. Sanford and W. M. Green. Vol. VI. W. C. Greene.

ST. AUGUSTINE, CONFESSIONS OF. W. Watts (1631). 2 Vols.

ST. AUGUSTINE, SELECT LETTERS. J. H. Baxter.

AUSONIUS. H. G. Evelyn White. 2 Vols.

BEDE. J. E. King. 2 Vols.

BOETHIUS: TRACTS and DE CONSOLATIONE PHILOSOPHIAE. Rev. H. F. Stewart and E. K. Rand.

CAESAR: ALEXANDRIAN, AFRICAN and SPANISH WARS. A. G. Way.

CAESAR: CIVIL WARS. A. G. Peskett.

CAESAR: GALLIC WAR. H. J. Edwards.

CATO: DE RE RUSTICA; VARRO: DE RE RUSTICA. H. B. Ash and W. D. Hooper.

CATULLUS. F. W. Cornish; TIBULLUS. J. B. Postgate; PERVIGILIUM VENERIS. J. W. Mackail.

CELSUS: DE MEDICINA. W. G. Spencer. 3 Vols.

CICERO: BRUTUS, and ORATOR. G. L. Hendrickson and H. M. Hubbell.

[CICERO]: AD HERENNIUM. H. Caplan.

CICERO: DE ORATORE, etc. 2 Vols. Vol. I. DE ORATORE, Books I. and II. E. W. Sutton and H. Rackham. Vol. II. DE ORATORE, Book III. De Fato; Paradoxa Stoicorum; De Partitione Oratoria. H. Rackham.

CICERO: DE FINIBUS. H. Rackham.

CICERO: DE INVENTIONE, etc. H. M. Hubbell.

CICERO: DE NATURA DEORUM and ACADEMICA. H. Rackham.

CICERO: DE OFFICIIS. Walter Miller.

CICERO: DE REPUBLICA and DE LEGIBUS: SOMNIUM SCIPIONIS. Clinton W. Keyes.

Ovid: Fasti. Sir James G. Frazer.

Ovid: Heroides and Amores. Grant Showerman.

Ovid: Metamorphoses. F. J. Miller. 2 Vols.

Ovid: Tristia and Ex Ponto. A. L. Wheeler.

Persius. Cf. Juvenal.

Petronius. M. Heseltine; Seneca; Apocolocyntosis. W. H. D. Rouse.

Phaedrus and Babrius (Greek). B. E. Perry.

Plautus. Paul Nixon. 5 Vols.

Pliny: Letters, Panegyricus. Betty Radice. 2 Vols.

Pliny: Natural History. Vols. I.–V. and IX. H. Rackham. VI.–VIII. W. H. S. Jones. X. D. E. Eichholz. 10 Vols.

Propertius. H. E. Butler.

Prudentius. H. J. Thomson. 2 Vols.

Quintilian. H. E. Butler. 4 Vols.

Remains of Old Latin. E. H. Warmington. 4 Vols. Vol. I. (Ennius and Caecilius.) Vol. II. (Livius, Naevius, Pacuvius, Accius.) Vol. III. (Lucilius and Laws of XII Tables.) Vol. IV. (Archaic Inscriptions.)

Sallust. J. C. Rolfe.

Scriptores Historiae Augustae. D. Magie. 3 Vols.

Seneca: Apocolocyntosis. Cf. Petronius.

Seneca: Epistulae Morales. R. M. Gummere. 3 Vols.

Seneca: Moral Essays. J. W. Basore. 3 Vols.

Seneca: Tragedies. F. J. Miller. 2 Vols.

Seneca: Naturales Quaestiones. T. H. Corcoran. 2 Vols.

Sidonius: Poems and Letters. W. B. Anderson. 2 Vols.

Silius Italicus. J. D. Duff. 2 Vols.

Statius. J. H. Mozley. 2 Vols.

Suetonius. J. C. Rolfe. 2 Vols.

Tacitus: Dialogus. Sir Wm. Peterson. Agricola and Germania. Maurice Hutton.

Tacitus: Histories and Annals. C. H. Moore and J. Jackson. 4 Vols.

Terence. John Sargeaunt. 2 Vols.

Tertullian: Apologia and De Spectaculis. T. R. Glover. Minucius Felix. G. H. Rendall.

Valerius Flaccus. J. H. Mozley.

Varro: De Lingua Latina. R. G. Kent. 2 Vols.

Velleius Paterculus and Res Gestae Divi Augusti. F. W. Shipley.

Virgil. H. R. Fairclough. 2 Vols.

Vitruvius: De Architectura. F. Granger. 2 Vols.

Greek Authors

ARISTOTLE: PHYSICS. Rev. P Wicksteed and F. M. Cornford. 2 Vols.
ARISTOTLE: POETICS and LONGINUS. W. Hamilton Fyfe; DEMETRIUS ON STYLE. W. Rhys Roberts.
ARISTOTLE: POLITICS. H. Rackham.
ARISTOTLE: PROBLEMS. W. S. Hett. 2 Vols.
ARISTOTLE: RHETORICA AD ALEXANDRUM (with PROBLEMS. Vol. II). H. Rackham.
ARRIAN: HISTORY OF ALEXANDER and INDICA. Rev. E. Iliffe Robson. 2 Vols.
ATHENAEUS: DEIPNOSOPHISTAE. C. B. GULICK. 7 Vols.
BABRIUS AND PHAEDRUS (Latin). B. E. Perry.
ST. BASIL: LETTERS. R. J. Deferrari. 4 Vols.
CALLIMACHUS: FRAGMENTS. C. A. Trypanis.
CALLIMACHUS, Hymns and Epigrams, and LYCOPHRON. A. W. Mair; ARATUS. G. R. MAIR.
CLEMENT OF ALEXANDRIA. Rev. G. W. Butterworth.
COLLUTHUS. Cf. OPPIAN.
DAPHNIS AND CHLOE. Thornley's Translation revised by J. M. Edmonds: and PARTHENIUS. S. Gaselee.
DEMOSTHENES I.: OLYNTHIACS, PHILIPPICS and MINOR ORATIONS. I.–XVII. AND XX. J. H. Vince.
DEMOSTHENES II.: DE CORONA and DE FALSA LEGATIONE. C. A. Vince and J. H. Vince.
DEMOSTHENES III.: MEIDIAS, ANDROTION, ARISTOCRATES, TIMOCRATES and ARISTOGEITON, I. AND II. J. H. Vince.
DEMOSTHENES IV.–VI.: PRIVATE ORATIONS and IN NEAERAM. A. T. Murray.
DEMOSTHENES VII.: FUNERAL SPEECH, EROTIC ESSAY, EXORDIA and LETTERS. N. W. and N. J. DeWitt.
DIO CASSIUS: ROMAN HISTORY. E. Cary. 9 Vols.
DIO CHRYSOSTOM. J. W. Cohoon and H. Lamar Crosby. 5 Vols.
DIODORUS SICULUS. 12 Vols. Vols. I.–VI. C. H. Oldfather. Vol. VII. C. L. Sherman. Vol. VIII. C. B. Welles. Vols. IX. and X. R. M. Geer. Vol. XI. F. Walton. Vol. XII. F. Walton. General Index. R. M. Geer.
DIOGENES LAERTIUS. R. D. Hicks. 2 Vols.
DIONYSIUS OF HALICARNASSUS: ROMAN ANTIQUITIES. Spelman's translation revised by E. Cary. 7 Vols.
EPICTETUS. W. A. Oldfather. 2 Vols.
EURIPIDES. A. S. Way. 4 Vols. Verse trans.
EUSEBIUS: ECCLESIASTICAL HISTORY. Kirsopp Lake and J. E. L. Oulton. 2 Vols.
GALEN: ON THE NATURAL FACULTIES. A. J. Brock.
THE GREEK ANTHOLOGY. W. R. Paton. 5 Vols.

GREEK ELEGY AND IAMBUS with the ANACREONTEA. J. M. Edmonds. 2 Vols.

THE GREEK BUCOLIC POETS (THEOCRITUS, BION, MOSCHUS). J. M. Edmonds.

GREEK MATHEMATICAL WORKS. Ivor Thomas. 2 Vols.

HERODES. Cf. THEOPHRASTUS: CHARACTERS.

HERODIAN. C. R. Whittaker. 2 Vols.

HERODOTUS. A. D. Godley. 4 Vols.

HESIOD AND THE HOMERIC HYMNS. H. G. Evelyn White.

HIPPOCRATES and the FRAGMENTS OF HERACLEITUS. W. H. S. Jones and E. T. Withington. 4 Vols.

HOMER: ILIAD. A. T. Murray. 2 Vols.

HOMER: ODYSSEY. A. T. Murray. 2 Vols.

ISAEUS. E. W. Forster.

ISOCRATES. George Norlin and LaRue Van Hook. 3 Vols.

[ST. JOHN DAMASCENE]: BARLAAM AND IOASAPH. Rev. G. R. Woodward, Harold Mattingly and D. M. Lang.

JOSEPHUS. 9 Vols. Vols. I.–IV.; H. Thackeray. Vol. V.; H. Thackeray and R. Marcus. Vols. VI.–VII.; R. Marcus. Vol. VIII.; R. Marcus and Allen Wikgren. Vol. IX. L. H. Feldman.

JULIAN. Wilmer Cave Wright. 3 Vols.

LIBANIUS. A. F. Norman. Vol. I.

LUCIAN. 8 Vols. Vols. I.–V. A. M. Harmon. Vol. VI. K. Kilburn. Vols. VII.–VIII. M. D. Macleod.

LYCOPHRON. Cf. CALLIMACHUS.

LYRA GRAECA. J. M. Edmonds. 3 Vols.

LYSIAS. W. R. M. Lamb.

MANETHO. W. G. Waddell: PTOLEMY: TETRABIBLOS. F. E. Robbins.

MARCUS AURELIUS. C. R. Haines.

MENANDER. F. G. Allinson.

MINOR ATTIC ORATORS (ANTIPHON, ANDOCIDES, LYCURGUS, DEMADES, DINARCHUS, HYPERIDES). K. J. Maidment and J. O. Burtt. 2 Vols.

NONNOS: DIONYSIACA. W. H. D. Rouse. 3 Vols.

OPPIAN, COLLUTHUS, TRYPHIODORUS. A. W. Mair.

PAPYRI. NON-LITERARY SELECTIONS. A. S. Hunt and C. C. Edgar. 2 Vols. LITERARY SELECTIONS (Poetry). D. L. Page.

PARTHENIUS. Cf. DAPHNIS and CHLOE.

PAUSANIAS: DESCRIPTION OF GREECE. W. H. S. Jones. 4 Vols. and Companion Vol. arranged by R. E. Wycherley.

PHILO. 10 Vols. Vols. I.–V.; F. H. Colson and Rev. G. H. Whitaker. Vols. VI.–IX.; F. H. Colson. Vol. X. F. H. Colson and the Rev. J. W. Earp.

PHILO: two supplementary Vols. (*Translation only*.) Ralph Marcus.

PHILOSTRATUS: THE LIFE OF APOLLONIUS OF TYANA. F. C. Conybeare. 2 Vols.

PHILOSTRATUS: IMAGINES; CALLISTRATUS: DESCRIPTIONS. A. Fairbanks.

PHILOSTRATUS and EUNAPIUS: LIVES OF THE SOPHISTS. Wilmer Cave Wright.

PINDAR. Sir J. E. Sandys.

PLATO: CHARMIDES, ALCIBIADES, HIPPARCHUS, THE LOVERS, THEAGES, MINOS and EPINOMIS. W. R. M. Lamb.

PLATO: CRATYLUS, PARMENIDES, GREATER HIPPIAS, LESSER HIPPIAS. H. N. Fowler.

PLATO: EUTHYPHRO, APOLOGY, CRITO, PHAEDO, PHAEDRUS. H. N. Fowler.

PLATO: LACHES, PROTAGORAS, MENO, EUTHYDEMUS. W. R. M. Lamb.

PLATO: LAWS. Rev. R. G. Bury. 2 Vols.

PLATO: LYSIS, SYMPOSIUM, GORGIAS. W. R. M. Lamb.

PLATO: REPUBLIC. Paul Shorey. 2 Vols.

PLATO: STATESMAN, PHILEBUS. H. N. Fowler; ION. W. R. M. Lamb.

PLATO: THEAETETUS and SOPHIST. H. N. Fowler.

PLATO: TIMAEUS, CRITIAS, CLITOPHO, MENEXENUS, EPISTULAE. Rev. R. G. Bury.

PLOTINUS: A. H. Armstrong. Vols. I.–III.

PLUTARCH: MORALIA. 16 Vols. Vols. I.–V. F. C. Babbitt. Vol. VI. W. C. Helmbold. Vols. VII. and XIV. P. H. De Lacy and B. Einarson. Vol. VIII. P. A. Clement and H. B. Hoffleit. Vol. IX. E. L. Minar, Jr., F. H. Sandbach, W. C. Helmbold. Vol. X. H. N. Fowler. Vol. XI. L. Pearson and F. H. Sandbach. Vol. XII. H. Cherniss and W. C. Helmbold. Vol. XV. F. H. Sandbach.

PLUTARCH: THE PARALLEL LIVES. B. Perrin. 11 Vols.

POLYBIUS. W. R. Paton. 6 Vols.

PROCOPIUS: HISTORY OF THE WARS. H. B. Dewing. 7 Vols.

PTOLEMY: TETRABIBLOS. Cf. MANETHO.

QUINTUS SMYRNAEUS. A. S. Way. Verse trans.

SEXTUS EMPIRICUS. Rev. R. G. Bury. 4 Vols.

SOPHOCLES. F. Storr. 2 Vols. Verse trans.

STRABO: GEOGRAPHY. Horace L. Jones. 8 Vols.

THEOPHRASTUS: CHARACTERS. J. M. Edmonds. HERODES, etc. A. D. Knox

THEOPHRASTUS: ENQUIRY INTO PLANTS. Sir Arthur Hort, Bart. 2 Vols.

THUCYDIDES. C. F. Smith. 4 Vols.

TRYPHIODORUS. Cf. OPPIAN.
XENOPHON: CYROPAEDIA. Walter Miller. 2 Vols.
XENOPHON: HELLENICA. C. L. Brownson. 2 Vols.
XENOPHON: ANABASIS. C. L. Brownson.
XENOPHON: MEMORABILIA AND OECONOMICUS. E. C. Marchant.
SYMPOSIUM AND APOLOGY. O. J. Todd.
XENOPHON: SCRIPTA MINORA. E. C. Marchant and G. W.
Bowersock.

IN PREPARATION

Greek Authors

ARISTIDES: ORATIONS. C. A. Behr.
MUSAEUS: HERO AND LEANDER. T. Gelzer and C. H.
WHITMAN.
THEOPHRASTUS: DE CAUSIS PLANTARUM. G. K. K. Link and
B. Einarson.

Latin Authors

ASCONIUS: COMMENTARIES ON CICERO'S ORATIONS.
G. W. Bowersock.
BENEDICT: THE RULE. P. Meyvaert.
JUSTIN–TROGUS. R. Moss.
MANILIUS. G. P. Goold.

DESCRIPTIVE PROSPECTUS ON APPLICATION

London **WILLIAM HEINEMANN LTD**
Cambridge, Mass. **HARVARD UNIVERSITY PRESS**